Classifications in their
Social Context

LANGUAGE, THOUGHT, AND CULTURE:
Advances in the Study of Cognition

Under the Editorship of: E. A. HAMMEL

DEPARTMENT OF ANTHROPOLOGY
UNIVERSITY OF CALIFORNIA
BERKELEY

Classifications in their Social Context

Edited by

ROY F. ELLEN and DAVID REASON
University of Kent at Canterbury

1979

ACADEMIC PRESS
LONDON   NEW YORK   SAN FRANCISCO
A Subsidiary of Harcourt Brace Jovanovich, Publishers

Academic Press Inc. (London) Ltd.
24–28 Oval Road
London NW1

US edition published by
Academic Press Inc.
111 Fifth Avenue,
New York, New York 10003

Copyright © 1979 by Academic Press Inc. (London) Ltd.

British Library Cataloguing in Publication Data
Classifications in their social context.
  – (Language, thought and culture).
  I. Classification
  I. Ellen, Roy F.
  II. Reason, David
  III. Series
  112   GN468.4   79–50312
  ISBN 0–12–237160–7

Printed in Great Britain by
W. & G. Baird Ltd,
Antrim, Northern Ireland

Contributors

Jacques Barrau   Sous-Directeur, Laboratoire d'Ethnobotanique et d'Ethnozoologie, Muséum National d'Histoire Naturelle, 57 rue Cuvier, 75231 Paris, Cedex 05, France

John Bousfield   Lecturer in Philosophy, Eliot College, The University, Canterbury, Kent CT2 7NS, England

Ralph Bulmer   Professor of Social Anthropology, University of Auckland, Private Bag, Auckland, New Zealand

R. G. A. Dolby   Senior Lecturer in the History, Philosophy and Social Relations of Science, Physics Building, The University, Canterbury, Kent CT2 7NR, England

Roy Ellen   Lecturer in Social Anthropology, Eliot College, The University, Canterbury, Kent CT2 7NS, England

Claudine Friedberg   Maître-Assistant, Laboratoire d'Ethnobotanique et d'Ethnozoologie, Muséum National d'Histoire Naturelle, 57 rue Cuvier, 75231 Paris, Cedex 05, France

Eugene Hunn   Assistant Professor of Anthropology, University of Washington, Seattle, Washington 98195, USA

John D. Kesby   Lecturer in Social Anthropology, Darwin College, The University, Canterbury, Kent CT2 7NY, England

Brian Morris   Lecturer in Social Anthropology, Goldsmith's College, Lewisham Way, New Cross, London 6E14 6NW, England

Alice Peeters   Maître-Assistant, Laboratoire d'Ethnobotanique et d'Ethnozoologie, Muséum National d'Histoire Naturelle, 57 rue Cuvier, 75231 Paris, Cedex 05, France

David Reason   Lecturer in Interdisciplinary Studies, Keynes College, The University, Canterbury, Kent CT2 7NP, England

Preface

"Classification" is a key concept in contemporary Western thought, figuring prominently in such apparently diverse fields of enquiry as anthropology, artificial intelligence, mathematics, history, biology, sociology, linguistics and philosophy. In each case, "classification" provides a topic for study, a methodological device and an explanatory principle. Where a concept appears to be so generally employed (seems, indeed, so necessary) in such a disparate range of disciplines, there is a clear and pressing need to scrutinize that concept, to put it to the question and to explicate and evaluate its various uses and usages. What is the logic of "classification"? What are its material, social and psychological determinants, correlates and corollaries? How, empirically, are "classifications" to be identified, elicited and described? How, theoretically, may they be compared and elucidated?

It was with these considerations in mind that, supported by the British Social Science Research Council, a two-day seminar on "Systems of Classification and the Anthropology of Knowledge" was held at the University of Kent at Canterbury in June 1977. Those who attended the seminar represented a wide range of disciplinary and substantive interests, although, by design, the papers presented tended more or less directly to relate their arguments to issues generally associated with the domains of "folk classification" and "scientific classification". Papers addressed current debates in anthropology (Morris, Ellen), proposed new directions for research (Barrau), provided ethnographic material (Kesby, Friedberg), considered examples of classifications devised in the historical past (Peeters, Dolby), and examined the nature of classification in relation to social practices of discrimination (Coxon, Bousfield, Reason). As the seminar proceeded, it became clear that each paper implicitly or explicitly related to the presuppositions and substance of the other papers, and, furthermore, that "classification" itself was by no means necessarily a unitary or unifying concept.

This volume contains revised versions of the papers pre-circulated and presented at the seminar, with the omission of Coxon's paper,* and with the addition of an essay by Ralph Bulmer. The paper by Eugene Hunn was presented *in absentia*. In general terms, they all relate to two major axes of debate. The first divides those who emphasize classification as a real stable conceptual order which reflects, grounds or governs social activity, from those who stress the priority of classifying understood as a situated, context-bound social activity itself. This latter view draws attention to classifications (the outcome of classifying) as being intrinsically matters of social construction. The other major axis of debate distinguishes those who argue for the logical and/or material necessity of classification for the analytical and/or practical comprehension of "the world", from those who are persuaded that classifications are a historically and/or socially specific possibility for grasping that world. The problems raised by this "quartering" of the concept are not resolved in this collection of essays; indeed, it is not clear whether, in the formulation given here, resolution is the proper goal of our considering them. Nevertheless, we hope that a valuable beginning has been made in sketching a territory for future exploration.

The success of the original meeting owed much to the critical presence of Edwin Ardener, Maurice Bloch, Marine Bouez, Stephen Feuchtwang, Ray Francis, Caroline Humphrey, Paul Jorion, Anne Sellar, Dan Sperber and Roy Willis. Doctor W. T. Stearn, formerly of the British Museum (Natural History), brought his own special expertise to bear on the proceedings, for which we are grateful. Rosalyne Pickvance helped with problems of translation. We acknowledge the financial assistance and helpful co-operation of the British Social Science Research Council and the Maison des Sciences de l'Homme in Paris. For the French participants the meeting was a sequel to the 1973 seminar on *Méthodes d'enquête ethnologiques sur la conceptualisation et la classification des objects et phénomenes naturels*, organized by Jacques Barrau and Maurice Godelier. Mary Douglas encouraged the project from its inception and so to her our last-but-not-least thanks are due.

May 1979   Roy Ellen
                                                        David Reason

* COXON, A. P. M. and JONES, C. L. (1979). Images and predication: the use of subjective occupational hierarchies. *Quality and Quantity.* **13**, 2, 121–40.

Contents

1

Introductory Essay

Roy Ellen

> Throughout nature, wherever man strives to acquire knowledge he finds himself under the necessity of using special methods, 1st, to bring order among the infinitely numerous and varied objects which he has before him; 2nd, to distinguish, without danger of confusion, among this immense multitude of objects, either groups of those in which he is interested, or particular individuals among them; 3rd, to pass on to his fellows all that he has learnt, seen and thought on the subject. Now the methods which he uses for this purpose are what I call the *artificial devices* in natural science,—devices which we must beware of confusing with the laws and acts of nature herself.
>
> Lamarck, 1963, p. 19

I

The above quotation, drawn from the *Zoologie Philosophique* of Jean-Baptiste Pierre Antoine de Monet de Lamarck, indicates succinctly a perennial problem in anthropology: the confusion of the order of nature with that imposed upon it by man. It is a problem which it shares with other sciences, but (as with sociology) is posed in a uniquely complex way. Historically, the problem of classifications in anthropology arose from the desire to assign physical and social man to groups arranged both spatially and through time. Underlying this has generally been some kind of evolutionary paradigm. The objections to such an enterprise are legion, but they commonly revolve around the accusation of stasis, the legitimacy of particular defining characteristics and categories, and the errors which arise from the assumption that groups with similar characteristics have a common origin. But whatever the complaint and however vigorous the assault, such classifications persist and for some workers remain a supreme objective. This is because they cannot be explained simply as indications of the primitive development of a science: they persist because they are necessary.

While we may defend classification as the logical prerequisite of comparison, generalization and explanation, it is difficult to justify some of the notions and theoretical underpinnings that have been perpetuated. Despite the sophistry, the objectives, procedures and problems still betray their intellectual origins in pre-modern natural history (Hempel, 1965; Ember, 1973). This approach is well illustrated in Radcliffe-Brown's conception of a *natural science* of society, where implicit evolutionism is obscured by social physiology (Radcliffe-Brown, 1957).

Radcliffe-Brown was positively pre-Lamarckian in his idea of species reflecting some basic immobility of nature. In terms of the history of science, he had much more in common with Tournefort and Linnaeus than with either Bonnet, Benoit de Maillet or Diderot, who viewed species as being more plastic (Foucault, 1970, p. 127). For Radcliffe-Brown, natural species and human societies were alike; both were closed, on-going self-perpetuating systems. In each case it was quite possible to arrive at *correct* descriptions and arrange them in *valid* typological relations, through observation, classification and generalization (Leach, 1976, pp. 14, 17). Edmund Leach has parodied this kind of classificatory activity, and the comparativism associated with it, in an elaborate, museological metaphor bridging 15 years. For him it is "butterfly-collecting", an antiquarian approach drawn from "fossils, rocks, insects, stuffed-birds . . . fixed entities, changeless, everlasting" (Leach, 1976, p. 8, 1961). We expect to find such things juxtaposed in the rigid spaces of cabinets, herbaria and zoological gardens; not in real life. It is a view founded in a set of ideas that is pre-genetic, pre-Darwinian and pre-molecular.

For Leach and for many others, there is a lack of fit between the ideal categories of classifications and the empirical discontinuities of nature. Paradoxically, this is a view which had its own origins in natural history rather than biology. Buffon, Bonnet and Lamarck all saw species simply as the end-products of applying the rules of taxonomic method. Like Aristotle and the Chinese Mohists of the Chou dynasty before them (Peck, 1965, pp. viii, *passim*; Needham, 1962, pp. 165–84), they recognized the difficulty of working out the principles of *natural* classification and the social element involved in fixing terminology and nomenclature. They were concerned with logical and artificial systems. That this is, in fact, the case, and that clear boundaries between species are not found by straightforward inference from empirical facts, has been amply confirmed by recent work in genetics and statistical biology. It is the very *idea* of species that is inherently imprecise. "The species of empirical reality lack objective homogeneity and are blurred at the edges; what is allocated to them is determined by definitions" (Leach, 1976, p. 17). And while all this finds more than an echo in the work of Lévi-Strauss, Foucault,[1] Mary Douglas, Leach himself, and their various acolytes, it seems to have gone unrecognized by Radcliffe-Brown.

II

The classifications so far considered, and the sense in which Radcliffe-Brown was employing them, have been described variously as observers', interpretative, operational, analysts', scientific and *etic*. They attempt to divide up the real world as perceived by the investigator. They are assumed to be objective and may be either the tools or end-product of a research project. It was only with the publication of "De quelques formes primitives de classification", published in the *Année Sociologique* for 1901–2, that classifications *themselves* really became a legitimate subject of ethnographic, philosophical and historical research. On this occasion, the key terms for categories were cognitive, cognized, perceived, conscious, native, "home-made" or *emic* (see e.g. Harris, 1969, pp. 568–604).

Although there are grounds for insisting that indigenous categories of kinship had earlier been subject to systematic analysis (Needham, 1971, pp. xxi–xxii), it is not simply a matter of convenience that we should see the contribution of Durkheim and Mauss as representing an important theoretical landmark. Few would now accept the extreme view that society, not the mind, is the prime model for the classification of nature; but that classifications generally *express* the societies within which they are elaborated is an inescapable verity. Over and above this, however, the importance of the work was to isolate classifications as an aspect of culture worthy of sociological analysis (Needham, 1963, p. xi).[2]

The ideas of Durkheim and Mauss on this subject have influenced contemporary thinking along two paths. The first is through the collective consciousness of the intellectualist Oxford tradition, by way of Lévy-Bruhl, Hocart and Evans-Pritchard; the second is via Lévi-Strauss. Among those writers who have consumed varying mixtures of this scholarly diet must be counted Leach, Douglas and Rodney Needham. I shall label these the sociologists or social constructionists.

In the meantime, ideas in America were shaping-up rather differently. Boasian particularism and a vigorous anthropological linguistics contrasted sharply with the general lack of interest in the categories of language (with the notable exception of Malinowski) in the British School (Ardener, 1971, p. ix). Via the descriptive linguistics of Sapir and Whorf, there developed a formal approach that was both detailed and, in its own terms, rigorous. This is usually termed ethnoscience, and among its most important exponents must be listed Conklin, Goodenough and Berlin (see Conklin, 1972). It has been characterized by an interest in semantic universals and general classificatory principles.

The results of research in these two areas have been as inadequate in some fundamental respects as they have been intriguing and stimulating in others. Those that have been sociologically sophisticated have often been technically and empirically weak, and those that have been technically and linguistically rigorous have frequently been sociologically naïve. The "sociologists" have paid attention to social concomitants with varying degrees of care, but have gone astray with the analysis of actual classificatory structures. They have made assumptions about "total" taxonomies, the existence of anomalies and semantic hierarchy where the evidence is unclear. On the other hand, the formalists have concretized words and categories, treating them as the only hard facts worthy of study; accessible reality is seen as items in abstracted classificatory systems which represent the mind in its pure state (Schneider, quoted in Douglas, 1975, p. 120). Sadly, we seem to know as little of the empirical details of Lele ethnozoology as we know of the sociology of Tzeltal botanical categories.

There have been two fairly recent developments which suggest some resolution of these stark alternatives. Firstly, classifications are being examined in a wider intellectual context with conscious attempts to link superficially distinct research problems: the history of ideas, structuralism, developmental psychology, phenomenology and ethnomethodology, social anthropology, language studies, theoretical biology and mathematics. Such tentative interconnections which do exist, largely as a result of a linguistic phase in social science, have by no means gelled into a recognizable and dynamic research network or distinctive field. It was partly the task of the seminar on which this volume is based to examine whether or not this putative convergence is likely to be fruitful and realizable, or if it is no more than a pious wish. Secondly, in a much more restricted anthropological sphere, there is some evidence that the formalists and social constructionists are beginning to come to terms with each other. In the field of ethnobiology, to which I shall largely restrict myself here, this is evident in the work of Ralph Bulmer, who has combined an almost pedantic concern for folk–zoological detail and accuracy, with a sophisticated treatment of both the structure of categories and their social context (Bulmer, 1967, 1970; and e.g. Bulmer and Tyler, 1968).[3] It may not be too optimistic to hope that these trends will nurture what Mary Douglas (1975, p. 21) has described as the synthesis of classificatory logic and transactions.

III

Much of the work on folk classifications of animals has been concerned with showing the extent to which they are similar to or different from phylogenetic schemes, in their structure, extensiveness and attention to detail. Perhaps motivated by assumptions concerning the psychological unity of mankind, both folk and scientific classifications are attributed with hierarchical taxonomic structures, suggesting common cognitive processes (Conklin, 1962; Kay, 1971). At the same time, and increasingly, other workers have shown that, in fact, in this and other respects, they are very different. Now, it seems to me that this has got us into something of a muddle, of much the same kind as that which has arisen over the degree of attribution of Western rationality to non-Western beliefs. Not only do such puzzles stem from false, or unhelpful, assumptions about the characteristics of particular systems, they also occur because the categories "folk classification" and "scientific classifications" are themselves problematic. This is well illustrated by the debate over the distinction drawn by Berlin and his associates between special purpose and general purpose schemes (Berlin et al., 1966; Bulmer, 1970; Berlin, 1974). Attempts to set out the general principles of classification and nomenclature in folk biology (e.g. Berlin *et al.*, 1973, pp. 215–16) are certainly useful for particular systems, but to make empirical generalizations about certain types assumes that variability is according to a limited number of well-understood criteria along parallel axes. What are the conditions which indicate the transformation from a folk classification to a scientific one, for example; and what are the characteristics of systems that cannot easily be assigned to either? Specifically, what of the criteria for classificatory systems falling outside the simple models of the formalists?

The restricted check-list approach exemplified by the work of Berlin and his associates cannot, then, cope with the wider dimensions of variation between systems. It tends not only to reify a particular kind of classification (that which we call taxonomic), but seems to claim that a large number of semantic fields are at all times similarly organized. That this is patently not so is made ridiculously obvious in the beautiful passage from Jorge Luis Borges which stimulated Foucault to write his *Les Mots et les Choses*. The reference is to "a certain Chinese encyclopaedia" which divides animals into categories:

(a) belonging to the Emperor, (b) embalmed, (c) tame, (d) sucking pigs, (e) sirens, (f) fabulous, (g) stray dogs, (h) included in the present classification, (i) frenzied, (j) innumerable, (k) drawn with a very fine camel hair brush, (l) *et cetera*, (m) having just broken the water pitcher, (n) that from a long way off look like flies.

(Foucault, 1970, p. xv)

That the example is either a complete fiction, or poorly translated from the original, or undecipherable through lack of knowledge of cultural context, may all be plausibly suggested. Equally, its authenticity might be attested to by seeing in it the scepticism of such sages as Chang Ping-Lin, for whom all possible classifications were unreal (Needham, 1962, p. 196). Strangely enough, and with all its logical paradoxes and Foucault's astonishment, the arrangement has a familiar ring for an anthropologist. Virtually all the animal categories and many of the combinations find parallels in known ethnographic schemes. The exception is "included in the present classification", and even this may exist in the perceived world with the aid of either mystical symbolism, the graphics of Maurits Escher, or the metaphysics of Borges himself. Now I am not being deliberately obscure here. I am trying to make the simple point that there are substantive areas and dimensions to classificatory space which remain unexplored (and perhaps unexplorable) by our present limited techniques, but which are nevertheless appropriate subjects for analysis.

What is required is some kind of meta-theory, or at least a meta-framework, which will bring order to this dizzy scene. But this is easier said than done. Some writers have already distinguished formally between different kinds of classificatory constructs: taxonomies, indices, keys, paradigms and typologies (Conklin, 1964, pp. 39–40), analytical (part–whole) and synthetic (class inclusive) forms (Conklin, 1962, pp. 131–2; Ellen, 1977, pp. 343–7) and so on. Others (e.g. Hunn, 1976) have worked on non-hierarchical models of organizing classificatory space. But many classifications combine several of these different forms. Further, such abstract analyses make little reference to features of the substantive context with which they might vary concomitantly. This requires a somewhat different perspective, and the key variables are not necessarily those emphasized in formal studies.

IV

In this section I look briefly at seven variables or groups of variables which may begin to provide us with analytical links between formal structures and social context. The list is incomplete, extremely provisional and many of the points have already been discussed in the literature, individually and in slightly different ways. They are: variability; arbitrariness; expression of inclusiveness; anomaly; structural complexity; terminology, nomenclature and taxonomy; and integration in semantic fields. They are discussed here with examples drawn from ethnobiology, but the generalizations can probably be applied more broadly.

Variability

Cognitive variability generally refers to relations between three variables: lexical items, the content of categories in scientific or other "objective" terms, and informants. Further elements could be added, such as knowledge of uses, but as yet this is an aspect which has not widely been considered. Moreover, although the incongruity between words and categories is well understood, it is generally assumed that the lack of congruence and the existence of covert categories can, in most cases, be ignored, or must inevitably be so if measurement is to be possible. Given this proviso we can distinguish between three basic kinds of variation:

a) variation in the relationship between lexical items (or categories) and scientific notation;
b) variation between individuals; and
c) variation according to rules appropriate to specific contexts.

These can be described, respectively, as *consistency, sharing* and *flexibility* (Ellen, 1979).

Consistency and sharing vary according to the material or social significance of the categories involved, the available aids for storing and arranging information—such as filing systems, libraries, training methods, catalogues, indexes, specialists, reference collections and illustrations, and the actual variations and complexities of fauna and flora. They are related to the social importance of conformity, either practically (Ellen, 1978a) or ideologically, and maintained through the process of social communication. Flexibility varies according to differing social and perceptual contexts within a society: classificatory structures in particular may vary according to the different purposes being served on separate occasions. It does not usually represent individualistic or deviant behaviour, but reflects social rules (e.g. Ellen, 1975).

Arbitrariness

Classifications can be ordered according to degree of arbitrariness. An arbitrary criterion, following Saussure, is one that is unmotivated. Thus, to classify dogs on the basis of their colour is less arbitrary than to do so on the basis of an alphabetical ordering of their names, for names are only signs. Here I extend this idea, such that by a less arbitrary classification we understand one that more adequately identifies a category *vis-à-vis* all others in the same set. So, to classify dogs solely on the grounds of colour is more arbitrary than to include also size and shape.

In practice, no classifications (limited as they are by material and cognitive space) can be formulated in terms of *all* natural discontinuities. Classifying requires the selection of features, on the grounds of manageability and significance. The number of distinctive features used in a classification varies according to information-handling techniques. To a large extent, folk classifications appear to be built up according to generalized conceptions of particular species (Ellen, 1979). but even here particular characteristics must be selected for emphasis, and those that are chosen vary for social and perceptual reasons. In his botanical taxonomy, Tournefort employed certain differentiae, not because they were the most obvious and useful parts of the plant, "but because they permitted a numerically satisfying combinality" (Foucault, 1970, p. 141). More arbitrary still are alphabetical classifications and other simple notations (such as numerals) based on abstract signs, including those not derived from the form of the species itself, but which are characteristics rather of the word or other sign used to denote it. Although some of these types are as old as written language itself, others are very recent innovations in European thought.

The fewer features considered the more arbitrary, in these terms, the classification. If we can employ a single feature the classification is logically most satisfying: all men classified by unique proper names, all animals classified by their diploid number of chromosomes, all plants classified according to the alphabetical order of their name: these are socially and cognitively efficient. They are aesthetically pleasing, too. Anomaly is excluded *a priori*. The problem is, of course, that the fewer the features adopted to distinguish categories, the less they reflect what is actually seen. But then that is not always the purpose of classifications. Some do purport to reflect reality (phylogenetic schemes), others simply to act as economical data-retrieval systems (such as library codes), and yet others to deliberately obscure it. Most classifications are, in fact, a bit of each.

The problems posed by single-feature schemes logically give rise to attempts to introduce schemes based on multiple features. Instead of employing a single feature which has different values for each item $(x(= a)_1, x(= b)_2, \ldots)$, a number of different features are chosen:

A	1	2	3	4	5
x	V_1	V_2	V_3	V_4	V_5
y	V_2	V_3	V_4	V_5	V_1
z	V_3	V_4	V_5	V_1	V_2

B	1	2	3	4	5
x	+	+	−	−	−
y	−	−	−	+	+
z	+	−	−	−	+

In any case, a decision has to be made as to whether the values assigned to them for each item are on a continuous scale (A) or whether they are to be listed on a simple binary (or conceivably ternary) basis (B).

The first alternative is difficult to implement in non-written systems, and is avoided in written systems wherever possible. It is easier to talk of "winged" in contrast to "legged", rather than degrees of "wingedness" or "leggedness". But even a continuous scale must be divided up into classes at some point, and this will always generate a binary structure. Such models have been the main means by which ethnographers, at least, have interpreted indigenous classifications. It is an approach which derives from formal treatment and has permitted the development of a rigorous, if largely unproductive, componential analysis.

In classifying items in which the number of utilized variables is large, the multiple-feature approach meets with difficulties. Isolating only a small number of characters might be misleading, and considering large numbers presents technical problems. In many folk classifications the problem of manageability is overcome by differentially rejecting certain attributes for each item, and I will discuss this matter further. In interpretative scientific schemes, modern hardware, such as the computer, has allowed the utilization of large numbers of attributes. Numerical taxonomy of this kind has been used by both biologists and archaeologists (Sokal and Sneath, 1963; Clarke, 1968). While such devices may reduce the complexity of a system, they are subject to finite limitations on the amount of information that can be encoded. The fallacy inherent in the phylogenetic system, then, is precisely this: that it seeks to reduce to linear order something which is, in fact, a complex reticulum virtually impossible to reduce to signs on a piece of paper. Indeed, among theoretical biologists doubts still exist as to whether or not there is an ideally perfect classification which may be accepted as the aim of taxonomy; and again, whether or not phylogeny can ever be fully expressed in classification. Clearly, here is a dilemma between a valid scheme and a useful one. Perhaps the best we can hope for is that different classifications should reflect different aspects of reality, as in the distinction between the evolutionary arrangement of homologous structures for the purposes of comparative morphology, and the grouping of organisms in an order of presumed evolutionary descent (McLean and Ivimey-Cook, 1956, pp. 2121–2).

The classifications considered so far in our discussion of "arbitrariness" have all been what Sneath has described as *monothetic*, i.e. the defining set of features is always unique (Sokal and Sneath, 1963, p. 13). Given the discriminatory inadequacy of those classifications made up of limited features and the impossibility or doubtful validity of those employing large numbers, contemporary biological taxonomies are something of a compromise. However, this is also true of what we know of folk classifications. One way in which we might distinguish the two is by the level at which the compromise has had to be made: folk classifications tend more towards the single-feature end of the continuum than do the scientific classifications.

Given the necessity of using some form of multiple-feature scheme, it is nevertheless clear that (a) the selected features are not always relevant or helpful for a particular discrimination and (b) it is difficult to operate schemes with a large number of attributes for each item. This, of course, is less so with written systems. Many folk classifications only become manageable through selectively rejecting attributes. Here, categories are not defined with reference to a limited set of features characteristic of and unique to each category, but are semantically primitive (Hunn, 1975a, p. 15); what Sneath has suggested we describe as *polythetic*. Such arrangements group items with the greatest number of shared features. Single features are neither essential to group membership nor sufficient to allocate an item to a group (Sokal and Sneath, 1963, p. 14). The idea is illustrated in the following much-reproduced form:

	1	2	3	4	5	6	7
x		a	b	c			
y				c	d	e	
z					e	f	g

Polythetic classification has been the subject of recent interest in disciplines other than biology; for example, anthropology (Needham, 1975) and philosophy, where it is akin to Wittgenstein's notion of "family resemblance" in ordinary language. This approach does not necessarily represent objective reality more faithfully, although the maximizing of informativeness requires increasing polythetism. Some biologists have seen it as a means of yielding "natural" taxa, but this only points to a difference between polythetic classification in scientific and folk systems. In the former it is associated with increasing information; in the latter it is a response to too much. Phylogenetic classification is always striving to be less arbitrary, but in folk systems this aim is absent. The notion of adequacy is a different one. Arbitrary polythetic systems are conveniently represented by the kinship categories investigated by Needham (1971), which are not necessarily a reflection of genetic relationships.

The co-ordinates of variation for arbitrariness, as discussed here, are illustrated in Fig. 1.

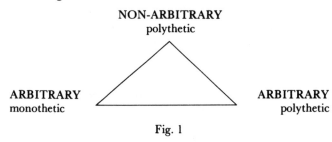

Fig. 1

Most classifications are generally mixtures of these different formal models. Although one may be dominant in individual schemes, it would be misleading to see any of them as representing the basic framework for folk systems. It is important to return to the idea that in many classification systems the items are seen as distinct entities rather than the sum of a specified number of distinctive characteristics. This is a view which is by no means confined to students of folk biology. Linnaeus suggested a list of biological families based on an intuitive feeling of affinity. As McLean and Ivimey-Cook (1956, p. 2121) point out, this is not necessarily a scientifically inferior process, but one which takes into account a large number of "qualitative sense data", expressed by the term "facies", many of which are either individually or cumulatively recognized by the observer as a sense-group which, for him/her, seems to entail a very strong presumption of "natural reality" (cf. Bulmer and Tyler, 1968; Ellen, 1979). In the sense of matching classificatory representations more closely with what is actually seen, such complex systems are probably less arbitrary than those that are logically consistent.

Expression of inclusiveness

Inclusiveness in phylogenetic classification is expressed essentially through an hierarchical metaphor involving linked notions of rank, level and contrast. This we know as taxonomy, an idea first made explicit in the history of European throught by Aristotle in his *Organon* and *Metaphysics*. The ruling principle is that "the highest genus is divided by means of differentae into subaltern genera, and each of these is then divided until the ultimate species is reached" (Peck, 1965, p. vii). It has been handed down through the Stoics, Porphyry and the Greek commentators to Linnaeus, from whom it passed into modern biological usage. The taxonomic approach gained such wide currency that a great many ethnographers assumed that it must also necessarily order the folk classifications they were beginning to describe and analyse. This assumption gave rise to the complex formal theories referred to in Section III.

Some recent work has cast doubt on the general applicability of this approach, gathering evidence to suggest that a taxonomy based on bounded semantic fields ordered exclusively by a hierarchy of inclusion is by no means always appropriate when it comes to the examination of folk systems (Frake, 1969, p. 132; Fox, 1975, pp. 118–19; Hunn 1976; Friedberg, 1968, 1970). This critique is, in part, a response to the so-called "special problems" of taxonomies, which are seen in many cases as simply artefacts of the method. Examples of these include multiple and interlocking hierarchies, extra-hierarchic relations, synonymy, homonymy, polysemy, anomaly, covert categories and residual taxa. As a result we are left with inelegant complications of formal models which, additionally, provide no basis for either distinguishing induction from deduction or explaining how taxa are actually generated (Conklin, 1969, pp. 41–57; Hunn, 1976, pp. 510–11, 19). Randall (1976) has criticized the model on the grounds that its assumptions about transitivity suggested incorrectly that elicited taxonomies represent structures involved in memory storage. Rather, he suggests, taxonomic trees are the results of classifying behaviour (see also Coxon and Jones, 1979).

It appears that many systems can be non-hierarchical while retaining the idea of contrast. An example of this is the scientific logic of the Chinese Mohist philosophers of the fourth and fifth centuries B.C. Although later logicians may have been working with an Aristotelian notion, the Mohist metaphor was in terms of "broad and narrow" (*ta hsiao*). Thus "animals of four feet" forms a "broader" group than does "oxen and horses", while the group of "things" is broader still. Everything is classified into broader or narrower groups. Similarly there is also the idea of "common point" (*chü*). Thus "oxen" and "horses" meet at a "common point" since they both have four feet. An analogy can be made with counting fingers; each hand has five, but one can take one hand as one thing (Needham, 1962, pp. 175–6). Similarly, we are told that the Nuer (being good Durkheimians) classify animals after the fashion of social groups: into *cieng*, local communities, and *thok dwiel*, descent groups (Evans-Pritchard, 1956, pp. 89–90). In this volume, Friedberg and Peeters discuss classifications which they claim can be represented more accurately as "networks". In other classifications, or partial classifications, not even the notion of contrast is present. Thus, rather than something being x or y, it is common for it to be more x than y, or more y than x. The idea of gradation eliminates distinct boundaries and has been suitably termed "fuzziness" (Lakoff, 1972). Thus we should speak of "shrubness" or "treeness", "birdness" or "snakeness" (Randall, 1976, pp. 549–51) as well as other phenomena, such as flexibility and consistency. This fits well with a polythetic conception of classification.

Anomaly

Classifications might also be ordered according to the degree to which they generate anomaly. In as much as all classifications are of varying degrees of arbitrariness, so they have a *potential* to create anomaly continually. Dan Sperber (1975a, p. 94) has reminded us that encyclopaedic knowledge is not without its incoherences and contradictions, but that life is concerned with a continuous effort to either avoid or correct them. In this sense anomaly is ubiquitous. However, it is important to distinguish genuine anomalies from those produced by careless use of the taxonomic method. Repeatedly, "anomalies" have been shown either to be spurious or culturally irrelevant (Hunn, 1975a, p. 310; Sperber, 1975b; Willis, 1974, p. 47); rather than falling between taxa they may be separate ones in their own right; rather than being negatively "anomalous" they may be positively *singular* (Ellen, 1972; Bulmer, Friedberg and Hunn, this volume). We must be careful not to invent anomalies where they do not exist. If we interpret as monothetic classifications those which are polythetic, or employ contrastive logic where concepts are "fuzzy", all sorts of problems are obviously going to arise. Whereas the inbuilt, rigorous logic of ethnographic method easily gives rise to anomalies, the informal logics of folk systems permit its avoidance.

Nevertheless, even given that the flexibility of folk classifications generally allows for the resistance of many potential anomalies, both in ethnobiological and phylogenetic schemes, the "higher" the order of categories involved the more likely they are to be evident. *Birds* fly by folk definition, but some that are otherwise perfectly good *birds* patently do not. For a long time in European biological thought *plants* were by definition autotrophic, although some are unable to manufacture their own energy. At the same time, though, we also find that anomaly can be more readily erased by sophisticated casuistry at higher rather than lower levels (Bulmer and Tyler, 1968).

Clearly there is variation in the appearance of anomaly, both between and within cultures. Nevertheless, everywhere the potential number of anomalies greatly exceeds the number that are recognized, let alone held to be significant and taken up in symbolic communication. Once anomalies have been set in their proper classificatory context we can then focus on their behavioural concomitants and make that all-important "frontal attack on the question of how thought, words and the real world are related" (Douglas, 1972, p. 29).[4]

Structural complexity

It is reasonable enough to assume that "complexity" must be an important variable linking the formal structure of classifications with their social context. But since this is a noun which may easily be applied to ideas that are simply unfamiliar it must be carefully defined.

Complexity here refers to three dependent subsets of variables:

i) the number of elements given classificatory recognition (usually by naming), expressed either absolutely or relative to natural species diversity, given some measure of degree of differentiation (Hunn, 1975b; Ellen, 1978);

ii) the number of levels in taxonomies, the number of categories at each level of class inclusion, and other related quantifiable characteristics (Berlin *et al.*, 1973). With classifications other than taxonomies *sensu stricto*, or if the taxonomic approach is rejected for folk systems, these characteristics can be described in other ways;

iii) with due regard to the cautionary advice already given concerning "special problems", complexity also refers to the existence of sub-classifications, keys, alternative schemes and so on.

These matters obviously tie in with the variables discussed already, e.g. flexibility and the number of features employed in making particular discriminations. Since much has already been written on this subject there appears little sense in repetition. It is clear that the careful delineation of selected semantic fields is a basic ingredient of any research strategy in this area.

Terminology, nomenclature and taxonomy

There has been great emphasis in the literature on meticulously dissecting and not confusing these three things, both in biological and folk classification (McLean and Ivimey-Cook, 1956; Conklin, 1962). However, there is considerable variation in the ways in which they are related in different systems. This has already come in for some discussion, particularly the extent to which terminologies (morphosyntactic features) are a guide to actual classificatory practice. Literacy effectively emphasizes the arbitrariness of the relationship between names and signs, and so we might reasonably expect the distinction between terms and taxa to be more important in scientific schemes. This is not so true for folk classifications, where naming and the meaning of names is generally more significant in both "mundane" and ideological classificatory contexts. The extremes of inseparability and total arbitrariness are rare. Much more common is a mixture of the two, and this we would expect since classification and speech are bound together intricately. So although it may be analytically important to distinguish between these phenomena, it would be misleading to assume that they always serve different purposes.

Integration in semantic fields

Finally, classifications might conceivably be ordered in terms of the degree to which semantic fields are autonomous. Although all non-literate classifications of an empirical nature possess contradictions, they are like some other systems in that in the absence of further inputs they tend towards symmetry and economy. This appears to be a cerebral condition for the efficient storage of information. The categorized items tend to be simplified to a cognitively satisfactory form (e.g.

Miller, 1956); distinctive features are restricted to the minimum neces-sary, and haphazard assemblages become ordered through binary oppositions (e.g. Lévi-Strauss, 1966, pp. 66–8). Thus, if particular fields possess such tendencies it is reasonable to expect groups of different fields in the same society, all things being equal, to *tend* towards a unity. All semantic fields are linked to others in some way, such as in the marginal overlap of content, but the degree to which they are integrated into a single system, through common organizing prin-ciples, metaphorical and symbolic links, does vary.

Durkheim and Mauss (1963, pp. 81–2) saw primitive societies as representative of ideal classificatory integration, but this specifically related to a "symbolic" level of experience, which was distinguished from the merely "technological". Although they are not entirely clear on this matter, their contention that "technological" schemes have no relation to "a first philosophy of nature" or "the origins of the logical procedure which is the basis of scientific classifications" has been refuted by modern work on folk classification. Rather than contrasting with one another, such classifications seem to merge, but the degree to which this is so varies, perhaps with the elaboration of "symbolic" schemes themselves. I return to this matter below.

V

It would be foolish to think that these variables fit neatly together, thereby allowing the construction of a simple typology. Though certain characteristics may reinforce one another because of their logical dependence and certain complexes may emerge under particular social circumstances, it is impossible to construct an infallible cross-cultural set of rules. In place of this I would argue the case for what might be called a classificatory substantivism.

I take it as axiomatic that all classifications are discursive practices situated in a given social matrix and general configuration of know-ledge and ideas (*epistemes*, ideologies . . .), and that they are products of specific histories (see Reason, this volume; Bourdieu, 1977). What we have relatively little systematic information on, and for which an effective framework has yet to be devised, are the various social condi-tions which determine and correlate with particular articulations of the variables discussed. Like the variables themselves, many of these social conditions are interdependent, but this should only assist us in locating particular classification–context linkages.

It is convenient to recognize two kinds of social condition: *situational* and *structural*, although I would shrink from giving this distinction any rigid analytical weight. Situational conditions reflect intracultural variation determined by either the *specific social context* of classificatory activity, or the *material or perceived content of different semantic fields*. Different social contexts may give rise to flexibility and differential consistency in the use of classifications which must be considered when eliciting their formal structure. Similarly, there are semantic field-dependent differences related to the phenomena being classified. On these grounds we would expect differences between natural species, cultural artefacts, social groups, abstract concepts and so on; and between analytic (part–whole) and synthetic (class inclusive) fields. This is not to deny that one type of field will influence the structure of another. We also find that particular kinds of natural species, because of either morphological or behavioural characteristics, have the effect of lessening inconsistency and flexibility (Ellen, 1979); and that particular objective arrays of species in a local environment will affect patterns observed in the classifications (Hunn, this volume).

Structural conditions are those that are predicted by specified social and economic relations, and the functions of those relations. One of the most important of these is the *division of labour*. The greater the specialization of work in society, the greater the scope for specialist-specific classificatory knowledge, and the greater the division of knowledge in classifications (see Bousfield, this volume). Complex occupational structures often result in the institutionalization of classification, as in craft guilds and professional associations. Not only does the subject-matter become group- or institution-specific, but also the ways of ordering that knowledge and its socialization. With institutionalization, too, come more strict beliefs about normal and deviant interpretations.

Although variation demonstrably exists according to particular function, attempts to group particular kinds of classification by gross functional attributes have been less successful. An example is the distinction made by Berlin and his associates (1966) between special-purpose and general-purpose schemes. Folk classifications are special, determined by specific subsistence and other culturally defined requirements; while scientific classifications are seen as general and logical, derived naturally from a consideration of all other data. Bulmer has argued the opposite (1970), and now Berlin (1974, p. 267) appears to agree that in this sense folk and scientific taxa are fundamentally alike. It is interesting that Berlin should choose to use the terms special-purpose and general-purpose in the way that he did, as in another sense they might have been used the other way round. Scientific classifications are developed by *specialist* groups in society for a highly esoteric purpose—the pursuit of knowledge itself. Folk classifications are generally not the product of groups of specialist minds, and must have general cognitive and social utility.

In Durkheimian theory, changes in the division of labour are linked to changes in the kind of *social integration*. Douglas (1966, p. 112) and Lévi-Strauss (1966, p. 138) have followed this line in attributing to "primitive society" an all-embracing, dynamic and undifferentiated world-view integrated through symbolic classification, in contrast to the partial, static, differentiated and relatively unintegrated ones of advanced societies. However, they differ from it—knowingly or unknowingly—in not distinguishing "technological" from "symbolic" levels of ordering experience (Morris, 1976, pp. 543, 553, and this volume; Bloch, 1977). The distinction does not seem to have been noticed either by some of the formalists; this misunderstanding underlies part of their critique of the sociologists (see Hunn, this volume).

There are two points which might be made here. The first is that the Durkheimian model is inadequate in the light of ethnography. Some politically complex societies seem to show a relatively high level of symbolic integration (China, the Incas, . . .), even on the admission of Durkheim and Mauss themselves; while some small groups of food collectors show fragmented and apparently unconnected classifications of natural species. Morris (1976, pp. 543–5, 552, and this volume) reports that the Hill Pandaram of South India employ classifications highly individualistically and that these are "largely independent of other aspects" of culture. There are no elaborate schemes of augury, animals and plants do not feature in ritual processes or ceremonial, and there is no totemic system. Not only are Hill Pandaram classifications limited in scope, but they are relatively unconcerned with systematization. They do not have a systematic knowledge of their natural environment clearly expressed in formal taxonomies. As I interpret it, this does not suggest that their knowledge is limited, that categories cannot be analysed as parts of a rational scheme, or that the *kinds* of categories are radically dissimilar from those found in other societies. These points have been raised seriously as objections to Morris's analysis (Berlin, n.d.). Rather than being concerned with abstract and generalized formal classifications, he is concerned with use, degree of sharing and the relationship to a wider realm of ideas and practices.

What seems to be important, then, are the various constraints and degrees of permissiveness associated with different social forms. In simple societies, scale and organization allow either alternative. But why this should be so—why certain communities have elaborate ideational patterns linking diverse aspects through symbolism into a single totality—is a crucial problem for investigation in its own right (Bloch, 1977; Morris, 1976, p. 544). In more complex societies, scale and organization act as constraints. So, whereas we may find surprising instances of symbolic integration, these tend to operate as parts of either subordinate or dominant schemes in ideologically plural societies, are reified in written doctrinal codes or relate to organizationally trivial levels of experience.

Societies of widely differing types often have a number of different classification schemes operating at both technological and ideological levels, but the range of variation is large. Although Durkheim and Mauss distinguished "technological" from "symbolic" classifications and report the Chinese system itself as being composed of "a number of intermingled systems", their argument assumes an unjustifiably neat correspondence between a uniform classification and the integration of society (Needham, 1963, pp. xviii–xix).

The second point is that the relations of the "technological" with the "symbolic" and the "mundane" with the "ritual", are genuinely problematic. Clearly, analytical demands enforce what may seem to be empirically distinct, but the total separation made by Durkheim and Mauss, which is supported by Bloch and Morris, is surely unwarranted. All so-called "mundane" classifications reflect relatively complex semantic fields, involving other fields, metaphorical extensions between them, and so on. Evans-Pritchard's discussion of Nuer colour terms for cattle derived from different animal species is a good example. The degree to which they are integrated will vary of course, but unless the distinctions are made explicit culturally there are no grounds for assuming them to be contrasted operationally. There are several ways in which the character of this interrelationship can be demonstrated.

One way is to emphasize the arbitrary location of boundaries drawn between the "mundane" and the "ritual", and the imprecision of the various terms used to designate these as substantively different types of classification. It seems that the distinction was used by Durkheim and Mauss to separate subsistence from non-subsistence spheres of activity, hence the use of the term "technological" for the former. Although this term is not entirely unambiguous, its suggested synonym "mundane" poses greater difficulties. I understand by this term such classifications that are derived from human practice on nature, whether this be "naturally" or socially constructed, rather than from the need to legitimate authority. But this world concerns spirits, as much as motor cycle spares, kinsmen as much as biota, time as much as topography and anatomy. The Nuaulu of eastern Indonesia recognize numerous spirit categories in much the same way as they recognize categories of animals. The way in which the fields are organized are similar and there is even an area of overlap where objectively invisible forms are grouped with visible ones, and vice versa (cf. Evans-Pritchard, 1956, p. 178; Douglas, 1975, p. 30, on "spirit animals"). Along with plants and animals, spirits inhabit the Nuaulu universe in every conceivable niche; in the same way that both flora and fauna threaten and help them, so spirits too have this basic ambivalent nature (cf. Kesby, this volume). The essential unity and continuity of supernatural and natural, visible and invisible taxa is also highlighted in the ambivalence shown over the correct classification of the numerous monsters in myths and stories.

Another way in which the interrelations between the "mundane" and "ritual" can be shown is that in both there exist essentially similar modes of information organization (Brown *et al.*, 1976). Although dualism originating in ritual can affect "mundane" schemes, dichotomous division is always at work in the ordering of categories of perception in both scientific (especially as keys) and folk classification (Bulmer, 1970, p. 1082; Bulmer and Tyler, 1968, p. 375). Such distinctions may form the basis of ideological oppositions. Symbolism can affect "mundane" categories; labels may evoke symbolic resonances and relations between species may be expressed through myth (Rosaldo and Atkinson, 1975, p. 50), but there is no predictability in such correspondences (Friedberg, this volume).

Then again, although the distinction between "mundane" and "ritual" fits quite well when dealing with terminal taxa or "natural

B

kinds" (Bulmer and Tyler, 1968), where there is a direct connection with observable reality; the arrangement of categories of higher order becomes increasingly prone to ideological invasion.

But to demonstrate empirical connections is not necessarily to undermine the theoretical or methodological significance of the distinction, any more than Weber's demonstration of the specific links between capitalism and protestant religon undermine either the distinction between base and superstructure, or Marx's separation of knowledge from ideology. It is because knowledge and ideology are conceptually different, and because methods have become somewhat confused with data, that there is some mutual enmity between the formalists' and sociologists' approaches to the study of classifications. The former have been concerned with "mundane" "technological" knowledge, with a view of culture which does not stress integration; the latter have been concerned explicitly with ideology, with a stress on symbolic integration (Bloch, 1977). It is also because there is an empirical overlap between method and data, knowledge and ideology, that Berlin, Bulmer, Douglas and others can present us with such apparently different explanations of the same thing. It is only when these various strands have been unravelled that we can talk legitimately of the logical primacy of knowledge over ideology, and the "perceptual" and "mundane" over the "ritual" and "symbolic".

It is reasonable to assume that the classification systems of all societies tend towards integration, economy and structural conformity between historically unique events. This is a feature of most social systems and sub-systems about which we are knowledgeable. But, equally, no system or sub-system can ever be a single, integrated totality; there will always be behavioural traits that do not "fit". This is both because socialization is never perfect—there is always a large element of individuality—and because societies and their environments change. And so we have the paradox that integration takes time, but time itself disintegrates.

Those social forces which encourage integration include social interaction itself, institutionalization and the relative importance of *social learning*. These are all devices which promote consistency, while having the inevitable consequence of promoting deviance and criticism. Although in all societies knowledge is based on personal experiences, its relation with that acquired through social learning varies. In small-scale food-collectors such as the Hill Pandaram the element of social learning is relatively small; in highly centralized state societies it may be paramount and enforced through specialized institutions such as schools. But it also seems to be related to a number of other dependent variables, such as the degree of symbolic integration, division of labour, scale, level of hierarchy and *literacy*.

Literacy is a key condition permitting greater complexity, quantitative elaboration and the recording of classificatory data for future use. Although there appear to be general properties of human thinking with regard to the number of items that the brain can handle at a given time (e.g. Miller, 1956), there is no similar limit imposed by written systems. In non-literate societies the entire content of cultural tradition, except artefacts, is held in memory. Purely oral discourse tends to emphasize group ideas and attitudes rather than those of the individual (Goody and Watt, 1968, p. 30). Language is learned in intimate association with community experience, individually through face to face contact. Information acquired in this way is stored in the brain, though much is generally forgotten. This is so, despite the possible use of mnemonic devices to assist information storage, such as formal speech, ritual recitation, music, professional remembrancers and the like (Goody and Watt, 1968, pp. 30–1).

The invention or introduction of writing may be critical in determining classificatory activity. Its potentialities, though, depend very much on the particular constellation of traits in the society concerned, such as the materials available, types of graphic form and means of organizing communication. Literacy—whether general or restricted—permits the construction of more elaborate schemes and the manipulation of letters, words and numbers, encouraging new directions in literature, art, mathematics and science; it also has uses in the sphere of social control. Literacy encourages reflective, analytical and sequential thought, the development of syllogisms, rigorous logics and the division of knowledge into autonomous specialist disciplines (Goody, 1968, pp. 17–18; Dolby, this volume). In fact, the cognitive products of written language are so pervasive that there is a tendency in European culture not to recognize them for what they are. As Whorf pointed out, European thought has been moulded from Aristotle to the present-day by a whole series of practices associated with the keeping of written records (Whorf, 1956, pp. 153, 238). It is also probable that the notion of taxonomic hierarchy is in part linked to attempts to represent classificatory relationships graphically and in writing.

With the signs of literate communication it is not always clear what is being signified. Meanings are not simply apparent through use, but are collected in dictionaries. Words acquire successive layers of historically validated meanings, whereas in oral communication the meaning of a word is ratified repeatedly in concrete situations, with vocal inflections and physical gestures. These combine to particularize its specific denotation and accepted additional usages. The process operates cumulatively and becomes more deeply socialized.

Literacy also reveals inconsistencies in classification. But the inconsistency of the totality of written material is less remarkable than its size and historical depth. Unlike the mind, it cannot unconsciously adapt and omit, and therefore the information it stores can only grow. Because there is no comparable means of elimination, no "structural amnesia", individuals cannot take part in a total cultural tradition as is possible in a non-literate society. Reading and writing are normally solitary activities. The degree of "semantic contact" is reduced. Because of this, culture may be more easily avoided and is also committed willy-nilly to an ever-increasing series of culture lags (Goody and Watt, 1968, p. 57). And because of all these things the ideologies and sets of knowledge of literate societies cannot possibly have, through elementary classifications, the same interconnection with other aspects of the social structure as is the case in small-scale societies (see Goody, 1968, p. 5).

Division of labour is closely linked to *social inequality*; the two phenomena reinforce each other and the first is a necessary historical condition for the latter. There are two aspects of inequality which must be considered here.

The first follows directly from the creation of different groups based on their relationship to the means of production. Classifications, knowledge and attitudes towards them, vary according to sex, age, occupation and class position. In small-scale societies, certain kinds of esoteric information are the property of descent groups or particular individuals of high status. Scientific biological classifications developed very much in the context of bourgeois European culture, where learning itself was an important social marker.

The second is that the types of inequalities and hierarchies present in a society shape wider structures and attitudes to classification, as well as the structure of classifications themselves. To paraphrase Marx, the dominant classifications are generally those of the ruling groups in society. They are part of an ideology with an important social control function. The various means by which classificatory uniformity is imposed therefore become critical: rote-learning, passing examinations and government control of communications and schools.

Inequalities can affect all social knowledge and often even the identification of natural species may be arrived at by deferring to the knowledge of a person of higher status, rather than of proven greater knowledge.

The extent to which a hierarchical notion of classification is itself a function of hierarchical systems of social order is still highly problematic. In some cases "taxonomy" fits well with hierarchical ideologies and in such a way that we might reasonably expect them to be related. I think it is not too fanciful to imagine this to be the case for Aristotelian Greece and post-Linnaean systematics. It may also be the case in some folk systems, such as Tzeltal. On the other hand, hierarchical social systems may have non-hierarchical classifications, as in Mohist China. What may be important, however, is the existence or otherwise of *any* hierarchical model as an idiom to express "natural" relationships, kinship, historical time and biota. This kind of argument would explain certain features in the schemes of the Hill Pandaram and other immediate-return food-collecting societies, where group structure is highly flexible and genealogical organization shallow, bound only by a few rules.

It is this kind of argument that Bloch has suggested specifically for "ritual" classifications, but it might well apply to "mundane" ones as well. In the realm of ritual classification, correspondences with social hierarchies are much more obvious and predictable. It has been suggested that binary opposition must be the correlate of hierarchy in any semantic theory (Fox, 1975, p. 118), but there is a danger here of confusing social inequality with metaphorical usages of "hierarchy", which, as we have seen, may be replaced by other means of expressing inclusivity. This is not to deny, though, that both may be intensified and elaborated through the development of particular kinds of hierarchy (insiders : outsiders; royalty : commoners; bourgeois : proletariat . . .)

Finally, there is *utility*. At a general, commonsense level it is easy to see a relationship between certain aspects of classification systems and the patterns of use. But while it is undeniable that such relationships exist, the extent to which they do so is highly variable; both in terms of the Nida–Conklin hypothesis, the idea that the vocabulary of particular fields expands in proportion to their social importance (see Hunn, 1975a; Ellen, 1975), and the relationship between structure and social use (Bulmer and Friedberg, this volume).

VI

The mix of variables in any given society will affect the structure, content and function of classification systems in terms of the variables listed in Section IV. But this does not say a great deal. To what extent is it justified to expect to find a series of correspondences in various aspects of a given ideology which include the classification systems of a society? How far can we really predict that particular kinds of societies and ideologies will give us particular kinds of classification systems?

Through cross-cultural analysis it is possible to demonstrate correlations between pairs of variables; between complexity and division of labour, literacy and arbitrariness, semantic field integration and social integration, and so on, linking the formal properties of particular classifications (Section IV) with the substantive ones of the societies in which they are found (Section V). If we could eliminate all other variables we might reasonably expect such *horizontal* pairs to show a regular correlation. The problem for the anthropologist, and one reason why I am suspicious of attempts to seek constant macro-relations between classifications and types of society defined in terms of vague and general criteria, is that it is not always possible to find predictable regularities in the *vertical* relations between variables. For example, literacy does not always accompany hierarchy, social learning is important in many oral cultures and not in others, and the same is true of literate cultures. Rigorous expression of inclusiveness may eliminate anomaly as well as generate it. The pattern observed and the extent to which particular pairs of correlations are evident depend upon the entire nexus of variables.

Having understood this it is then possible to proceed to analyse the organization of classifications in particular cases and, for particular semantic fields, how these might affect discontinuities in the structures of different kinds of field and how we might distinguish these objectively in the first place. Thus, there is still much to be discovered about the structural and sociological differences between classifications of living species compared with physical objects, abstract concepts and systems of signs. In such investigations it is not always helpful if we are tied to ideological distinctions *a priori*, such as those between "scientific" and "folk".[5] Inevitably, such an enterprise also involves an investigation into methods of demarcating boundaries of semantic fields, areas of overlap and fuzziness. Then there is the question of the logical and historical primacy of different fields, and the processes which create new ones. There is the issue of variation, both in the ultimate sense of the number of different constructions that can be put on any one field (cf. Douglas, 1975, p. 10), what determines this and what the limits (if any) are; and also variation in the sense of how this is defined by any one society. The degree of ambiguity of cognitive norms and the extent to which they are endorsed for a particular semantic field vary over time and from one field to another. New information will be accepted more easily the more it accords with current cognitive and technical norms and the more widespread the agreement as to what those norms are (Mulkay, 1972, pp. 16–17).

This paper has been concerned, then, with the social nature of classification, though not the simple social determination of cognition espoused by either Durkheim or (in his very different way) Whorf. Neither is it an apology for the despair of historical particularism. In fact, I have suggested a marriage between the formal and the sociological approaches. This does not involve a denial of the validity of research and speculation on the cerebral aspects of classifying, the seeking of pan-human invariants and evolutionary generalities (e.g. Berlin, 1970); it simply emphasizes the complexity of the social variables and the subtle relationships between them and the genetic predisposition of the brain. The rigid dichotomy between mind and material world, between mode of representation and represented, breaks down at this point, and it is no good seeking solace in a hopeless and fallacious social relativism (Macrae, 1976; Bloch, 1977, p. 282). Our categories may well be socially constructed and yet still refer to the real world (Engels, 1934). Perhaps part of the difficulty is that classifications are not, in the last instance, "things" at all (Bourdieu, 1977; Reason, this volume), but are simply the objectification of a process: classifying. However, in so much as we treat them as things, and I think this is unavoidable, it is the examination of less ideologically complex systems (those we describe as either "mundane" or "technological") that can be among the most helpful processes used to reveal that "hidden architecture" of subtleties, asymmetries and indeterminacies in structure, dynamics and operation (Lehrer, 1974, p. 325) which is characteristic of all semantic fields. It follows that these also provide a convenient focus for the investigation of more fundamental philosophical issues.

Empirical generalizations and phenomenological descriptions of the association between classification and social form in different societies are undoubtedly useful, but the resulting typologies are inevitably superficial. It is insufficient and misleading to embark upon intellectual paper-chases to reveal "inner essences" through their reflection in classifications. The possible outcomes, like those for certain kinds of structuralist analysis, are as numerous as the anthropologists on the job. They should certainly not pass for causal explanation, which can only be found in specific studies of the mechanisms operating in empirically observable schemes.

Notes

1. Foucault (1972) has objected to being bracketed with structuralists and those of a structuralist persuasion, and in a sense he is correct. In so far as he is a substantivist he could never be a Lévi-Straussian, but in so much as he seeks to unearth the "structure" of an *episteme* which is internally consistent and has a logical structure related to language form, it is understandable that Leach (1976) should mistake him for one. After all, Foucault himself has remarked that "structuralism is not a new method; it is the awakened and troubled consciousness of modern thought" (1970, p. 268); a characterization that might well be applied to his own *oeuvre*.

2. Some of the obvious objections to Durkheim and Mauss are given by Rodney Needham (1963). Bloch (1977) has recently taken up the subject again, but is surely mistaken in believing that there has been no theoretical challenge before his own (see also Hunn, 1976, and this volume; Worsley, 1956).

3. Within ethnobiology, Bulmer (1974, pp. 79–81) has identified a number of fairly distinct orientations—lexicographic, formal, social, biological and natural–historical. With typical modesty he places himself in this latter category. While amateur natural history may have been his initial motivation, he is now more of a vigorous hybrid, confirming his own remarks on the overlap between these areas. It seems to me that this is an increasing trend with, for example, biologists making significant contributions to the anthropological literature (e.g. Dwyer, 1976a, b).

4. Despite a great deal of attention in the literature there is still much to be discovered about anomalies. Most work has so far been on morphological and behavioural anomalies, as represented by Douglas's pangolin, Bulmer's cassowary and Borge's *Imaginary Beings*. But there are also those created by the use of language. Among such *semantic* anomalies are the paradoxes of Hui Shih in *Chuang Tzu*, e.g. the propositions "the tortoise may be longer than a snake" (longevity) and "white dogs may be black" (eyes) (Needham, 1962, p. 197). We might add "blackbirds may be white" (albino) or metaphors such as "The White House is Red" (politically) (see also Sperber, 1975a).

5. This is not to deny differences between "folk" and "scientific" classifications, for a denial would undermine the possibility of an anthropology of knowledge. But stark oppositions generally contrive to obscure the historical and structural continuity between the two. Dissimilarities tend to be substantive rather than formal: a technical concern about objectivity and utility. For example, folk systems are generally related to a conception that knowledge may accumulate but in the end is finite and cannot change; science is not so strictly bound by this view, although the conceptions of certain kinds of scholar (those we label "empiricists") may approach it.

There are several good reasons, then, for paying attention to early scientific schemes (Peeters, this volume), but one of immense importance is precisely their transitional and heterogenous nature; they have not been swallowed up by an all-consuming phylogeneticism. Thus, Foucault (1970, p. 39) tells us that Buffon expressed astonishment on discovering that the work of a naturalist like Aldrovandi contained such an inextricable mixture of exact description, reported quotations, fables without commentary, remarks dealing indifferently with the animal's anatomy, its use in heraldry, its habitat, its mythological value, or the uses to which it could be put in medicine. Such a hotchpotch comes as no surprise to the practical ethnographer of folk biology in contemporary, small-scale, non-literate societies. Schemes such as Aldrovandi's do not represent bad science but parts of rational, ideological constructions of knowledge for the societies that produced them.

References

ARDENER, E. (1971). Introductory essay: social anthropology and language. In "Social Anthropology and Language" (Ed. E. Ardener). Ass. Social Anthrop. Monogr. No. 10. Tavistock, London.

BERLIN, B. (1970). A universalist – evolutionary approach in ethnographic semantics. In "Current Directions in Anthropology" (Ed. A. Fisher). Bull. Am. Anthrop. Ass., 3, 3–18.

BERLIN, B. (1974). Folk systematics in relation to biological classification and nomenclature. Ann. Rev. Ecol. Sys., 4, 259–71.

BERLIN, B. (n.d.). "Whither the savage mind?—Yonder, classifying and well, as is its nature". Unpublished manuscript.

BERLIN, B., BREEDLOVE, D. and RAVEN, P. (1966). Folk taxonomies and biological classification. Science, 154, 273–5.

BERLIN, B., BREEDLOVE, D. and RAVEN P. (1973). General principles of classification and nomenclature in folk biology. Am. Anthrop., 75, 214–42.

BLOCH, M. (1977). The past and the present in the present. Man (N.S.), 12, 278–92.

BORGES, J. L. with GUERRERO, M. (1969). "The Book of Imaginary Beings" (Revised, enlarged and translated by N. Thomas di Giovanni in collaboration with the author). Jonathan Cape, London.

BOURDIEU, P. (1977). "Outline of a Theory of Practice" (Trans. R. Nice), Cambridge Studies in Social Anthropology No. 16. Cambridge University Press, Cambridge.

BROWN, C. H. et al. (1976). Some general principles of biological and non-biological folk classification. Am. Ethnol., 3, 73–85.

BULMER, R. (1967). Why is the cassowary not a bird? A problem of zoological taxonomy among the Karam of the New Guinea highlands. Man (N.S.), 2, 5–25.

BULMER, R. (1970). Which came first, the chicken or the egg-head? *In* "Échanges et Communication: mélanges offerts á Claude Lévi-Strauss" (Eds J. Pouillon and P. Maranda), Vol. 2. Mouton, The Hague, Paris.

BULMER, R. (1974). Memoirs of a small game hunter: on the track of unknown animal categories in New Guinea. *J. d'Agric. trop. bot. appl.*, **21**, 79–99.

BULMER, R. (1975). Folk-biology in the New Guinea highlands. *Soc. Sci. Inform.*, **13**, 9–28.

BULMER, R. and TYLER, M. J. (1968). Karam classification of frogs. *J. Polynesian Soc.*, **81**, 472–99, 82–107.

CLARKE, D. (1968). "Analytical Archaeology". Methuen, London.

CONKLIN, H. C. (1962). Lexicographical treatment of folk taxonomies, *Intern. J. Am. Linguistics*, **28**, 119–41. *In* "Problems in Lexicography" (Eds F. W. Householder and S. Saporta), Publication 21. Indiana University Research Center in Anthropology, Folklore and Linguistics, Bloomington. Reprinted (1969). *In* "Cognitive Anthropology" (Ed. S. Tyler).

CONKLIN, H. C. (1964). Ethnogenealogical method. *In* "Explorations in Cultural Anthropology" (Ed. W. H. Goodenough). McGraw-Hill, New York.

CONKLIN, H. C. (1972). "Folk Classification: A Topically Arranged Bibliography. Department of Anthropology, Yale University.

COXON, A. P. M. and JONES, C. L. (1979). Images and predication: the use of subjective occupational hierarchies. *Quality and Quantity*, **13**, 121–40.

DOUGLAS, M. (1966). "Purity and Danger". Routledge and Kegan Paul, London.

DOUGLAS, M. (1972). Self evidence. *Proceedings of the Royal Anthropological Institute of Great Britain and Ireland for 1972*.

DOUGLAS, M. (1975). "Implicit Meanings: Essays in Anthropology". Routledge and Kegan Paul, London and Boston.

DURKHEIM, E. and MAUSS, M. (1963). "Primitive Classification" (Trans. R. Needham). Cohen and West, London.

DWYER, P. D. (1976a). Beetles, butterflies and bats: species transformation in New Guinea folk classification. *Oceania*, **46**, 188–205.

DWYER, P. D. (1976b). An analysis of Rofaifo mammal taxonomy. *Am. Ethnol.*, **3**, 425–45.

ELLEN, R. F. (1972). The Marsupial in Nuaulu ritual behaviour. *Man (N.S.)*, **7**, 223–8.

ELLEN, R. F. (1975). Variable constructs in Nuaulu zoological classification. *Soc. Sci. Inform.*, **14**, 201–28.

ELLEN, R. F. (1977). Anatomical classification and the semiotics of the body. *In* "The Anthropology of the Body" (Ed. J. Blacking). Academic Press, London and New York.

ELLEN, R. F. (1978a). Restricted faunas and ethnozoological inventories in Wallacea. *In* "Nature and Man in Southeast Asia" (Ed. P. A. Stott). School of Oriental and African Studies, London.

ELLEN, R. F. (1978b). "Nuaulu Settlement and Ecology: An Approach to the Environmental Relations of an Eastern Indonesian Community". Verhandelingen van het Koninklijk Instituut voor Taal-, Land- en Volkenkunde No. 83. Martinus Nijhoff, The Hague.

ELLEN, R. F. (1979). Omniscience and ignorance: variation in Nuaulu knowledge, identification and classification of animals. *Language in Society*, **8** (2).

EMBER, M. (1973). Taxonomy in comparative studies. *In* "A Handbook of Method in Cultural Anthropology" (Ed. R. Naroll and R. Cohen). Columbia University Press, New York and London.

ENGELS, F. (1934). "The Dialectics of Nature". Progress Press, Moscow.

Evans-Pritchard, E. (1956). "Nuer Religion". Clarendon Press, Oxford.
Foucault, M. (1970). "The Order of Things: An Archaeology of the Human Sciences". Tavistock, London.
Foucault, M. (1972). "The Archaeology of Knowledge". Tavistock, London.
Fox, J. J. (1975). On binary categories and primary symbols: some Rotinese perspectives. In "The Interpretation of Symbolism" (Ed. R. Willis), Ass. Social Anthrop. Stud. No. 2. Malaby, London.
Frake, C. O. (1962). The ethnographic study of cognitive systems. In "Anthropology and Human Behaviour" (Eds T. Gladwin and W. C. Sturtevant). The Anthropological Society of Washington, Washington. Reprinted (1969). In "Cognitive Anthropology" (Ed. S. Tyler). Holt, Rinehart and Winston, New York.
Friedberg, C. (1968). Les méthodes d'enquête en ethnobotanique. Agric. trop. Bot. appl., 15, 297–324.
Friedberg, C. (1970). Analyse de quelques groupements de végétaux comme introduction à l'étude de la classification botanique Bunaq. In "Échanges et Communications: Mélanges Offerts à Claude Lévi-Strauss" (Eds J. Pouillon and P. Maranda), Vol. 2. Mouton, The Hague, Paris.
Goody, J. (1968). Introduction. In "Literacy in Traditional Societies" (Ed. J. Goody). Cambridge University Press, Cambridge.
Goody, J. and Watt, I. (1968). The consequences of literacy. In "Literacy in Traditional Societies" (Ed. J. Goody). Cambridge University Press, Cambridge.
Harris, M. (1969). "The Rise of Anthropological Theory: A History of Theories of Culture". Routledge and Kegan Paul, London.
Hempel, C. G. (1965). Fundamentals of taxonomy. In "Aspects of Scientific Explanation" (Ed. C. G. Hempel). Free Press, New York.
Hunn, E. (1975a). The Tenejapa Tzeltal version of the animal kingdom. Anthrop. Quart., 48, 14–30.
Hunn, E. (1975b). A measure of the degree of correspondence of folk to scientific biological classification. Am. Ethnol., 2, 309–27.
Hunn, E. (1976). Toward a perceptual model of folk biological classification. Am. Ethnol., 3, 508–24.
Kay, P. (1971). On taxonomy and semantic contrast. Language, 47, 886–7.
Lakoff, G. (1972). Hedges: a study in meaning criteria and the logic of fuzzy concepts. In "Papers from the eighth Regional Meeting, Chicago Linguistic Society", Chicago.
Lamarck, J. B. (1963). "Zoological Philosophy, an Exposition with Regard to the Natural History of Animals" (Translated with an introduction by H. Eliot). Hafner Publishing Company, New York and London.
Leach, E. (1961). "Rethinking Anthropology". L.S.E. Monogr. Social Anthrop. No. 22. Athlone, London.
Leach, E. (1976). "Social Anthropology: A Natural Science of Society?" From the Proceedings of the British Academy No. 62. Oxford University Press, Oxford.
Lehrer, A. (1974). "Semantic Field and Lexical Structure". North Holland, Amsterdam.
Lévi-Strauss, C. (1966). "The Savage Mind". Weidenfeld and Nicolson, London.
McLean, R. C. and Ivimey-Cook, W. R. (1956). "Textbook of Theoretical Botany", Vol. 2. Longmans, London.
Macrae, D. (1976). The naming of names (review of "Implicit Meanings" by Mary Douglas). Observer Review, 25 January, 30.
Miller, G. (1956). The magical number seven, plus or minus two: Some limits on our capacity for processing information. Psych. Rev., 63, 81–97.

MORRIS, B. (1976). Whither the savage mind? Notes on the natural taxonomies of a hunting and gathering people. *Man (N.S.)*, **11**, 542–57.

MULKAY, M. J. (1972). "The Social Process of Innovation: A Study in the Sociology of Sciences". Macmillan, London.

NEEDHAM, J. (1962). "Science and Civilization in China: 2. History of a Scientific Thought". Cambridge University Press, Cambridge.

NEEDHAM, R. (1963). Introduction. *In* "Primitive Classification" (Eds E. Durkheim and M. Mauss) (Trans. R. Needham). Cohen and West, London.

NEEDHAM, R. (1971). Introduction. *In* "Rethinking Kinship and Marriage" (Ed. R. Needham), Ass. Social Anthrop. Monogr. No. 11. Tavistock, London.

NEEDHAM, R. (1975). Polythetic classification: convergence and consequences. *Man (N.S.)*, **10**, 349–69.

PECK, A. L. (1965). Introduction. *In* "Aristotle: Historia Animalium" (Trans. A. L. Peck). Heinemann, London.

RADCLIFFE-BROWN, A. R. (1957). "A Natural Science of Society" (Foreword by Fred Eggan). The Falcon's Wing Press, Glencoe, Illinois.

RANDALL, ROBERT (1976). How tall is a taxonomic tree? Some evidence for dwarfism. *Am. Ethnol.*, **8**, 229–42.

ROSALDO, M. with ATKINSON, J. M. (1975). Man the hunter and woman: metaphors for the sexes in Ilongot magical spells. *In* "The Interpretation of Symbolism" (Ed. R. Willis), Ass. Social Anthrop. Stud. No. 2. Malaby, London.

SOKAL, R. R. and SNEATH, P. H. (1963). "Principles of Numerical Taxonomy". Freeman, San Francisco and London.

SPERBER, DAN (1975a). "Rethinking Symbolism" (Trans. Alice L. Morton). Cambridge University Press, Cambridge.

SPERBER, DAN (1975b). Pourquoi les animaux parfaits, les hybrides et les monstres sont-ils bons a penser symboliquement? *L'Homme*, **15**, 5–34.

WHORF, B. L. (1956). "Language, Thought and Reality". Massachusetts Institute of Technology Press, Boston.

WILLIS, R. (1974). "Man and Beast". Paladin, London.

WORSLEY, P. (1956). Emile Durkheim's theory of knowledge. *Sociol. Rev.*, **4**, 47–62.

2

The Rangi Classification of Animals and Plants

John D. Kesby

I

The universe as experienced by the Rangi

The Rangi live at the southern end of the mass of hill-country which begins in the north beside the Lake Rudolf depression, and then extends southwards till it dies out, in Rangi country, north of the Gogo plains. Most of the Rangi live in the Kondoa District of Tanzania. There are about 150,000 of them, mostly engaged in intensive farming. They speak a Bantu language, although their area of the Tanzania Rift Highlands is linguistically complex, and none of their immediate neighbours speak a language even remotely related to the Bantu group.

Certain features of their country are important since they limit the Rangi view of what exists to be classified. I shall have to return to these features in more detail later, but it is worth stressing at this point that, unless Rangi go to the coast to work, they never see the sea. There is no Rangi word for the sea, nor for sharks nor whales nor other sea creatures. Furthermore, there are no large lakes in Rangi country, and only two small lakes. The seasonal swamps (*mbuga* in Swahili, *nyiha* in Rangi) are all small; and the streams are rarely full of water, all of them being dry or else mere trickles most of the time. The only large river near to Rangi country is the Bubu (called Dudu by Rangi, who have adopted the Alagwa name for it) and even that never reaches the sea, but dies out in an extensive swamp to the south, in Gogo country. In spite of this relative shortage of water, Rangi do attach some importance to water creatures, as I shall show later, even though there used to be no fish in their country, and they have no indigenous word for fish.

Turning from their surroundings to their perception of these surroundings, Rangi assume that all events, good or bad, stem ultimately from the activity of God (*Mulungu*). Human prosperity depends utterly upon God's power to provide food, health and children. Only the Roman Catholics, a minority of Rangi, have abandoned the major annual ritual at the beginning of the wet season, which entails the sacrifice of a black sheep in each locality, so that the rains will be good and the year go well. Also, only the Roman Catholics have abandoned the occasional sacrifices to the ancestral dead (*varimu*) in times of trouble, such as individual illness. Although the power of God, expressed in part through ancestors, is everywhere, and does everything, God is associated especially with the sun, the sky and the tops of high hills.

Given that food, health and children are supremely desirable (*-aboha* in Rangi), drought, famine, illness and barrenness are supremely undesirable (*-aveha*). These disasters come about through an interference with the proper links between people and God, either through immoral conduct or through sorcery (*usave*). In discussing animals further on, I shall have to draw these distinctions between desirable and undesirable features of experience, as well as between sky and earth, and between water and earth.

For the Rangi, as for other peoples, the sources of divine power or, more cautiously, ultra-human power,[1] lie outside their local community and indeed outside the world of humans altogether. God is linked with the sky, above the earth, and the whole body of *varimu* are associated especially with the uninhabited areas of hill and bush country, away from the fields and houses of the named settlements. Rangi are not clear whether all the *varimu* were once living people. Possibly they once were. At present, however, most of them have lost their individual identity and the links between the *varimu* and living Rangi are maintained by visitations in dreams from recognizable dead kinsmen, for instance a grandfather, and by sacrifices made by Rangi to the *varimu*, when occasion demands. The recognizable dead among the *varimu* are thus mediators, both in the sense used by Lévi-Strauss, and in that used by Christian theologians, between people, on the one hand, and the ultra-human powers, ultimately vested in God, on the other.

This distinction between divine power, from sky and hills and bush, and the relative powerlessness of the human communities, who need but cannot provide that power, implies a distinction between "outside" and "inside", between ultra-human and human. A very elegant example of this inside–outside dichotomy has been given by Middleton (1960) for the Lugbara.[2] As with the Lugbara, Rangi see the local community and human affairs as orderly and moral, whereas divine power is unpredictable and ambivalent, bringing both weal and woe. Those *varimu* who are not known ancestors could bring disaster as well as blessing, and it is the prerogative of both God and the ancestors to punish people who have offended them in some way by causing something nasty, like illness, to happen to the offenders. The "outside" is associated with ambivalent power and with unpredictable events. Significantly, adultery, that is disorderly copulation, is said by Rangi to occur in the bush, whereas coupling between people married to each other is regarded as taking place inside houses, that is in the human, not the ultra-human, zone.

Less impressive than the superhuman powers are neighbouring human groups. Rangi recognize all the nearby language-groups, for example Sandawe and Burunge, and have a name for each of them. There is no hostility as such towards any of them, and before 1900, apparently, much of the fighting in which Rangi were involved was between Rangi groups, and not between Rangi and non-Rangi. Rangi see neighbouring groups as people like themselves, except that they recognize that Maasai (*Vuumba*) and Datoga (*Vamang'ati*)[3] have a different (i.e. wholly pastoral) way of life. Hence Rangi express reservations about marrying into these two ethnic groups, but, in fact, some Rangi do intermarry with them.

Not only are non-Rangi groups recognized and named, but there are also different groups acknowledged within the Rangi. Haubi Basin people regard Rangi in the Kolo area as Alagwa, and not true Rangi, and they consider Rangi in the Mondo area to be Burunge. As opposed to the people of the "outside", there are the people "inside" one's own moral community. These are divided into *vanduu* (=*vanduhu* in Kolo area), kinsmen, and *vakuyu*, neighbours. Between "insiders" and "outsiders" the "mediators", as everywhere, are the people who marry between the small local communities.

Each of these small communities, effectively between 100 and 200 people, has as its setting (the "stage" on which they live their lives): the cycle of the seasons; of day and night; and also the cardinal directions. These events are all "outside" the activities of the community. Directions are geared to the sun's path, from east to west. Here there is a vague, but only vague, connection between, on the one hand, the east, life and birth, and, on the other, the west and death. Many peoples are much more explicit about these connections than are the Rangi.

At present, Rangi usually describe north and south by the Swahili terms, but until recently they called the north *umbuwe*, country of the Mbowe, and the south *uoo*, country of the Gogo, that is by the names of foreign groups, thus, perhaps only incidentally, linking human to cosmic events.

The times of day are named according to the position of the sun, but the sun does not define the year, which is recognized as the completion of a full cycle of wet and dry seasons, and of sowing and harvest. There are twelve months in the year, and these are defined by the waxing and waning of the moon. One explicit link between people and the rhythm of the universe is the Rangi description of a menstruating woman: *alwiire mweri*, "she is ill month/moon".

Rangi astronomy seems to be rudimentary, the only terms which I can discover being those for the sun, moon, stars, very bright stars, and the Pleiades. The sun is the supreme visible expression of God, but is not itself a person. A further link between the human community and super-human universe is that one of the names for colour-patterns in cattle is *irunyenyeri*, which refers to *nyenyeri*, the stars, and connects domestic animals ("inside") to the sky ("outside"). I shall come back shortly to the colour-patterns of domestic animals. In addition to the major events of the seasons and the sky, Rangi name types of both country and soil. On a much smaller scale, there usually[4] are some inanimate objects which are "inside" the community. These are man-made utensils and also houses. Rangi have a large vocabulary for these objects. For instance, they have different words for each of the types of wooden posts and poles from which they construct the walls and roofs of houses.

The remaining named features of the Rangi universe are the animals and plants, the domestic forms on the "inside", and the great majority on the "outside". Along with many other African peoples, for example the Nuer and Dinka,[5] Rangi have a complex vocabulary of names for colour-patterns on domestic animals. An impression of the degree of detail of this vocabulary may be gained from Table 1.

TABLE 1

Colour-patterns of domestic animals

A. Cattle

1) *irunyenyeri*	white back; brown expanses and brown spots on sides and legs	Derived from *nyenyeri*, stars.
2) *irutumbiri*	"blue" with black head and shoulders	Derived from *ntumbiri*, the vervet monkey.
3) *irufunde*	"blue"	Derived from *funde*, the shamba rat.
4) *irunyala*	?	Derived from nyala, the striped grass mouse.
5) *njiru*	Black	(The literal meaning of the stem -*iru* is black or dark).)
6) *njēru*[6]	white or pale, e.g. white with fawn blotches	(The literal meaning of the stem -*ēru* is white or pale.)

((7) and (8) refer not to colours, but to the shape of the horns.)

7) *irankorongo*	with the horns pointing forward and down	
8) *na mpēmbe ndee*	with upright horns; the connection between birds and upwards is important	(Literally: with horns birds.)

B. Goats

1) *irupici*	?	Derived from *mpici*, hyena.
2) *kisēne*	black head and neck, with a mixture of brown; white middle; black hindquarters; black legs, with a mixture of brown	This is connected with *njiva nkusēne*, the speckled pigeon, the link being their common colour-pattern.
3) *arankundu*	(literally: "red")	

C. Chickens

1) *iruvee*	grey, with darker barring	Derived from *luvee*, the lanner falcon and other falcons which have roughly this colouring.

There is one outstanding feature which recurs in the examples given in this table, and that is the use of wild creatures and even stars as models for the names of domestic animals, for instance in *iruvee* and *irunyenyeri*. This is another mediating link between "inside" and "outside", just as the sacrifice of a domestic sheep is an offering from the "inside" to the "outside". In this connection, it is worth noting that chickens are called by a term relating to birds, while cattle and goats are named after mammals. This is important in the light of the distinction between mammals and birds (*"vanyama"* and *ndee*), and between "below" and "above". I shall return to these themes later.

In addition to names linked to "outside" features, there are terms which are simply colour-categories: "black", "white", "red", or rather approximations to these colours. The Rangi only have three terms for colours, and all colours come under one of the three categories. I shall return later to this theme also.

A third observation worth making at this point is that the prefix *a-* in *arankundu* (B(3) in Table 1) is the one used for people, and implies a special connection between people and goats: goats are more like people than are either birds or snakes, for instance. Indeed, the use of the plural prefix *va-* in *"vanyama"* implies a special connection between people (*vantu*) and all mammals, but again I shall have to return to this point later.

Having noticed the symbolic link between "inside" and "outside" in the colour-patterns, this is an appropriate place at which to mention totems, since above all these share this "mediating" aspect, bridging the gap between "inside" and "outside". They are objects of the "outside" which are intimately linked with groups of people on the "inside". However, I need only to register the relevance of totems, since the Rangi have none.

Before passing on from domestic animals, it remains for me to comment on one further aspect of the links between them and wild creatures. Rangi have three different words for excreta. *Maavi* refers to the excreta of almost all animals, including people and the highly inauspicious hyenas. *Maavi* is nasty and to be avoided, and contrasts with the droppings of sheep and goats (called *mbibia*, sing. and pl.) which are benign and inoffensive, and the dung of cattle (*ntohe*),[7] which is positively beneficial, being stored and used as fertilizer on the fields. No Rangi farmer objects to getting dung on his hands, although he would certainly object to touching *maavi*. This distinction is not unusual. Indeed it recurs throughout Africa and Eurasia, reaching its highest intensity in India, where cattle dung is positively purifying; and it can be perceived in the different emotional toning of the English words "shit" and "dung". However, it is worth mentioning here because the distinction highlights the special status of cloven-hoofed, cud-chewing domestic animals in their mediating, even priestly, position between people and the dangerous "outside".

II

Animals and plants in a "three-tiered" universe

It is with the dangerous "outside" that most animals and plants are connected. I would like to leave the details of the Rangi classification of these to a later section, and to concentrate now upon the major features in the Rangi view of these creatures. In the first place, a great number of animals and plants are named by the Rangi, at least 250 animals and a similar number of plants.[8] The named animals are not only creatures which may be eaten, and not only these plus others used either as raw materials, or in medicine, or perceived as symbolically significant. Indeed, the great majority of names are those of creatures with no resounding significance in Rangi perception. Among animals, *mpici* (hyena), *muundi* (sheep), *njoka* (snake), *satu* (python), *luuvu* (chameleon) and *nkungu* (owl) are highly significant; but there is nothing about the words for them, in either pattern or phonetic features, to set them apart from the vast majority of other, and much less significant, names.

The Rangi have no word for "animals" as such, nor for "plants", but they do have six categories into which most living creatures are grouped, and these are:

ndee	birds and bats
"*vanyama*"	mammals, except bats and people
makoki	"creeping things"[9]
samaki	fish
miti	woody and large plants
masambi	small plants

I am convinced that *samaki* is a relatively new category, and that the term "*vanyama*" has been borrowed recently from the Swahili (*wanyama*) for a category which was, one hundred years ago or less, only implicit, although real, and unnamed.

In addition to these explicit categories, there are others which cut across them, but which are not apparent from the names themselves. These implicit categories are:

above and below;
night and day;
water and land.

They provide subdivisions within the explicit categories. As I shall try to show in the next section, there are, for instance, *ndee* of the night, of the water, of the land below and of the sky above.

At this point it is indeed possible to jump ahead of the evidence in the next section and, for the sake of clarity, suggest a pattern of significant animals which reflects the way in which the Rangi perceive the main features of their surroundings. Such a pattern takes the form shown in Table 2.

TABLE 2
Significant animals

Night (inauspicious)	Day (auspicious)
Ndee owl	eagle
"*Vanyama*" hyena	lion, leopard/sheep
Makoki snake	python

At this stage I am leaving out the finer divisions introduced by the implicit above–below-water categories, but I will come back to these.

When talking to Rangi I found that the important animals were prominent because of their repeated interest in them, and because of the way in which they talked about them. Also, when I was gathering together their words for animals and plants, the major categories, which are explicit, sprang to my attention. On the other hand, I would not have noticed the "outside–inside" distinction if I had not been struck by the Lugbara picture presented by Middleton. In the same way my attention was drawn to another feature of the Rangi's implicit categories by the much more overt schemes of other peoples in different parts of the world.

In Table 2 I have shown three categories, namely, *ndee*, "*vanyama*" and *makoki*. These correspond very closely with a distinction which occurs in all the major cultural regions of the world, although not necessarily in all known societies, and that is the division of events and objects into:

those of the sky;
those of here, where people are;
those more lowly than people.

These "tiers" of experienced reality are affirmed explicitly by most, or all, Siberian forest peoples, such as the Tungus and Yakut; and there seem to have been animals associated with each level, although contact with Russians has somewhat eroded these details.[10]

The three physical-cum-metaphysical levels are widely known among South American wet forest peoples. For many of these, eagles, jaguars and anacondas are linked with the sky, the earth and the waters, respectively. As I hope to show in the next section, the Rangi equivalent would be: eagles (and other soaring birds), lions and leopards, and pythons.

In order to emphasize here the widespread incidence of this "tiered" pattern, it is worth mentioning three Pacific examples, none of which have been demonstrated explicitly by the writers who report the relevant details. In New Caledonia, among Houailou and other groups, there is a pattern:[11]

frigate-bird
shark
gecko = sea-snake

The same pattern, with a modification, occurs on San Cristobal (and other eastern Solomon Islands):[12]

frigate-bird
shark
snake

In both these cases, the absence of mammal predators to fill the "like people" role has led these faunally impoverished people to put the shark in the jaguar–leopard niche.

The same is particularly true of the faunally poor Mejprat of Western New Guinea. For them the pattern is:[13]

hornbill
cassowary
python

Here, cassowary fills the "here on earth, similar to people" role, in the absence of any large mammals, apart from people and domestic pigs.[14]

I hope to justify this excursus to areas outside Africa when I discuss the Rangi classification in detail. At this point I want only to assert that Rangi are normal, and fit into this widespread human awareness of above–earth–below/waters.

III

The Rangi criteria for explicit and implicit classification

Turning from the grand design of the universe to the details of the Rangi's view of animals and plants, I would like to go back to their six major categories:

ndee	birds and bats (90 terms, at least)
"vanyama"	mammals, except bats and people (80 terms, at least)
makoki	"creeping things" (80 terms, at least)[15]
samaki	fish (2 terms)
miti	woody and large plants (100 terms, at least)
masambi	small plants (100 terms, at least)[16]

Rangi classify animals and plants into groups of only two, occasionally three, different orders of magnitude. They group most living creatures into the six major categories, and each of these, except *samaki*, contains a large number of named minor categories. *Samaki* is, it seems, a recently introduced category, and it is hardly a major category at all. I hope to show shortly that it can be seen best as being merged with *makoki*. In the case of some, but not most, minor categories, there is a sub-division. Thus there are four named types of dove within the category *njiva*, and at least six types of snake within the category *njoka*. If *samaki* is merged in *makoki*, then it contains two sub-categories. Some people may prefer to see the scheme rather differently, with terms like *njiva* and *njoka* occupying a middle position between major category and minor categories.

In having only two or three "levels" of classification, the Rangi scheme differs strongly from that of Linnaeus and, *a fortiori*, from

Linnaeus' contemporary followers, the professional taxonomists, who recognize twelve to twenty, or more, "levels" of grouping. Kingdoms contain phyla; phyla, classes; classes, orders; orders, families; families, genera; and genera contain species; but this is only a skeletal classification, since there are divisions, tribes, super-species and geographical varieties still to be considered.

However, although unlike a Linnaean scheme, the Rangi pattern is fairly close to Aristotle's version, and to the version of all European vernaculars. Indeed, it seems likely that all vernacular classifications are either two-tier or three-tier, and that the many-tiered, refined, Linnaean version is unusual to the point of uniqueness.[17] Implicitly, however, Rangi do subdivide the major categories, and group the categories within them; but this does not alter the essentially two-tier arrangement, since the process is implicit and there are no terms to denote the groups so formed.

If we consider the six major categories, we can see that they are familiar to us already, because they coincide, to a large extent, with European vernacular classifications. *Ndee* are set apart by their ability to fly, and then set apart from the flying *makoki* (the insects), by being warm-blooded. I suspect that what strikes the Rangi, though, is not their warm-bloodedness but the fact that their blood is red, i.e. like people's blood. However, no Rangi has ever commented to me on this topic. Like some European peoples, the Rangi classify bats and birds in one category. In Europe, it is naturalists, and not peasants, who see bats as mammals and therefore distinct from birds. From this it follows that Rangi and Europeans alike attach no great importance to feathers. Birds have feathers and bats have fur, but both are *ndee* to the Rangi.

Unlike the term *ndee*, "*vanyama*" is very rarely used by the Rangi, and this leads me to conclude that in the recent past the mammals (apart from bats and people) were an implicit category and that this is still largely true. "Vanyama" is borrowed from the Swahili *wanyama*, and borrowed well within the last hundred years. Indeed, I have never heard old or middle-aged men use the term. However, there is no Rangi term which "*vanyama*" has replaced, the significance of this being, I infer, that "*vanyama*" are creatures like people and therefore need no special term. It is the alien categories which require explicit qualification.

To Rangi, the resemblance between "*vanyama*" and people is most strikingly seen in their having red blood, in their genitals and in their manner of giving birth. However, to say that they are more like people than are, say, *ndee* or *makoki* is not to say that people are *"vanyama"*. That would be insulting to Rangi, as such comparisons usually are in other societies. The category *vantu* is separate from the six major categories. Implicitly, *vantu* are the subjects who do the classifying, and not the objects which are classified. Hence, I have excluded them from the account of classification.

In regarding people as a separate, unique category, the Rangi are in accordance with the vast majority of people the world over. Here again, the uniqueness of the post-Linnaean naturalists has to be emphasized. To them, *Homo sapiens* is a mammalian species, not part of a category "people" which is equal in taxonomic status to the category "mammals". Even so, the majority of, if not all, naturalists feel unconsciously the same demarcation as do the Rangi and other peoples: that is, people are unique. They are subjects, not objects; they are classifiers and not classified.

The third major category, *makoki*, includes creatures very unlike people. They correspond closely to the "creeping things" of the Authorized Version of Genesis. Insects, as naturalists call them, spiders, slugs and snails are all *makoki*, and so are lizards and snakes. Even small mammals, such as the slender mongoose (*Herpestes sanguineus*), are sometimes called *makoki*, but only rarely. Most Rangi regard small mammals as belonging to the (implicit) category *"vanyama"*.

Makoki are always small, compared with people, and are always low on the ground. Even the ones which can fly, such as butterflies and winged termites, are low on the ground when they *are* on the ground. Also, they are not red-blooded, or not visibly so, as are *"vanyama"* and *ndee*.

In this connection, there is a difference in both scale and emphasis between the Rangi classification and that of contemporary taxonomists. *Makoki* has the same status as *ndee* and *"vanyama"*, but whereas in contemporary taxonomic schemes birds and mammals are two distinct classes, the category *makoki* includes representatives of many different classes and even phyla. The phyla Platyhelminthes, Annelida, Mollusca and Arthropoda are all *makoki*, as are the vertebrate classes Batrachia and Reptilia.

The Rangi place much more importance on birds and mammals than on any other class of animals and this is clear from their detailed vocabulary. They have a word for elephant, one for jackal buzzard and one for spider. By taxonomists' standards, the elephant is one species, the jackal buzzard is one species, and spiders are an order, with probably hundreds of species in Rangi country. It is true that some words for birds and mammals indicate a group of species, rather than just one. An example is *mwevi*, meaning medium-sized-dark-coloured-bird-of-prey, which includes the black kite and marsh harrier. Even so, the difference in emphasis is consistent. There are more words for mammals and birds than for members of any other class of animals.

Jumping slightly ahead, it is worth noticing here that there are more words for flowering plants than for all the other kinds of plants and fungi put together. Some species of fungi are named, but I know of no term for fungi as a group, nor have I found names for either mosses or ferns. The Rangi pay more attention to flowering plants than to other types.

Once again, it is the naturalists and taxonomists who are unusual. In all languages where there is evidence available, and except in areas where these forms are scarce, mammals, birds and flowering plants are more richly named than are any other groups of organisms; and it seems likely that this will be found to be true of all languages. Very simply, it seems that birds and mammals strike most people as more like people than are other animals and therefore they attract attention; while flowering plants, with their varied colours and shapes, lend themselves to symbolic interpretation much more than do most other plants. Birds, mammals and flowering plants are also relatively large.

I shall need to return to the plant categories later, but at this point there remains the animal category *samaki*. Within living memory, the Rangi borrowed this term for fish from Swahili. When middle-aged men were boys, the term for fish was *soompa*, which the Rangi had most likely borrowed from the Sandawe[18] some time between 1880 and 1900, when they were acquiring fish from the Sandawe in trade-exchanges. If this is so, there remains the problem of what the Rangi term was for fish before they acquired the word *soompa*. At that time there were no fish in Rangi country, but there were fish in the Bubu River to the west. Middle-aged Rangi men still say that formerly they were not allowed to eat fish, although they do now. Further, they were not allowed to eat fish because fish are snakes (*njoka*); and this earlier attitude to fish coincides exactly with that of the Gogo and of other peoples of the Eastern Rift Highland zone. It seems likely, therefore, that around

1870, or before, the Rangi word for fish was *njoka* and, since *njoka* are *makoki*, fish were included in *makoki*. In this case, *samaki* cannot be treated as a major category but only as a sub-category within *makoki*, and this fits neatly with the distinction between above, here and waters/below, which I have discussed in the previous section and which I must shortly discuss further.

There are, then, three major categories of what, in English, are called animals. There are also two of plants. Their distinguishing feature, when contrasted with the three animal categories, is that, although alive and showing growth, they do not move as the animals do. The plants are then distinguished from each other, *miti* being large and/or woody and *masambi* being small and non-woody.[19] However, these criteria are quite implicit in the Rangi classification, as are all the others I have mentioned. It is I and not the Rangi who state them explicitly.

Another implicit feature is that *ndee* fly and are associated therefore with the air; *"vanyama"* are terrestrial and like people in most respects; and *makoki* are terrestrial, but intensely unlike people. Furthermore, the outstandingly important *makoki* include snakes (*njoka*) and python (*satu*). Although the Rangi themselves have given me no lead on this theme, people in different parts of the world repeatedly associate snakes with the earth and with water. This is true of great numbers of ethnic groups in both North and South America, other parts of Africa, India, China, New Guinea and Australia. I conclude that it is justifiable to maintain, as I have already done in the previous section, that implicitly Rangi are saying:

ndee	above
"vanyama"	here
makoki	below/water

The distinction between *makoki*, creeping things, and *samaki*, fish, is very recent, as I have tried to show, and the Rangi formerly experienced animals in three rather than four categories. With the adoption of the term *soompa*, and then *samaki*, the Rangi moved slightly towards the Hebrew four-category scheme of Genesis (1:20–5).[20] However, even in Genesis the waters are intimately linked, as they are universally in snakes, with lowly creatures, below people.

The classification is further complicated, because the three categories of animal are each represented by two highly significant animals, one of them auspicious and the other inauspicious, as in Table 2. As I have pointed out already, this inferred scheme is not fantastic because it is remarkably close to more explicit schemes of peoples in other parts of the world. The only truly dubious features of it are: the eagle, since I have not heard Rangi explicitly attach great importance to eagles; and, by contrast, the chameleon, which is the one highly significant animal not featured in the scheme.

The silence of the Rangi about eagles and other large soaring birds of "the above" is worth noting since other African peoples, e.g. the Nuer, clearly and explicitly attach great importance to these birds.[21] However, it must be significant that the Rangi will not eat them.

The chameleon, I suspect, merges with *njoka* (snakes), although the Rangi are not explicit about this issue. If I am right, there is a clear parallel to the situation in New Caledonia, where geckoes and sea-snakes are symbolically interchangeable.[22]

Given these points, the scheme is that owls are the inauspicious aspect of the above, paralleled by auspicious eagles, and probably the other large soaring birds. Among the animals most like people, hyenas are expressions of extreme evil, notably of the ultimate human wickedness of *usave*, sorcery. Hyenas are balanced out by lions and leopards, and in a special sense by sheep, which cleanse people from defilement by being sacrificed, presumably in people's stead: a life for a life, or a life for lives.

Sheep are linked explicitly with pythons in the farewell "*Lwata satu na muundi*", "tread python and sheep", and pythons represent the auspicious aspect of the below, which the Rangi associate implicitly with water. The malign aspects of *makoki*, below and water are *njoka*, snakes in general (but not pythons).

However, this does not exhaust the implicit classification within the five main categories, since the division above–here–below/water recurs *within* these explicit categories. I have not been able to detect any such further division within the plant categories, *miti* and *masambi*. No plants that I have come across are associated with the above, although it would be worth discovering the Rangi, and other African peoples', attitudes to mistletoes (Loranthaceae), which are associated with the above by some West European peoples, like the Gauls and Britains of the first century A.D. Also, although some plants grow in water in Rangi country, for instance *Typha latifolia*, the reed-mace, I have found no trace of a clustering of certain plants as specifically plants of the water.

Similarly, in the case of *makoki*, I cannot detect any subdivisions of the category. Most insects fly, but they are not seen high up in the sky as some large birds are, and no Rangi that I have met attach any importance to the fact that some *makoki* are water animals.

Among the *"vanyama"*, however, there are traces of a subdivision of the major category. Among mammals, bats are the outstanding candidates for placing in the above, since they fly; but bats are *ndee*, to the Rangi, not *"vanyama"*. On the other hand, hippopotami are known to Rangi and are associated with water. Although none of them live permanently in Rangi country, a hippopotamus wanders into the area from time to time, and there is a Rangi term for them, *ntoromondo*. Their association with water, symbolical as well as actual, was brought out when I was asking a group of men at Kolo the name for crocodile (*mamba* in Swahili). They hesitated. Actually, there are no crocodiles in Rangi country; but they were eager to put a name to them and the one they favoured was *ntoromondo*. To them, in some way, crocodiles and hippopotami are the same. Presumably, the link is that they are both large animals of the water. Eventually, though, they agreed that *ntoromondo* are hippopotami, and that there is no Rangi word exactly equivalent to the Swahili *mamba*. The Nuer again provide a parallel, since they attach some importance to the hippopotamus as representative of the water, and any babies which resemble hippopotami are put into the water, this being their proper element.[23]

Earlier in this section I have said that *"vanyama"* is the major category of creatures which are most like people. Sheep are sacrificed on behalf of people and hyenas represent human wickedness in its ultimate form, sorcery. Not surprisingly, the Rangi and their Alagwa neighbours regard eating hyenas with disgust; and they also feel that they may not eat leopards and lions, vervet monkeys and baboons.[24]

Presumably, vervets and baboons should not be eaten because they are so like people. Leopards and lions, on the other hand, represent majestic authority and are, if anything, more akin to the above than are any other *"vanyama"*. Their position is thus comparable to that ascribed to them by numerous other African peoples, for instance the Nuer[25] and the Banyang.[26] A parallel example from outside Africa is the position of the jaguar in the experience of tropical American peoples, which I mentioned in the previous section.

Implicitly, then, the *"vanyama"* major category, itself the middle term in the explicit tripartite tiering of the universe, is divided into the same three tiers internally, with lions and leopards "above", sheep and hyenas "here", and hippopotami "in the water", and implicitly, therefore, "below". This internal division is much clearer when we look at the *ndee*.

In the course of collecting the names of birds, I was struck by the haphazard way in which the Rangi attributed certain names to various water birds. The same name served different Rangi for birds of different orders. For instance, *njoēra* was, on various occasions, the red-bill (duck), the red-knobbed coot and the blacksmith plover. At the time,[27] I felt that it meant that most Rangi are unfamiliar with water birds and their names, and this is probably true. However, while writing out the names later, it struck me that the Rangi attitude is that as long as it is a water bird and they put a water bird's name to it, then that is good enough. I infer from this that to the Rangi water birds are a cluster, albeit implicit, within the *ndee*.

Another smaller cluster, of only four names, are the *ndee* of the night, including bats and the inauspicious owls (*nkungu*). These night birds are opposed to the day birds, as hyenas and snakes are opposed to sheep and pythons.

The birds of the day are then arranged in three tiers, with water birds quite clearly separate "below", large soaring birds, like storks and eagles, "above" and the remainder "here", where people are.

The five major categories, then, are distinguished from each other on the basis of their being either mobile or immobile. The two immobile among them, *miti* and *masambi*, are differentiated on the criteria of size and woodiness; while the three mobile groups, *ndee*, "*vanyama*" and *makoki*, are differentiated spatially, as being of the above, here, and of the below/water, respectively.

Turning from the major categories to the minor, it is necessary to make two preliminary observations, one about the Rangi and the other about their country. Rangi country is thickly inhabited and surrounded on all sides by areas of almost empty woodland. As a result there are many woodland animals which are abundant on the margins of Rangi country, but not where the majority of the Rangi actually live. Few Rangi see many lions, elephants, buffaloes or rhinoceroses. The only antelope at all abundant in areas settled by the Rangi is the little dikdik, and some birds, such as the grey hornbill, *Tockus nasutus*, are abundant in the woodlands, but not seen in the settled areas.

I have mentioned previously another limitation on Rangi experience imposed by their country: there is very little permanent surface-water, and hence no hippopotami, and no names even for crocodiles and fish. Another group of candidates for the below/water category, namely the otters, are also missing from Rangi country because of the shortage of surface-water.

As a result of the features of their country, the Rangi have a great deal of experience of some animals and plants and much less of others, so that they can name some with much more confidence than others. Age is also important. Small boys are, on the whole, good informants, being alert and lively, with good eyesight, but they are relatively lacking in experience. Middle-aged men, on the other hand, have far more experience, but often poor eyesight. However, if boys and middle-aged men agree in the naming of an animal or plant, the identification is more secure.

One very important feature of Rangi knowledge is that some individuals are much better informed than others, and can identify more animals and plants than can others. All Rangi can put creatures into the major categories in which they belong, but many are unable confidently to put a name to every animal or plant which they see. The situation is thus analogous to that in Europe, where naturalists are better informed than the majority of people, and where, even in rural areas, some men know much more about the local wildlife than do their neighbours. After I had been in Rangi country for two years and more, some men regarded me as knowledgeable because I knew the Rangi names of birds better than they did.

It is important to bear in mind that knowledge of the living creatures about them is not evenly distributed among the Rangi, but that the relatively knowledgeable and the relatively ignorant alike rely on the same criteria in telling one minor category or folk "species" from another.

These criteria are familiar to Europeans. The three which are always important are size, shape and colour. There are only three Rangi terms for abstract colour, as I have noted already, and they can be crudely translated as "black", "white" and "red". More precisely, however, the stem /-iru/ means dark-coloured, /ēru/ means light-coloured and /-nkundu/ means in the red—orange—yellow range.

For some animals, too, the sound which they make is critical in their identification. This applies to some birds, some orthopterous insects and to the cicadas. In these instances the names are usually, or perhaps always, onomatopoetic. Two examples of overtly onomatopoetic names are *ncēle*, applied to a species of black cricket, and *nkududu*, the slate-coloured boubou. I have not come across any examples of either animals or plants where the critical factor in their identification is their smell.

Granted the underlying agreement on criteria, I must stress again that some Rangi know more about animals and plants than do others. On one occasion a middle-aged man called a drongo *nkududu*. We both saw it but it made no sound, so he was unable to hear that it did not make the *nkududu* noise, as made by the true *nkududu*, namely the slate-coloured boubou. Both birds are black, of about the same size and shape, and the mistake was easily made. However, the birds look and behave differently in detail. Some Rangi, and most European bird-watchers familiar with African birds, would not have confused them. Greater experience makes the observer familiar with the idiosyncratic details, the "jiz", that separates one bird from another.

It would be tedious and unnecessary to go through a large number of names showing how they are discriminated by means of the criteria which I have outlined. As an example, I will take the cluster of water birds which I mentioned earlier in this section. In this instance, eleven names are used for a group of birds which includes at least sixty-two species, according to European naturalists. As I have noted already, there is a significant overlap in the use of these names, but it is possible to discover a pattern from the information given by the Rangi who are best informed about water birds (Table 3).

TABLE 3

The Rangi classification of water birds

	Dark	Dark and Light	Light
Very large		(Wading) *mpohe* (Swimming) *ibata*	
Large	*ikomanjoka*	*nkoromēro*	
Medium-sized (wading)	{ *ing'ang'a* *nkune* }	{ *kinkurinkuri* *ikongolimambo* }	*munyanke*
	(separated by sound)	(separated by sound)	
(swimming)	*njōēra*		
Small	*kidukwi*		

In the same way it is possible to infer a pattern of falconiform birds. Excluding the very distinctive secretary bird, which may not even be falconiform, the Rangi have six terms which they apply variously to the raptors which they see. There are at least thirty-six species of this group in Rangi country, and these are named according to size and colouring. Thus the term *mwevi*, already mentioned, refers to raptors which are medium-sized and dark-coloured, while *luvee* is used of the lanner falcon, peregrine and African hobby, which resemble each other in colouring and shape, although differing in size. *Ihungungu* is most often used of the jackal buzzard, although it is sometimes applied to other large and strikingly marked birds of prey.

A more complex pattern is presented by the small passerine birds. The sunbirds, with their distinctive long curved beaks, are clearly set apart by the Rangi from other small passerines, and so are those species which have long tails, for instance the paradise and straw-tailed whydahs. However, these exceptions still leave a large number of species to name. Rangi employ about twenty terms for the great mass of the small passerines, although there are at least eighty species of this group in the area. The names seem to refer to fixed points of reference in the small passerine complex, but are used by extension for other rather undistinctive but similar species.[28] One firmly fixed point is the term *kidwedia*, applied consistently to *Cisticola chiniana*, the rattling cisticola, whose call the name represents. Small brown birds which are not heard to make any sound are also readily called *kidwedia*. Other important focal groups, with names attached, are the yellow weavers (*Ploceus*) and the red-and-black bishops (*Euplectes*).[29] Even though the European naturalist may consider that most of the Rangi discriminate inadequately between small passerines, twenty terms in common use shows some degree of refinement.

IV

Conclusions

In the light of Rangi knowledge, there are a number of conclusions which, however obvious they may seem, are worth emphasizing.

1) The Rangi, like most or all other peoples, have a very large vocabulary of names for animals and plants, that is, some five hundred

terms, probably many more. However, the distinctions between the creatures so named are based upon a few simple criteria.

2) Most living creatures known to the Rangi are divided between five major categories:

Three of these are of mobile creatures (animals in English) and two are immobile (plants). The immobile are divided between *miti* and *masambi* on the basis of size and/or woodiness.

3) The mobile creatures (animals) are divided spatially and coincide with: the above, here and below/water. Furthermore, this tripartite spatial division occurs implicitly *within* the two categories *ndee* and *"vanyama"*.

4) Within each of the major categories are numerous minor categories, or folk "species", some of which are divided further by Rangi. These "species" are distinguished from each other on the basis of three criteria: size, shape and colour. In the case of some birds and insects, sound is the critical diagnostic feature.

5) The Rangi have only two, or at most three, "levels" of classification, namely the major and the minor categories, and sometimes further subdivisions of the minor categories. In this respect they differ from post-Linnaean naturalists and taxonomists, but they resemble all other groups of people whose classifications have been even partially investigated.

6) Lying behind the explicit Rangi ordering of animals and plants is the unspoken assumption of a division between "inside", where "we" are, and an "outside", which is alien. On the "inside", the people of the community are feeble compared with the overwhelmingly powerful forces of the "outside"; and they perform rituals, hoping thereby to keep themselves from being crushed by those forces. I have to say "hoping" because the performers of the rituals appreciate that the initiative lies not with them, but with the ultra-human powers.

Naming the features of experience is a minimal ritual, establishing contact between people and the essentially uncontrollable features of experience, which are felt to be "outside" "us". Naming events or objects does not, in their own view, give the Rangi power over them. The initiative remains ultra-human and not human. However, it is necessary to be in contact with uncontrollable external events, or else the classifiers know nothing which is "not-us", and hence, lacking anything with which to contrast themselves, lose all sense of their own being.

Notes

1. Lienhardt (1961, pp. 28, 29).
2. Middleton (1960, pp. 230–8).
3. The letters *ng'*, with apostrophe, represent the sound at the end of English "sing".
4. They are inanimate unless animated "miraculously", as the British would say, by ultra-human power.
5. Evans-Pritchard (1934); Lienhardt (1961, pp. 10–15).
6. The letter $\bar{e}$ represents the vowel in English "then".
7. *Ntohe* is the dung as it drops from the beast. When it has been stored in a heap it is called *ncukuru*. In writing Rangi terms the letter c has the value of the consonants in English "church".
8. I suspect that these figures could be doubled by prolonged travelling with the Rangi in areas of dry woodland well away from the settled areas.
9. Genesis 1:24, Authorized Version.
10. For a thorough but wooden coverage of the Siberian details, see: Holmberg (1964, reprint, Part 2, pp. 317, 318, 439, 440, 498–518). Eliade has relied heavily on the Siberian peoples for his book "Le Chamanisme" (e.g. 1964), and information on the "three-tiered" cosmos occurs repeatedly throughout.
11. Leenhardt (1930, pp. 184–94). In the light of the information in this account, compared with that on neighbouring south-west Pacific peoples, I feel justified in finding this pattern in New Caledonia, although the writer himself does not stress this point. The same applies to my view of Fox's and Elmberg's accounts.
12. Fox (1924, pp. 236–40, 267–76).
13. Elmberg (1968, especially pp. 219, 223, 227, 278, 279).
14. Bulmer (1967) comments on this unbirdlike role of the cassowary in a New Guinea symbolic scheme, that of the Karam (Kalam).
15. *Makoki* can be subdivided into taxonomists' categories as:
    Reptiles (15 terms, at least);
    Batrachians (one term, at least);
    Insects (50 terms, at least);
    Arachnids (4 terms, at least);
    Myriapods (one term, at least);
    Molluscs (2 terms, at least, i.e. slug and snail);
    Annelids (2 terms, at least, i.e. earthworm and leech).
16. The Rangi also have at least six terms for different forms of fungi, but they do not seem to have a term for fungi in general. However, they may recognize fungi as an implicit category.
17. Berlin *et al.* (1973).
18. The Sandawe themselves had probably borrowed the term from the Rimi some time before 1870.

19. It is worth noting that large numbers of *miti* take the prefixes *mu-* and *mi-*, respectively, in the singular and plural, and that large numbers of *masambi* take the prefixes *i-* and *ma-*.
20. This is a five-category scheme if domestic animals are separated from wild mammals (Genesis 1:24, 25). Such a pattern is still consistent with the Rangi criteria, since Rangi implicitly do the same as the Hebrews. Another variation in categories, but with similar criteria to those of the Rangi, occurs among the Gimi (Glick, 1964), and yet another, but again with similar criteria, among the north-eastern Thai (Tambiah, 1969), where water creatures are separated from creeping things, as among the Hebrews.
21. Evans-Pritchard (1956, pp. 3, 88, 90).
22. Leenhardt (1930, pp. 184–6).
23. Evans-Pritchard (1956, pp. 84, 89, 98).
24. Unlike the Rangi and Alagwa, the Sandawe used to eat all four of these kinds of mammals, although they have given up eating them since their reliance on hunting has diminished and they have become relatively more dependent on farming for a livelihood.
25. Evans-Pritchard (1956, pp. 290–3), where the leopard-skin worn by the priest shows his powerful connection with God and the above.
26. Ruel (1969, pp. 49–59).
27. I was with the Rangi from 1963 to 1966.
28. Hunn (1976).
29. A very distinct group, readily recognized by most Rangi and not included in the 20 terms mentioned, are *vinandau* (singular: *kinandau*), which comprises the swallows, martins and swifts, birds resembling each other closely in appearance and habits, but belonging to two separate orders.

References

BERLIN, B., BREEDLOVE, D. E. and RAVEN, P. H. (1973). General principles of classification and nomenclature in folk biology. *Am. Anthrop.*, 214–42.
BULMER, R. (1967). Why is the cassowary not a bird? *Man (N.S.)*, **2**, 5–25.
DIAMOND, J. (1966). Zoological classification system of a primitive people. *Science*, **151**, 1102–4.
ELIADE, M. (1964) (English Trans.). "Shamanism". Routledge and Kegan Paul, London.
ELMBERG, J. E. (1968). "Balance and Circulation". Monogr. Series No. 12. Ethnological Museum, Stockholm.
EVANS-PRITCHARD, E. E. (1934). Imagery in Ngok Dinka cattle names. "Bulletin of the School of Oriental Studies", London Institution, Vol. VII, Part 3.
EVANS-PRITCHARD, E. E. (1956). "Nuer Religion". Clarendon Press, Oxford.
FOX, C. (1924). "Threshold of the Pacific". Routledge and Kegan Paul, London.
GLICK, L. B. (1964). Categories and relations in Gimi natural science. *In* "New Guinea, the Central Highlands" (Ed. J. B. Watson). *Am. Anthrop.* Special Publication.
HOLMBERG, U. (1964) (reprint). "The Mythology of All Races, Vol. IV: *Finno-Ugric, Siberian*". Cooper Square, New York.
HUNN, E. (1975). A measure of the degree of correspondence of folk to scientific biological classification. *Am. Ethnol.*, **2**, 309–27.

HUNN, E. (1976). Towards a perceptual model of folk biological classification. *Am. Ethnol.*, **3**, 508–24.

LEENHARDT, M. (1930). "Notes d'Ethnologie Néo-Calédonienne", Travaux et Mémoires VIII. Institut d'Ethnologie, Paris.

LIENHARDT, R. G. (1961). "Divinity and Experience". Clarendon Press, Oxford.

MIDDLETON, J. (1960). "Lugbara Religion". Oxford University Press, London.

RUEL, M. J. (1969). "Leopards and Leaders". Tavistock, London.

TAMBIAH, S. J. (1969). Animals are good to think and good to prohibit. *Ethnology*, **8**, 423–59.

3

Mystical and Mundane in Kalam Classification of Birds

Ralph Bulmer

This paper examines the relationship between the everyday, general purpose classification of birds by the Kalam of the New Guinea Highlands and their attribution of ritual or mystical significance to certain categories of birds. It suggests that the material and mystical attributes of birds are closely integrated in Kalam thinking, so that in a sense mystical significance is built into, or partially expressed by, the general classification. However, one can also identify birds of mystical significance as either the most salient (frequently, the largest) species in the Kalam classificatory groups in which they occur, or as being singular in some aspect of their behaviour relevant to man, and in this respect distinguishable either from all other birds, or from all other birds in the lower-order categories to which they belong.

In a previous paper (Bulmer, 1978) I argued that while it is very true that animals are "good to think", *which* particular animals are thought about, either as totems or otherwise ritually significant, is not unrelated to which of them are good to eat. Thus I attempted to demonstrate, in the case of the Kalam of the New Guinea Highlands, that those creatures which are salient in the everyday, general purpose classification of the people (a classification which is demonstrably related, in part, to economic evaluations) are also, by and large, those marked for totemic and other forms of ritual recognition. An important point to note in this argument is that is not necessarily the animal kinds whose individual members have the highest economic value which are chosen—though in some instances this is the case; even less is it the animal kinds which contribute most, in gross, to the economy, which are marked. What does appear to be the case, at least for the Kalam, is that it is the animals which are either the most salient representatives of classes that are collectively of some positive or negative material significance, or which are the most unusual members of these classes, which are ritually marked. Put another way, what Douglas (1966) and Tambiah (1969) might regard as "anomalous animals" certainly show some tendency to be ritually marked; but so also do the animals which are the most prominent and notably "typical" representatives of their groups; creatures which, in some respects, bear analogous positions to the "type species" of Linnaean genera.

In this argument I was building on Radcliffe-Brown who, in my view, was, with certain qualifications, right when he stated, in that well-known and much-criticized passage, that,

any object or event which has important effects upon the well-being (material or spiritual[2]) of a society, or anything which stands for or represents any such object or event, tends to be an object of the ritual attitude.

(Radcliffe-Brown, 1952, p. 124)

In this previous paper I was also questioning an assertion by Peter Worsley (1967, pp. 153–6), based on his presentation of material from the Aborigines of Groote Eylandt, that there is no connection between everyday classifications of animals and plants, and their totemic classifications.

I made a further point in the same paper, which also derives ultimately from Radcliffe-Brown, that if one is trying to understand the ascription of particular animals to a particular ritually significant series (e.g. "clan totems", narrowly defined), then one needs to review all ritually significant series in the culture concerned, and the extent to which these appear to be mutually exclusive. Such an examination should yield additional understanding of the principles of selection for each separate, or overlapping, list.

The purpose of this paper is to consider two criticisms which have been levelled at the previous one. I shall take one of them quite briefly, the other at some length.

The first, raised initially by Lester Hiatt, concerns the degree of circularity in my exposition of the relationship between ritual marking and taxonomic status. Might one not as well suggest that ritually marked creatures assume taxonomic salience, as that taxonomically salient creatures tend to be ritually marked? The second, raised most cogently by Peter Dwyer, questions the objectivity of my judgements of "taxonomic salience".

The short answer to the first criticism is that in so far as everyday, or general purpose, classifications and ritual classifications can be distinguished from each other, a two-way relationship between them must be expected; and, depending on how important animals are in everyday contexts, the contribution of the categories of everyday experience will vary. Thus one might expect that in hunting and gathering societies the contribution of everyday knowledge and classifications of animals and plants will normally be very great; whereas in societies which have changed with time so that direct interaction with wild nature is not a significant part of everyday experience, ritual and symbolic associations of animals may both bear little relation to the natural behaviour of the creatures concerned, and go so far as to dominate everyday classifications of them. We should recall Evans-Pritchard's (1956, p. 135) comments on the continuing importance of big game animals in African totemic belief long after they have become locally extinct. There is a pretty thin line between some of these creatures and Leach's (1954, pp. 112–13) Kachin *baren* and, for that matter, dragons—Chinese, Welsh, St George's or otherwise.

However, in the present context we may note that in his 1929 discussion of totemism, Radcliffe-Brown was restricting himself to the Australian Aborigines and to other hunting and gathering societies. He was arguing the positive case that animal and plant species which are significant in the lives of hunting and gathering peoples tend to be the objects of the ritual attitude, not, I think, trying to explain why, in the case of peoples with other types of economy, certain animals which are of no everyday significance may retain ritual importance.

Thus, from now on I shall restrict myself to a consideration of the second criticism, which is concerned with the problem of *objectively* defining taxonomic salience. I shall consider only birds: I have little to add to the information on other animals of ritual importance which is included in my previous paper.

The list of birds which I present now (see Table 1) is based on a re-examination and amplification of my fairly complex and extensive data on this topic undertaken by one of my long-term Kalam assistants, Ian Saem Majnep, and myself, when Saem visited New Zealand for three months in 1974–75. At that time we drafted a book called *Birds of my Kalam Country*, the main text of which is provided by Saem, who also decided what birds should go together in each chapter, and in what order the chapters should appear.

TABLE 1

Birds of ritual or mystical importance

1) "Super-totems", i.e. taxa subject to avoidance (of killing, eating, naming) at certain times by all Kalam, in relation to most important horticultural activities: cassowary; harpy-eagle.

2) "Totems", i.e. taxa which many Kalam must respect at all times (not kill or eat) on account of hereditary associations: sooty owl; flying fox.

3) Transformations of human souls in dream experience:
    (a) as mens' souls: five species of lories, one of which, the Papuan lory, is also subject to nest avoidance; typical goshawks (two species);
    (b) as womens' souls: three species of long-tailed birds of paradise, especially greater sicklebill.

4) Messenger-manifestations of ghosts:
    willie-wagtail; pied chat; mouse-warbler; the first two of which are never eaten (partly because they are unclean birds) and should also not be killed.

5) Omens:
    (a) of death: king parrot, and possibly also some other rare parrots. (Also, in some contexts, totems, e.g. (2) above, and Papuan lory, 3(a) above).
    (b) of ill-success in hunting: king parrot; owlet-nightjars; black-mantled cuckoo-shrike; black fantail (sometimes); friendly fantail (sometimes).

6) Manifestations of witchcraft:
    magpie-lark/river-flycatcher; slatey thicket flycatcher; wild duck; cuckoo-dove (sometimes); black fantail (sometimes); "spirit-whistler" (? migratory waders) (sometimes; alternatively interpreted as manifestation of ghosts).

7) Significant in ritual:
    (a) named in male beauty ritual chants: five species of lories; zoe fruit pigeon; racquet-tailed kingfisher; friendly fantail;
    (b) named in war-ritual; goshawk; pitohui;
    (c) plumage used in marriage ritual: woodswallow;
    (d) hunted and cooked in initiation ritual: boobook owl.

8) Other mystical significance:
    (a) association with taro: mountain pigeon;
    (b) association with seasons: rainbow bird;
    (c) significant in dream experience, as indicator of success in self-decoration: boat-billed flycatcher.

In attempting to explain why it is that the species listed in Table 1 are ritually or mystically significant, I shall first outline the formal taxonomy which the Kalam apply to birds; then discuss the extent to which what I call "the principle of natural taxonomy" is recognized by the Kalam; then put forward what I presently see as the main factors by which groups of birds are distinguished and evaluated, and individual species or species-like taxa are evaluated by the Kalam.

The Kalam with whom I have worked apply some 180 terminal taxa (smallest standardly named categories) to the different kinds of flying birds and bats which they place in the primary taxon (largest named category) *yakt*. Cassowaries, which are very large flightless birds, are not normally regarded as *yakt*; but they are certainly associated with birds and in some contexts, e.g. name taboo, the cassowary can be referred to as "the large bird", which is why, after some debate, Saem included a chapter on the cassowary in our book.

The formal taxonomy is shallow. The majority of terminal taxa are immediate subdivisions of "*yakt*", e.g. the white cockatoo is just *wtay* or *yakt wtay*; but in about 30% of cases the immediate, named subdivisions of *yakt* have two or more named divisions themselves; and just one or two of these subdivisions are further subdivided, so that in these very restricted areas the formal taxonomy has four levels.

All but a very few kinds of birds are eaten by the Kalam at least occasionally, and many kinds are highly esteemed as foods. Some 40 kinds have plumage that is valued for personal adornment, and a few have other parts with either ornamental or technological uses. A sizeable minority of Kalam men and boys are enthusiastic and highly competent bird hunters, and these tend to be very knowledgeable about birds; but any Kalam would have a knowledge which would at least equal, and probably exceed, that of the average Western European country-dweller.

I have asserted in earlier publications (e.g. Bulmer, 1970, 1974) that, as far as vertebrate animals are concerned, the Kalam have a very good appreciation of natural species, in that, in the overwhelming majority of cases where they are dealing with creatures with which they are reasonably familiar, they recognize the distinctiveness of what modern scientific zoologists identify as "species". This is quite simply because, in any restricted geographical area, the majority of vertebrate species are readily distinguishable from each other by a large number of characters of appearance and behaviour, so that if one is hunting them or in other ways consciously interacting with them with any intensity, the recognition of species differences is virtually inevitable.

It is important for my present argument to make the further point that the Kalam are well aware of certain groupings higher than the species, in which a number of species (which are in fact in most cases related in zoological "genera" or "families") share a complex of morphological and behavioural characters. Notable examples, where the Kalam appreciate the association of four or more related species are: hawks and falcons; parrots; and within the parrots, lories, or lorikeets, i.e. nectar-feeding smaller parrots; pigeons; "typical" nectar-feeding, long-beaked honey-eaters; and medium sized birds of paradise and bower birds. I must stress that they do not have standard names for these "natural" groups—they are what Berlin calls "covert categories" or "complexes" (Berlin *et al.*, 1968, 1974, pp. 59–61)—but their reality in Kalam thinking is unquestionable. Saem's chapter contents (see Appendix) illustrate this. On the other hand, where a "natural" group of only two or three species exists in Kalam territory, and there are many of these also, both within and outside the covert categories I have mentioned (e.g. cuckoos, cuckoo-shrikes, quails and kingfishers, which are not in the larger covert groups; and goshawks, cuckoo-doves and medium sized birds of paradise of *Lophorina* and closely related genera, contained within them), Kalam do tend to have names for them—and the named groups thus constituted account largely for these areas of the formal taxonomy which have three or four levels.

These "natural" taxonomic groups and covert categories above the level of the species are important to my argument, as when the Kalam are discussing and defining such groups, they tend to do so by taking the *largest typical species* as the reference point for comparison. Where they do not take the largest as the reference point, it is almost always the case that the largest is either very much less familiar than some other kind, or it is atypical of its group in certain respects other than size; or where both these conditions apply.

For example, among pigeons the largest is the zoe fruit pigeon (*Ducula zoeae*), and they do sometimes name this species first and use it as their reference, but it is rare locally, and usually they take the largest common pigeon instead, the mountain pigeon (*Gymnophaps albertisi*), which is abundant. Among the honey-eaters, the largest typical common ones are the sibling species Reichenow's melidectes (*Melidectes rufocrissalis*) and Belford's melidectes (*M. belfordi*), and they name these first. There is a larger species, the New Guinea friar bird (*Philemon novaeguineae*), which is also quite familiar to them, but this is atypical of the group in a number of respects, in its appearance and behaviour.

The same pattern appears when the Kalam discuss other groups of fauna—mammals, reptiles, frogs, grasshoppers. Thus I feel confident in asserting the following proposition: "In Kalam animal classification, within any formally recognized taxon or covert category, size, other things being equal, implies salience".

Granted that, in the chapters of Saem's book, birds are grouped in terms of several other principles which I shall proceed in a moment to discuss, as well as in terms of natural taxonomy (that is, the grouping of phenomena in terms of degrees of general similarity based on multiple criteria), it is still instructive to note that of the fourteen chapters in which the species discussed vary significantly in size, eight start with accounts of the largest included; three more with the largest member of the main sub-group of birds discussed; and in only three chapters is a bird which is not the largest in either of these senses taken first.

How might one interpret the rating the Kalam give to size? Obviously large birds have more meat and feathers on them than small ones. Further, assuming that all classification is anthropocentric, one may note that larger birds also approximate more closely to the size of man than do small ones; and, perhaps more significantly, in human society parents are larger than children, elder siblings are larger than younger, and men are larger than women. As in many other Melanesian societies, both mature adult males in the prime of their lives, and also leaders in the community, regardless of their physical size, are referred to, literally, as "big men" (*b yob*).

However, natural taxonomy and relative size are not the only principles which underly Kalam discrimination and evaluation of birds and other creatures. Several others may be inferred and I shall discuss briefly six of these. These are:

1) forest birds are to be distinguished from, and more highly evaluated than, birds of the open country;
2) arboreal birds are to be distinguished from, and more highly evaluated than, terrestrial birds;
3) birds which eat clean food are to be distinguished from, and more highly evaluated than, birds that eat dirty food.

(These first three principles are related to each other.)

4) Birds are to be distinguished in terms of their spontaneous interaction with man, i.e. those that either consistently or inconsistently approach man spontaneously are accorded special significance;

5) brightly plumed birds are to be distinguished from dull-plumaged birds;

6) nocturnal birds are to be distinguished from diurnal birds.

I will elaborate a little on each of these six points.

1) The forest–cultivation, or forest–human settlement, opposition is a very important one in Kalam thinking and is stated explicitly in myth and ritual. It is linked to oppositions between wild–domestic, hunting–gardening, clean–dirty and male–female. By definition, almost all hunting, which is a male activity, takes place in the forest.

Kalam distinguish forest birds, *ytk yakt*, from open country birds, *mseŋ yakt*; but by no means all species fall neatly into these divisions. However, the majority can be categorized reasonably well and all the species which are quantitatively important in hunting (certain honey-eaters and pigeons), and most which are individually significant (e.g. hawks), even if taken infrequently, are "forest birds". On the other hand, the "natural groups" of birds that the Kalam recognize are bisected by this division in some cases. Thus some hawks are forest birds and some are open country birds; to a lesser extent, the same applies to the pigeons, and, to a greater extent, to the typical honey-eaters; rails, woodcock and snipe, which the Kalam regard as a covert natural category, are found in forest and open country, though each of the different "species" of the two named "generic" taxa which constitute this group (rails: woodcock and snipe) is restricted to one or the other; in contrast, many small, named generic taxa such as those applied to cuckoo-doves, brush-cuckoos, and swiftlets and swallows, have members which span both ecological zones. However, the important natural groups of parrots (and lories), long-tailed birds of paradise, and medium sized birds of paradise and bower-birds, are exclusively forest categories.

If one wished, one might generalize this forest–open country opposition into a "principle of ecological association", noting that the Kalam also isolate, for example, "beech forest birds" within "forest birds", and "water-side birds" and "grassland birds" within "birds of the open country".

2) Arboreal birds are distinguished from terrestrial birds, and arboreal birds themselves are graded according to whether they dwell in the tops of the trees or in the middle or lower foliage. There are two apparent reasons for this: hunting techniques applied in their capture and cleanliness of feeding habits, which I will discuss in a moment. Men, but neither women nor little boys, climb trees, and they do so with great skill. Climbing to the birds that nest highest up, or to hides from which to shoot birds which feed on the blossom or fruit in the highest branches, is both prestigious and economically productive.

3) Birds which eat clean food are more valuable than those that eat dirty food. It is implicit in the Kalam world-view than man (or, perhaps, woman) is the most polluting element in the environment, and human excrement, decomposing human flesh and, in some contexts, human blood, are the most polluting substances. Some birds are alleged actually to eat excrement and decomposing human corpses: these are regarded as totally inedible; but so are birds, other than domestic fowls, that eat worms, maggots and insects around human settlements. In general, carrion eaters and feeders on worms, terrestrial insects and rats are unclean, though progressively less so, depending on how far removed are their habitats from human settlement. Those that feed on arboreal and aerial insects are not considered unclean, though they do not rate as highly for human food as those that feed on fruit and blossom from high up in the forest trees. The carnivorous birds, the hawks, falcon and owls, are finely subdivided into those that feed basically on arboreal mammals, and which are thus themselves completely clean; those that prey on other birds, i.e. the goshawks; those that eat substantial proportions of insects, lizards and terrestrial mammals which live distant from human settlements; and those that eat carrion and the dirty rats, insects and other small creatures living near human settlements.[4]

4) The spontaneous interaction of certain kinds of birds with man is a topic I discuss elsewhere (Bulmer, n.d.). The ways in which birds and some other creatures interact spontaneously with man, or are interpreted as doing so, is a consideration which is, I think, neglected by Lévi-Strauss

in his extended answer to Radcliffe-Brown's question "Why all these birds?" (Lévi-Strauss, 1963, Chapter 4). Essentially, my argument is that birds of mystical importance are likely to include representatives of two broad groups: those that normally maintain a considerable distance from man (many may be relatively rare) and which are selected for complex reasons, but, when encountered unexpectedly, are likely to be interpreted in highly mystical ways; and those that interact regularly and spontaneously with men and whose mystical significance derives mainly from the nature of this interaction. These in turn are divided into those that are common, relatively fearless of men and have calls or songs which readily lend themselves to anthroposonic or anthropovocoid interpretation; and those that are either fairly rare, or at least cautious in their approach, and which men see as interacting with them in an unpredictable and mysterious way. In the case of the Kalam, two of the commonest unclean-feeding birds around human settlements approach man relatively fearlessly—the willie-wagtail and the pied chat—and they call at men in the gardens and near the homesteads. In the forest the mouse-warbler does this. These are manifestations of ghosts, and in the case of the pied chat and the mouse-warbler, which chatter in a human-like way, they bring messages. On the other hand, the birds that habitually, but nevertheless unpredictably and mysteriously, approach and often startle men, and then disappear in an elusive way, are witches.

5) I have said that the plumes of some forty kinds of birds are used by the Kalam for self adornment. Evaluations are based partly on colour and colour-pattern, size, other aesthetic qualities, and durability. Their value in external trade is also a factor and does not correlate closely with evaluation for local use. Availability is also important. The Kalam like their dance teams to dress with some measure of uniformity and, to that extent, certain plumes which are scarce, but not too scarce, are in great demand, notably those of the yellow, or lesser, bird of paradise (*Paradisaea minor*). Interestingly, the yellow bird of paradise does not appear to have any significant mystical value for the Kalam. Part of the reason may be that it is not a local bird; but it may also be partly that in the regions where it is found, between half and two day's walk from the Upper Kaironk settlements, it tends to be a very common and conspicuous bird, both in the settlement areas and in the forest. The same is also true of the white cockatoo (*Cacatua galerita*),

which is quantitatively very important in Kalam head-dress ornaments, but which appears to have no mystical significance, and the
saxony (*Pteridophora alberti*), the one species of bird of paradise which is
locally present and fairly common in the Upper Kaironk forests, and
used widely in dance regalia. In other cases in which birds are very
important both in ceremonial regalia and mystically, it is hard to
estimate quite what the relationship is between the two factors. For
example, eagle (*Harpyopsis*) plumes are the most valued of all—is this
because the eagle is the most notable of birds? Or is the eagle the most
notable of birds partly because of the size and splendour of its barred
brown and white tail and wing plumes, and its white breast feathers?
And is the Papuan lory (*Charmosyna papou*) given high mystical status
because of its brilliant, multicoloured plumage, including the green
and red which, according to Saem, are the best colours for male
ornaments? Or is it also because it lives in the tops of trees in the high
mountain forest, feeds on the cleanest of all foods, is particularly shy
and mysterious in its habits, and is one of the greatest challenges to the
skill of the hunter?

6) Little needs to be said about the diurnal–nocturnal categorization. Most wild mammals are nocturnal and, therefore are opposed to
man and domestic animals (with partial exception of the dog). Most
birds are diurnal, but a minority are nocturnal, and it is perhaps not
surprising that several of these species are accorded mystical
significance.

There are of course other ways in which the Kalam classify birds, e.g.
into local v. non-local or exotic; but granted that the six dimensions I
have listed are not "refined"—for several of them can be partially
reduced to others in the list—I would argue still that they provide us
with a set of grids by which we can isolate both salient groups and
salient species other than simply in terms of natural taxonomy.
Let me now illustrate how these principles are invoked, by just one
particular Kalam, Ian Saem Majnep, in what is admittedly hardly a
traditional Kalam cultural activity, namely the ordering of chapters for
an ornithological monograph (see Appendix). While it is highly impro-
bable that any other Kalam would order his list of birds in precisely the
same way that Saem does, and while his working with myself and other
expatriate anthropologists and naturalists (intermittently for ten

years) unquestionably affects his approach to his task, I do not think
that there is any significant general feature of his classification which is
out of line with the thinking of the generality of members of his society.
It will of course be interesting to see the reaction of other Kalam to his
book, when they have the opportunity to read it.

There are two general principles which obviously underly the order
of Saem's chapters, i.e. the placing of groups of birds of high collective
economic and mystical importance at the beginning and end of the
work; and his ordering of habitat groups, which is very much from the
point of view of the hunter.

Turning to the principles I have discussed, the following observations may be made.

1) We may note first that Saem keeps the widely recognized covert
categories together as groups, for example lories in Chapter 4, typical
honey-eaters in Chapter 6, pigeons in Chapter 8 and diurnal raptors in
Chapter 20.

2) Regarding the forest–open country dimension, we can see that
the first seven chapters (4–10) and 21 deal basically with forest birds;
11–14 and 17 with birds of the open country; 18 and 19 with exotic
birds; and 15, 16 and 20 with groups established on criteria that
override geography and spatial ecology, i.e. natural taxonomy and
also, in the case of Chapter 16, nocturnal habit.

In so far as Chapters 4–10, notably 6 and 10, include a few species
which are predominantly non-forest birds, this also is accounted for by
Saem's following natural taxonomy and including open-country birds
that are similar both morphologically and behaviourally to the forest
species which constitute the majority in the natural groups. Similarly,
Chapters 11 and 13 include certain species which are essentially forest
birds and others that straddle forest and open country, so that one
cannot say that either habitat is the more characteristic; and the
inclusion of these can again be accounted for by natural taxonomy.

3) Within the seven chapters devoted mainly to forest birds, 4, 5, 6
and 8 are devoted largely to natural taxonomic groups, though in 4, 5
and 8 arboreality and feeding habits are also stressed. Chapters 6, 7 and
9 are sub-groups of forest birds which are essentially defined more

narrowly by arboreality and feeding patterns, in ways which make a great deal of sense from the point of view of the bird-hunter.

4) The five chapters devoted to birds of the open country divide them in terms of ecological and behavioural associations: waterside birds (Chapter 14), aerial birds (Chapters 12, 13, 17) subdivided according to whether or not they perch and/or nest in trees, and a residue of grassland, garden and arboreal birds (Chapter 11), after many species that could also have been included here have been placed in earlier chapters for other reasons.

5) Of the non-local birds (Chapters 18 and 19), the yellow and red birds of paradise are treated separately for their unique plumage and high economic value. However, Saem notes in his text that they behave similarly to the long-tailed birds of paradise of the forest.

6) In the present context, Chapter 20, on the diurnal raptors, is of interest in two different ways. Firstly, Saem said that he had great difficulty in deciding where to place this chapter. These birds are very important, so they had to come either at the beginning or at the end of the book. He eventually opted for the end. Secondly, he was tempted to break down this one long chapter into several shorter ones, each dealing with a group of hawks distinguished by their characteristic prey and life-style: eagle and buzzard in one chapter, the goshawks in another, and the kites, harrier and brown hawk into one or two more. He wavered over this: and this was the one occasion when I consciously influenced him in his decisions as to chapter contents and chapter order, indicating that in my view it seemed more appropriate to leave them together. His inclination to "split" reflects both the high interest he has in this group, and the importance the Kalam in general attach to a bird's feeding habits.

I should add that in many places in his text Saem points to relationships between species he discussed in one chapter and others that he discusses elsewhere, and in some cases notes that he has necessarily been arbitrary in placing them where he does.

Thus, making the crudest of counts, one may say that "natural taxonomy" is invoked in almost every one of these eighteen chapters, and could be seen as a major organizing principle in at least six of them;

the forest–open country dimension is significant in the definition of thirteen chapters; the vertical–horizontal dimension (aerial; high arboreal; middle arboreal; terrestrial) is relevant to the definition in at least six chapters; feeding habits could be seen as a defining principle for nine chapters; plumage value for three or four; and nocturnality two.

In conclusion, to return now to my central topic, the determination of "salience" in the general-purpose and essentially non-mystical classifications of birds by the Kalam. I suggest that salience attaches both to groups of species and to individual species within groups. I would regard as salient those "natural" groups valued on account of size or plumage or both (hawks, long-tailed birds of paradise, pigeons, parrots and lories); and the largest typical representatives of these groups as particularly salient (eagle, greater sicklebill, zoe fruit-pigeon *or* mountain pigeon, Papuan lory).

I would also suggest that we may regard as salient any bird which is the largest, typical species of any sizeable, "non-natural" group based on a combination of the criteria of habitat (both spatial and vertical dimensions being considered) and feeding habits: e.g. arboreal frugivores, arboreal insectivores, terrestrial insectivores, aerial insectivores, nocturnal insectivores and nocturnal carnivores. Such a list would again include the zoe fruit pigeon or mountain pigeon, but also black-hooded cuckoo-shrike, chestnut rail, woodswallow, boobook owl and sooty owl.

Turning back to Table 1, most of the species listed under points 1, 2, 3, 5, 7 and 8, are thus accounted for, and only *one* species, the chestnut rail, has so far been named which appears to have *no* mystical associations. A little special pleading which I am prepared to provide if requested, will plausibly account for nearly all the remainder, in 1, 2, 3, 5, 7 and 8.

However, the birds in 4 and 6, ghost-messengers and witch-birds, cannot be accounted for thus. Here the additional consideration of spontaneous interaction with man has to be invoked: the most important of these species are those that interact with man either consistently and relatively fearlessly (ghost-messengers) or do so mysteriously and unexpectedly (witch-birds).

In this paper I have not made much use of the Douglas–Tambiah propositions about taxonomic anomaly. One can perhaps construct a plausible argument that cassowary, flying fox and possibly also the wild duck (a witch-bird) are taxonomically anomalous to the Kalam, though I am not sure how far a category can be considered to be anomalous when it is as important in its own right as cassowary. I do not myself see anomaly as being a highly significant factor in accounting for which birds have mystical significance to the Kalam, except in so far as the unusual behaviour directed towards man by certain species is regarded as anomalous. Which leads me to ponder if the most crucial characteristic of the anomalous pangolin might not be its singular response to the hunter, that of rolling up in a ball like a hedgehog.

Although I am still by no means satisfied with my formulation of the argument, I hope I have at least conveyed some of my reasons for remaining convinced that birds and other animals are not selected randomly as totems and for other forms of ritual and mystical marking.

A partly analogous case might be that of the investigator who set himself the task of deciding how appointments to university teaching positions had been, and were being, made by reviewing, on the one hand, the successful applicants and their qualities and qualifications and, on the other, the files of applicants from which they had been selected. How far had the following been considered: academic qualifications such as degrees; previous teaching experience; being well-known personally to the appointments committee; choice of the right referees; nationality, race and sex; and how far had contingencies of timing affected decisions?

A review of this kind might well persuade one that evaluations in terms of explicitly acknowledged criteria of academic merit did not adequately account for all appointments, but one would probably have to admit still that selection appeared not to have been entirely random.

Notes

1. Revised version of a paper delivered in the Department of Anthropology, University of Sydney, on 10 July 1975, and subsequently circulated as Working Paper No. 45 of the Department of Anthropology, University of Auckland under the title "Totemism and Taxonomy: Part II".

2. "Spiritual" is the slippery term in this proposition. If "spiritual well-being" is "morale", then, of course, this is precisely what ritual symbols do affect; but if the impact of ritual use and reference is included, the statement becomes tautologous. Possibly what Radcliffe-Brown had in mind were phenomena such as either natural landmarks, or flora and fauna characteristic of a people's territory, recognition of which affects their morale. However, in such cases, might one not argue

that these phenomena *stood for* the territory, or its divisions, and thus for something that is of material significance?
3. I am very grateful to both these critics for prodding me into trying to clarify my arguments.
4. Saem's original proposal was to place these groups in three or four different chapters of *Birds of my Kalam Country*, see Appendix below.

References

BERLIN, B., BREEDLOVE, D. E. and RAVEN, P. H. (1968). Covert categories and folk taxonomies. *Am. Anthrop.*, **70**, 290–9.

BERLIN, B., BREEDLOVE, D. E. and RAVEN, P. H. (1974). "Principles of Tzeltal Plant Classification". Academic Press, New York and London.

BULMER, R. N. H. (1970). Which came first, the chicken or the egg-head? *In* "Échanges et Communications: Mélanges offerts à Claude Lévi-Strauss a l'Occasion de son 60ème Anniversaire" (Eds J. Pouillon and P. Maranda). Mouton, Paris.

BULMER, R. N. H. (1974). Folk biology in the New Guinea Highlands. *Soc. Sci. Inform.*, **13**, 9–28.

BULMER, R. N. H. (1978). Totems and taxonomy. *In* "Australian Aboriginal Concepts" (Ed. L. Hiatt). Aust. Inst. Aboriginal St., Canberra.

BULMER, R. N. H. (n.d.). Birds and men's souls. Mimeo version of talk given at Australian Museum, Sydney, 8 July 1975. Dept. of Anthropology, University of Auckland.

DIAMOND, J. M. (1972). "The Avifauna of the Eastern Highlands of New Guinea". Nuttall Ornithological Club, Cambridge, Mass.

DOUGLAS, M. (1966). "Purity and Danger". Routledge and Kegan Paul, London.

EVANS-PRITCHARD, E. E. (1956). "Nuer Religion". Oxford University Press, Oxford.

LEACH, E. R. (1954). "Political Systems of Highland Burma". Bell, London.

LEACH, E. R. (1964). Animal categories and verbal abuse. *In* "New Directions in the Study of Language" (Ed. E. H. Lenneberg). MIT Press, Cambridge, Mass.

LÉVI-STRAUSS, C. (1963). "Totemism". Beacon, Boston.

MAJNEP, I. S. and BULMER, R. N. H. (1977). "Birds of my Kalam Country". Auckland University Press/Oxford University Press, Auckland/Wellington.

RADCLIFFE-BROWN, A. R. (1951). The comparative method in social anthropology. *J.R.A.I.*, **81**, 15–22.

RADCLIFFE-BROWN, A. R. (1952). "Structure and Function in Primitive Society". Cohen and West, London.

RAND, A. L. and GILLIARD, E. T. (1967). "Handbook of New Guinea Birds". Weidenfeld and Nicolson, London.

TAMBIAH, S. J. (1969). Animals are good to think and good to prohibit. *Ethnology*, **8**, 424–59.

WORSLEY, P. M. (1967). Groote Eylandt totemism and *Le Totemisme aujourd'hui*. *In* "The Structural Study of Myth and Totemism" (Ed. E. R. Leach), ASA Monogr. No. 5. Tavistock Publications, London.

Appendix: Ian Saem Majnep's ordering of birds in *Birds of my Kalam Country* (Majnep and Bulmer, 1977)

NOTES

i) Kalam synonyms are excluded from this list.

ii) Taxa marked with asterisks are of ritual or mystical significance.

iii) Taxa marked with daggers are defined by Saem in ways which do not correspond to general usage of other Upper Kaironk Valley men consulted.

iv) Kalam names in brackets are mentioned by Saem as applied by some other men to species which he describes, though he either disagrees with, or will not vouch for, their application.

v) Zoological species names in brackets refer to species not explicitly described by Saem, but which have been identified by the editor and assigned by other Kalam men to taxa Saem names.

vi) Where Saem explicitly recognizes more than one division of a terminal taxon, but does not name them, these are numbered (i), (ii), etc.

vii) Where glosses referring to age, sex or polymorphism are unbracketed, these follow explicit distinctions Saem makes; where they are bracketed, these indicate the editor's, and not Saem's, assessment of biological correspondence.

viii) Latin names follow Rand and Gilliard (1967), except in the case of certain whistlers (Pachycephalinae), honey-eaters (Meliphagidae) and berry-peckers (Decaeidae), where revisions in Diamond (1972) are followed.

ix) English names follow Rand and Gilliard (1967) in the main, though in a few cases either alternatives provided by Diamond (1972) or innovations by the editor are used.

Chapter 4 "Birds which men's souls can turn into (i.e. that represent men, in dream experience)". (Lories and other local parrots; nuthatches.)

kob	Papuan lory, *Charmosyna papou*—mature birds with much red in their plumage (mature non-melanistic males)
tabal	Papuan lory, *Charmosyna papou*—collective term (most often applied to prepared skins)
* kañm	Papuan lory, *Charmosyna papou*—with yellow rumps (mature non-melanistic females)
sg	Papuan lory, *Charmosyna papou*—immature birds (especially of melanistic phase)
cmgan	Papuan lory, *Charmosyna papou*—dark birds with red on rump only (mature or near-mature melanistic males)
adwg	(i) Dusky lory, *Pseudeos fuscata* (ii) Rainbow lory, *Trichoglossus haematodus*
* gaslŋ	Yellow-billed mountain lory, *Neopsittacus muschenbroeki*
* kamaygs	Orange-billed mountain lory, *Neopsittacus pullicauda*
* wdn-ṅg	Tearful lory, *Oreopsittacus arfaki*
* jbog	Little red lory, *Charmosyna pulchella*
byay	Striated lory, *Psittueteles goldiei*
tmwk-yakt	? Yellow-fronted blue-eared lory, *Charmosyna placentis*

(*godmay-ket*)	Pygmy striated lory, *Charmosyna wilhelminae*
mayap	(i) Brehm's tiger parrot, *Psitacella brehmi*
	(ii) ? Madarasz's tiger parrot, *P. madaraszi*
*kablamneŋ	Papuan king parrot, *Alisterus chloropterus*
spsep	(i) ? Papuan sitella, *Neositta ? chrysoptera*
	(ii) Pink-faced nuthatch, *Daphoenositta miranda*
	(iii) Pygmy parrot, *Micropsitta ? bruijni*

Chapter 5 "Birds in which women show themselves (i.e. that represent women, in dream experience)". (Long-tailed birds of paradise.)

*gwlgwl	Greater sickle-bill, *Epimachus fastosus*—mature males
*jbjel	Lesser sickle-bill, *Epimachus meyeri*—mature males
galkneŋ	Greater and lesser sickle-bills, *E. fastosus* and *E. meyeri*—females and immature males
*ksks	Stephanie bird of paradise, *Astrapia stephaniae*—mature males
bdoŋ	Stephanie bird of paradise, *A. stephaniae*—females and immature males

Chapter 6 "Birds that feed at flowering trees". (Typical honey-eaters; mistletoe-bird.)

nol	Reichenow's melidectes, *Melidectes rufocrissalis*
alŋawnm	Belford's melidectes, *Melidectes belfordi*
golyad	Cinnamon-breasted wattle-bird, *Melidectes torquatus*
kb	Grey honey-eater, *Pycnopygius cinereus*
kb-slk	Honey-eaters of the *Meliphaga analoga* group
kojway	Black-throated honey-eater, *Meliphaga subfrenata*
ky	Brown-backed streaked honey-eater, *Ptiloprora guisei*
sep	Myzomela honey-eaters (*Myzomela* spp.) and mistletoe-bird, *Dicaeum* sp.
sep kalom	Adult male red-collared myzomela, *Myzomela rosenbergi*
sep bys	female and immature male red-collared myzomela, *M. rosenbergi*
sep mwmloj-kab-ket	Mistletoe-bird, *Dicaeum geelvinkianum*
ywak	(i) New Guinea friarbird, *Philemon novaeguineae*
	†(ii) ? Meyer's friarbird, *Philemon meyeri*
	((iii)) (New Guinea oriole, *Oriolus szlayi*)

Chapter 7 "The families of birds that feed on *gwŋ* Pipturus fruit". (Melipotes honey-eaters, certain berry-peckers and birds of paradise, and the bower-bird.)

memneŋ	Common melipotes, *Melipotes fumigatus*
maldapan	Berry-peckers, *Melanocharis versteri*, (*M. nigra*), *Rhamphocaris crassirostris*
maldapan yb	Fan-tailed berry-peker, *Melanocharis versteri*
maldapan mosb	Fan-tailed berry-peker, *M. versteri*—males
maldapan gs	(i) Fan-tailed berry-peker, *M. versteri*—females
	(ii) Spotted berry-peker, *Rhamphocaris crassirostris*—males

maldapan kl	Spotted berry-pecker, *Rhamphocaris crassirostris*—females
kabay	Certain birds of paradise, *Lophorina* sp., *Parotia* spp., *Loria* sp., (*Diphyllodes* sp.), (*Cicinnurus* sp.), (*Cnemophilus* sp.—females and immature males), (*Paradisaea rudolphi*)
kabay kl	Superb bird of paradise, *Lophorina superba*—females and immature males; (magnificent bird of paradise, *Diphyllodes magnifica*—females and immature males)
kabay bl-bad	Superb bird of paradise, *L. superba*—mature males
kabay pok	Six-plumed birds of paradise, *Parotia lawesi* (and ? *P. carolae*)—females and immature males
kabay wog-dep	Six-plumed birds of paradise, *P. lawesi* (and ? *P. carolae*)—mature males
kabay gs	Loria's bird of paradise, *Loria loriae*—females and immature males; (sickle-crested bird of paradise, *Cnemophilus macgregori*—females and immature males)
kabay mosb	Loria's bird of paradise, *L. loriae*—mature males
(*kabay asdal*)	Blue bird of paradise, *Paradisaea rudolphi*; magnificent bird of paradise, *Diphyllodes magnifica*—mature males; king bird of paradise, *Cicinnurus regius*—mature males)
kwŋb	Gardner bower-bird, *Amblyornis macgregoriae* and sickle-crested bird of paradise, *Cnemophilus macgregori*
kwŋb bl-bad	Gardner bower-bird, *A. macgregoriae*—mature males
kwŋb neb	Gardner bower-bird, *A. macgregoriae*—females and immature males
kwŋb pok	Sickle-crested bird of paradise, *Cnemophilus macgregori*—mature males
n̄opd	Saxony bird of paradise, *Pteridophora alberti*
n̄opd kolman	Saxony bird of paradise, *Pteridophora alberti*—mature males
n̄opd neb	Saxony bird of paradise, *Pteridophera alberti*—females and immature males

Chapter 8   "The families of birds that come to places where there are stones that they can break up small and swallow".

*malg	Mountain pigeon, *Gymnophaps albertisi*
koct	White-fronted fruit-dove, *Ptilinopus rivoli*
koct btep-sek	White-fronted fruit-dove, *Ptilinopus rivoli*—adult males
koct amam	White-fronted fruit-dove, *Ptilinopus rivoli*—females
gadmab	Ornate fruit-dove, *Ptilinopus ornatus*
gadmab btep-sek	Ornate fruit-dove, *Ptilinopus ornatus*—adult males
waymn	Great cuckoo-dove, *Reiwardtoena reiwardtsi*
*kwwt	Cuckoo-doves, *Macropygia* spp.
kwwt twn	Amboina cuckoo-dove, *Macropygia amboinensis*
†*kwwt yb*	Black-billed cuckoo-dove, *M. nigrirostris* (adults)
†*kwwt sapolkod*	Black-billed cuckoo-dove, *M. nigrirostris* (immature) (most Kalam distinguish only two kinds of *kwwt*, not differentiating *kwwt yb* from *kwwt sapolkod*, so that this taxon corresponds exactly with *M. nigrirostris*).
*koptt	Zoe imperial pigeon, *Ducula zoeae* (and ? red-breasted imperial pigeon, *D. chalconota*)
mokbel	? White-breasted ground-dove, *Gallicolumba* ? *jobiensis*

Chapter 9   "Birds of the inner foliage".

sñeñ	Cuckoo-shrikes, *Coracina* spp.
*sñeñ twn	Black-hooded cuckoo-shrike, *Coracina longicauda*
sñeñ skoy	Black-bellied cuckoo-shrike, *C. montana*
swalwal	Stout-billed cuckoo shrike, *C. caeruleogrisea*
wet	Black-throated thicket-flycatcher, *Poecilodryas albonotata*
wlmeñ saky	White-winged thicket-flycatcher, *Peneothello sigillatus*
koŋds	Typical smaller whistlers, *Pachycephala schlegeli,* ? *P. soror, P. modesta, P. rufiventris dorsalis*
koŋds yb	Schlegel's whistler, *P. schlegeli* and ? Sclater's whistler, *P. soror*
koŋds todymady	Brown-backed whistler, *P. modesta,* and white-bellied whistler, *P. rufiventris dorsalis*
slek-yakt	Blue-capped ifrit, *Ifrita kowaldi*
*jolbeg	Fantails, *Rhipidura atra* and *R. brachyrhyncha*
jolbeg mosb	Black fantail, *R. atra*—males
jolbeg pok	Black fantail, *R. atra*—females; (and rufous fantail, *R. brachyrhyncha*)
*ttmñ	Friendly fantail, *Rhipidura albolimbata*
*smlsmlnap	Boat-billed flycatcher, *Machaerirhynchus nigripectus*
ytem-klekley	? Black monarch, *Monarcha axillaris*
pnes	Microeca flycatchers, *Microeca papuana* and *M.* ? *griseoceps*
pñepk	Slaty-chinned longbill, *Toxorhamphus poliopterus*
walkobneŋ	Mountain white-eye, *Zosterops novaeguineae*
sjweywey	Tree-warblers, *Gerygone ruficollis* and *G. cinerea;* ? thornbill, *Acanthiza murina*
kamay sjweywey	(i) Red-necked tree-warbler, *Gerygone ruficollis* (ii) ? Grey tree-warbler, *G. cinerea*
kaby-kas-ket	? Grey-headed warbler, *Gerygone chloronota*
peñbyn	Leaf warbler, *Phylloscopus trivirgatus*
jeptpt	Fidgiting flycatcher, *Eugerygone rubra*
tbwm-kab-ket	Tit berry-pecker, *Oreocharis arfaki*
tbwm-kab-ket nonm	Mountain berry-pecker, *Paramythia montium*
gwpñ-magl-ket	Mottled whistler, *Pachycephala leucostigma*
bajj	Parrot-finch, *Erythrura trichroa*

Chapter 10   "Terrestrial birds". (Rails, woodcock and snipe, ground-dove, quails and certain babblers, warblers and flycatchers of the forest floor and low undergrowth.)

koŋak	Forbes's chestnut rail, *Rallicula forbesi*
koŋak sd-ket	? Slate-breasted rail, *Rallus pectoralis*
kñopl ＿	Woodcock, *Scolopax saturata*
kapy-knopl	? Snipe, *Gallinago* spp.
bleb	Beccari's ground-dove, *Gallicolumba beccari*
kwyŋ	Swamp quail, *Synoicus ypsilophorus*
kabpet	King quail, *Coturnix chinensis*
kawslog	False-pitta, *Melampitta lugubris*
*kosp	Mountain mouse-warbler, *Crateroscelis robusta*
señŋ	Wren-warblers, *Sericornis* spp. esp. mountain wren-warbler, *S. nouhuysi*; (mountain straight-billed honeyeater, *Timeliopsis fulvigula*); ploughshare tit, *Eulacestoma nigripectus*

seññ yb	Large mountain wren-warbler, *Sericornis nouhuysi*
skek	(i) ? Papuan wren-warbler, *S. papuensis*
	(ii) ? Buff-faced wren-warbler, *S. perspicillatus*
seññ twmd-bad-sek	Ploughshare tit, *Eulacestoma nigripectus*—males
seññ mwlk-sgy	Ploughshare tit, *Eulacestoma nigripectus*—females
*plη	Slatey thicket-flycatcher, *Peneothello cyanus*
gopkob	? Lesser New Guinea thrush, *Amalocichla incerta*
(gopkob)	High mountain eupetes, *Eupetes leucostictus*
sweg	Rufous-naped whistler, *Pachycephala rufinucha*

Chapter 11   "Birds of the open country".

twwη	Pheasant-coucal, *Centropus phasianinus*
gac	Grass-warbler, *Megalurus timoriensis*
*koñmayd	Willie-wagtail, *Rhipidura leucophrys*
*wlmeñ	Pied chat, *Saxicola caprata*
lbg	Schach shrike, *Lanius schach*
sbaw	Brush cuckoos, *Cacomantis pyrrhophanus*, *C. variolosus*, (*C. castaneiventris*)
sbaw mseη-ket	Grey-breasted cuckoo, *C. variolosus*
sbaw kamay-ket	Fantailed cuckoo, *C. pyrrhophanus*
sloj	Black and white fairy wren, *Malurus alboscapulatus*
kaj-meg	Tailor-bird, *Cisticola exilis*
plolom	(i) Sacred kingfisher, *Halcyon sancta*
	(ii) ? Mountain yellow-billed kingfisher, *Halcyon megarhyncha*
*nyolelegp	? a small flycatcher
dη	Mannikin, *Lonchura spectabilis*
*wobob	Black-headed pitohui, *Pitohui dichrous*

Chapter 12   "Those birds that perch high in the lopped trees".

cpnabgw	Mountain peltops flycatcher, *Peltops montanus*
*kackac	Greater woodswallow, *Artamus maximus*

Chapter 13   "The kinds of birds that just fly constantly around".

mmañp	Swiftlets, *Collocalia* spp., and swallow, *Hirundo* sp., especially glossy swiftlet, *C. esculenta*
sskl	(i) Pacific swallow, *Hirundo tahitica*
	(ii) Larger swiftlets, e.g. Whitehead's swiftlet, *Collocalia whiteheadi* and, often, mountain swiftlet, *C. hirundinacea*
ymanηn pl-pat	Moustached swift, *Hemiprocne mystacea*

Chapter 14   "Birds that fly above the water".

*ñay	New Guinea mountain duck, *Salvadorina waigiuensis*
(kon ñay)	? Cormorant, *Phalacrocorax* sp. or spp.
gwlmly	? New Guinea bittern, *Zonerodius heliosylus*
*jjgayaη	Magpie-lark, *Grallina bruijni*; (and river flycatcher, *Monachella muelleriana*, sometimes distinguished as *kotleg*)

n̄gogpagog	Grey wagtail, *Motacilla cinerea*
*joly	Racquet-tailed kingfisher, *Tanysiptera* ? *galatea*

Chapter 15 "Birds of Darkness". (Owls, frogmouths, owlet-nightjars and nightjars.)

*sagal	Sooty owl, *Tyto tenebricosa*
skayag	Grass owl, *Tyto capensis*
*mwmjel	Boobook owls, *Ninox* spp., especially Papuan boobook, *Ninox theomacha*, and possibly also smaller frogmouth, *Podargus ocellatus*
mwmjel wagn-sek	Papuan boobook, *Ninox theomacha*
mwmjel magy-nokom	? Lesser Papuan frogmouth, *Podargus ocellatus*
mwm	Giant frogmouth, *Podargus papuensis*
pow	Owlet-nightjars, *Aegotheles* spp., and forest nightjar, *Eurostopodus* sp.
pow yb	Large owlet-nightjar, *Aegotheles insignis*—dark phase
pow pok	Large owlet-nightjar, *Aegotheles insignis*—rufous phase
*kwlep	(i) Mountain owlet-nightjar, *Aegotheles albertisi* †(ii) Archbold's nightjar, *Eurostopodus archboldi*
wogn̄alam	White-tailed nightjar, *Caprimulgus macrurus*

Chapter 16 "Those kinds of birds that constitute the family which vomits up the food that they have eaten". (The bats.)

*alp	(i) Spinal-winged Bat, *Dobsonia moluccensis* (ii) All large fruit-bats or "flying-foxes" (iii) All bats
mokol	"Typical" flying-foxes, *Pteropus* spp.
cekl	(i) Blossom bat, *Syconycteris crassa* (ii) All small bats
cekl pok	Blossom bat, *S. crassa*—with rufous fur (? immature)
gwbn̄	? Tube-nosed bats, *Nyctimene* sp. or spp.
wnln̄	Small insectivorous bat sp. or spp.

Chapter 17 "When this bird comes, we say that the season of the sun has arrived".

*byblaw	Rainbow-bird, *Merops ornatus*

Chapter 18 "Birds of the warm lowlands".

kaywl	Hornbill, *Aceros plicatus*
koben	Victoria crown pigeon, *Goura victoria*
wtay	White cockatoo, *Cacatua galerita*
bley	Wattled brush turkey, *Aepypodius arfakianus*
abownm	Brown-collared brush turkey, *Talegalla jobiensis*
yabagay	? Common scrub hen, *Megapodius freycinet*
ydam	Pesquet's parrot, *Psittrichas fulgidus*
gwmgwm	? Palm cockatoo, *Probosciger aterrimus*

kaganm	Bare-faced crow, *Gymnocorvus tristis*
plag	Shovel-billed kingfisher, *Clytoceyz rex*
†*gokal*	Roller, *Eurystomus orientalis* (alternatively, the New Guinea oriole, *Oriolus szalayi*. cf. Chapter 6, *ywak*)
(*gokob*)	Black-headed butcher-bird, *Cracticus cassicus*
*cpsawey	? migratory wader spp.

Chapter 19 "The Yellow and the Red Birds of Paradise are birds that are different from all others".

yabal	Yellow, or lesser, bird of paradise, *Paradisaea minor*
pkaŋ	Yellow bird of paradise, *P. minor*—females and immature males
añgoym sgy	Yellow bird of paradise, *P. minor*—fully mature males
tay	Red bird of paradise, *Paradisaea raggiana*

Chapter 20 "The families of birds which variously take furred animals, birds, snakes, lizards and carrion". (The diurnal raptors.)

*dwk	Harpy-eagle, *Harpyopsis novaeguineae*
skwb	Long-tailed buzzard, *Henicopernis longicauda*, and at least one other unidentified hawk
skwb goblad	Long-tailed buzzard, *H. longicauda*
†*skwb kawl-kas-ket*	Unidentified hawk sp.
god	(i) Meyer's goshawk, *Accipiter meyerianus*
	†(ii) ? Grey goshawk, *A. novaehollandiae*
	(iii) ? Peregrine falcon, *Falco peregrinus*
*ccp	"Typical" goshawks, esp. *A. fasciatus* and *A. melanochlamys*
ccp kamay-ket	(i) Black-mantled goshawk, *A. melanochlamys* (? mature plumage)
	†(ii) Black-mantled goshawk, *A. melanochlamys* (? immature plumage)
ccp mseŋ-ket	Australian goshawk, *A. fasciatus*
dmŋawt kosbol	? Spotted marsh harrier, *Circus spilonotus*
aŋmt	Black kite, *Milvus migrans*
kolm	Red-backed kite, *Haliastur indus*
glegl	Brown hawk, *Falco berigora*
(*ñgaglagl*)	? Osprey, *Pandion haliaetus*

Chapter 21 "The Cassowary". (Not normally considered to be a "bird" (yakt).)

*kobty	Cassowaries, *Casuarius bennetti*, and *C. unappendiculatus*
kobty mosb	Dwarf cassowary, *C. bennetti*—adult
kobty gs	Dwarf cassowary, *C. bennetti*—juvenile
kobty mok malam	Dwarf cassowary, *C. bennetti*—mature adult with bright wattles
kobty gwlgyn	Large lowland cassowaries, probably *C. unappendiculatus*

4

Socially Significant Plant Species and their Taxonomic Position Among the Bunaq of Central Timor

Claudine Friedberg

Scarcely a dozen years ago Sturtevant predicted that the study of all the folk classifications in a given society would enable us to know its culture, since: "A culture itself amounts to the sum of a given society's folk classifications" (Sturtevant, 1964, p. 100). This amounted to a declaration of faith in the "new ethnography". However some claimed (e.g. Keesing, 1972) that the "new ethnography" was stillborn, having borrowed models from linguistics in which the linguists themselves no longer believed. For Keesing, culture forms a whole, to be segmented only with great difficulty:

If we describe a cognitive code, it should not be to avoid analyzing who does what and why. It should be to help us make sense of the complexity of social behaviour, not retreat from it. Anthropologists do not need more compartmentalization within their field—they need systematic modes of integration. They need to develop a paradigm within which a cognitive model of culture can be systematically *related to* sociological, biological, ecological, and other realms, not simply abstracted from them.

(Keesing, 1972, p. 325)

Away from American "think tanks", researchers (including those from the United States itself) have continued the task of ethnology. In France, for example, where we have stayed faithful to the idea of the ethnologist as a "one-man band" going into a society to study it in its totality, investigations of folk classifications are most frequently under-taken as part of general ethnological surveys or ethnological enquiries in the widest sense (Dournes, Ferry, Friedberg, MacDonald, Martin, Revel-MacDonald, Sperber, Tornay, etc.): this is in part due to the Maussian tradition, but perhaps also to lack of funds. I am not suggest-ing that we cease the study of folk classifications but that we rethink them. The discussion about the validity of the new ethnography origi-nates frequently in a misunderstanding concerning objectives. Is the aim to know more about a particular human community, to draw from it more general data about the functioning and evolution of a certain type of society, which is the usual aim of the ethnologist? Or is it to pursue knowledge of the activity of the universal human mind, as a researcher like Berlin would claim?

Researchers do not even agree in what they mean by classification or taxonomy. For some these terms designate systems in which different groups or taxa are found in hierarchical relations of inclusion; whereas the Greek term *taxis*, from which the word "taxonomy" is formed, simply signifies "arrangement", stipulating nothing about the form of the arrangement. In order not to prejudge the different types of classification which one may encounter in different human com-munities, it seems to me wiser to stick to a vague definition of the terms classification and taxonomy in relation to objects which we find in nature, viz. the way in which a particular society orders the discon-tinuity of the natural world. However, the notion of discontinuity is itself very subjective, and this is demonstrated sufficiently by the juxtaposition of two quotations from Lévi-Strauss and Buffon:

... the diversity of species furnishes man with the most intuitive picture at his disposal and constitutes the most direct manifestation he can perceive of the ultimate discon-tinuity of reality.

(Lévi-Strauss, 1966, p. 137)

To build a system, or an arrangement, in brief a general method, everything must be included in it; the whole must be divided into different classes, the classes into genera; the genera into species, and all this, according to an order in which accident necessarily enters. But nature works through unknown graduations and consequently cannot lend itself entirely to these divisions, since it shifts from one species to another, through imperceptible shades. ...

(Buffon, 1752, pp. 17–18)

Between a fir-tree and a cabbage the discontinuity is obvious, but theoretically one could set up a succession of plants which, by imper-ceptible changes, would enable us by starting from any one of these species to arrive at a common ancestor. Many of these plants have now disappeared and the twin game of evolution and natural selection has left us a natural world in which there exists a greater or lesser degree of discontinuity between species. What interests the ethnologist is to know how this greater or lesser discontinuity is perceived and how it is expressed. For example, in the classification of the Bunaq of Lamaknen considered below, there is only one representative of the class[1] Equisetales, the horsetail, which was very abundant in the Palaeozoic past. However, it is not as isolated in the Bunaq classification as it would be in the scientific classification, being categorized as similar to the *Casuarina*; the whole plant, which is herbaceous, resembles a branch of this tree. By contrast, as we shall see later, *Mallotus philippensis*, which is one of many representatives of the family Euphorbiacae, is considered as a separate plant in the folk classification.

Whatever the way in which a population orders the natural objects which surround it, this order cannot be independent of the particular environment in which the population lives. But the ethnologist generally is only concerned with those objects in the environment that play a role in the cultural life, material or otherwise, of the population. The question thus arises: why those and not others?

Lévi-Strauss's demonstration of the importance of species that are "good for thinking" has undermined the belief that only useful plants and animals could be distinguished by man, and the prime question has now become: why is a particular plant or a particular animal the object of intellectual speculation? Thus certain scholars came to study the position occupied in a particular society by socially marked species in the total classification of natural objects. Mary Douglas's brilliant work, starting from the abominations of Leviticus, seemed to inaugurate a new direction of research by establishing a cause-and-effect relation between taxonomic anomaly and impurity. However, as Bulmer has pointed out that:

It would seem equally fair . . . to argue that the pig was accorded anomalous status because it was unclean as to argue that it was unclean because of its anomalous taxonomic status.

(1967, p. 21)

The question here is that of the reality of the relations between the order which a population establishes in nature and the rest of its culture. Unfortunately, our knowledge of this subject is still very patchy.

On the subject of symbolism, Sperber rightly asserts that

It is necessary . . . not to proceed from certain symbolic animals to a demonstration that they are taxonomically abnormal, but to do the opposite, take a complete taxonomy and view all the anomalies which permit . . . symbolic traits.

(1975, p. 11)

This means, in particular, that it is those who have collected classifications who are in a position to study the relations between classifications and the role given in the culture, as a whole, to the plants and animals which are their objects, rather than those who seek an explanation for the use of a particular species and then look for it in a taxonomy constructed for the purpose.

One now appreciates all the more the systematic research undertaken by Bulmer to discover the extent to which animals having a particular place in each category of vertebrates recognized by the Kalam are given special significance.[2] His studies have led him to the conclusion that among the Kalam, totemic species or those which are the object of a ritual attitude are not chosen randomly from the total fauna, but after a pre-selection based on criteria of prominence in the taxonomic plan—for example, that of being the largest animal in a category. For Bulmer the relations between totemism and taxonomy are reciprocal and classifications are influenced by cultural factors (including language), as well as biological and biogeographical ones.

Nevertheless, it is regrettable that it is animals that are almost always the object of this kind of study and rarely plants. Thus we always remain enclosed in a biblical version of nature where plants are neither honoured in Noah's Ark, nor in the abominations of Leviticus.

It is not possible here to undertake a full "Bulmerian" analysis of the only folk classification of plants for which I can claim some competence, that of the Bunaq of Timor. Rather, I shall do yet again what I advise against: that is, take a certain number of socially marked plants and examine their classificatory position. In order to reduce the drawbacks of this approach I have taken the widest possible range of the various possible cases, more to demonstrate the problems which arise in such an analysis than to formulate any new theory.

The Bunaq

The Bunaq[3] occupy the mountains of central Timor. They are swidden cultivators whose basic food is maize, rice being a special food reserved for rituals and guests. Tubers traditionally constituted an extra food, especially in the fields. The primary social unit is the House, *deu*.[4] At birth, each Bunaq enters the House of his mother. There are two types of marriage: in one, the most common, residence is uxorilocal, the husband continuing to belong to his own House but the offspring of the couple entering the House of the woman; in the other, the woman and her offspring leave her House in order to join that of her husband. The offspring of the different Houses of wife-givers are always distinct within a given House; these are the *dil*. For the most part, inheritance is matrilineal and follows the *dil*. The basic territorial and political unit is the village, grouping a number of Houses which do not always occupy an equal position in the hierarchy.

Here we are concerned principally with the Bunaq of Lamaknen (Kabupaten Belu). These Bunaq believe, for the most part, that their ancestors came from elsewhere and settled in Lamaknen after having chased out or killed the original inhabitants, the *melus*. Their genealogy systematically bears no trace of cross-breeding with the *melus*.

The Bunaq have a mythical and genealogical history recorded in texts in verse, and in particular in the *bei gua*, "the footsteps of the ancestors", which are recited in many circumstances and are part of the common culture. However, the specialist "masters of speech", the *lal gomo*, are responsible for the collective memory. In accordance with a phenomenon very widespread in the region, the texts are formed of two hemistichs, between whose terms there exists a correspondence which varies from synonymy to opposition. This correspondence is known by everyone and in the public, sung recitations the *lal gomo* limit themselves to giving the first hemistich which the crowd answers with the second. Thus the plants figuring in the mythical texts or rituals are always associated in pairs, and this is taken into account in this article.[5]

Bunaq classification of plants

In Bunaq classification, plants appear to be organized more according to a complex web of resemblances and affinities in which individual plants can belong to several categories, rather than according to a tree-like system of hierarchical categories and mutual exclusion (Friedberg, 1968, 1970, 1974). Nevertheless there are certain categories which are included entirely in wider ones, but there are no superior

D

taxa corresponding to what Berlin calls *life form*. Among the Bunaq, the notions of trees, *hotel*, herbs, *u*, and lianas, *mun*, belong to the system of identification rather than to the system of representation.

In such a classification, the intermediary plants between two or more groups take on special significance. These categories shift depending on whether or not suitable plants exist in the local flora to perform this role. For this reason, there are variations between the classifications of different villages, chiefly between the villages of High and Low Lamaknen. The former is situated between 600 and 1100 metres, the latter is below this, down to the Maliana plain, which is at an altitude of only 200 metres. Mythical and ritual traditions vary considerably from one place to another, and I emphasize that the data mentioned here have nearly all been gathered at Abis in High Lamaknen.

I am not concerned here with food plants and the hierarchy of their uses; nor shall I discuss in general the role of plants in myths, but for the species discussed I shall mention what is said about them in myths. First, I will rapidly review the plants which are the most socially marked among the Bunaq, the betel and the areca nut; then I shall discuss some plants used ritually; and, finally, I shall consider the problem of prohibitions.[6]

The betel and the areca nut

The two plants in the betel quid are the first whose social use becomes evident to a person staying for the first time in Lamaknen. In fact, the exchange of betel is the prelude to all social relations.

Betel and areca are cultivated plants. The first, *molo*, is planted at the foot of trees with a diameter of around 40 cm, which the plants climb as they would stakes. When the betel grows well and is not harvested too often, it soon covers the trunk of the tree like ivy. It is for this reason that the betel is placed is placed in the category of *netel$_1$ dutula$_2$* "root$_1$ to place oneself$_2$", containing epiphytic plants and parasites. In this category *molo* is considered to form a special group with *lemel*, a term designating the *Raphidophora*, the climbing aroids. This group is labelled *netel$_1$ hotel$_2$ hene$_3$*, "root$_1$ tree$_2$ to hold$_3$", because these are plants which start to grow from the ground and only then climb the tree.

The areca, *pu*, belongs to the category of *hotel$_1$ upan$_2$ gutu$_3$*, "tree$_1$ with$_3$ (a term designating the petioles of the palm leaf and banana tree)$_2$".

This morphologically defined category has a sociological existence; in fact it appears in the list of the plants whose exploitation the "guardians of the products of the land" have the duty of limiting, and which they must protect from fire and from cutting.

Although there is no general term to designate them, the palms are grouped together in the following order: *hoza*, the coconut, *pu*, the areca, *dilu*, the palmyra, *hak*, the *Corypha*, *tueq-kubus*, the sugar palm and *nawa leru*, *Caryota* sp.

Neither the betel nor the areca, therefore, occupy a particular position in the classification. However, in myth they are considered the mother and father of all plants, because they were created first in heaven. Despite this, the plant species created in myths are limited; starting from the original betel, only varieties of the same plant appear, whereas all the (admittedly few) palms are born from the areca.

In fact, associated with this myth of the origin of the betel and the areca nut in the first moment of creation, is the division between the soft, the betel, and the hard, the areca nut; the first symbolizing flesh, the second bone and eventually trees. I cannot expand here on this symbolism which conforms exactly to the position of the two plants in the classification (the betel being in the category of plants needing a support and the areca in a group of woody plants). Anyway, it tells us nothing further about the subject treated here.

Plants used for spraying seeds in fertility rituals

In the Bunaq system of symbolic representation, coldness is connected with fertility. On several occasions it is necessary to cool the plants symbolically; in particular, a seed-cooling ritual takes place before sowing. For this, water, coconut milk (if available), and the blood of a young pig—an animal considered to be cold—are used. A small branch is used as a sprinkler, frequently a branch of *kabokeq*, *Ficus septica* Burm.

This shrub is also considered cold. However, there is no category of "cold" plants in Bunaq botanical classification. In fact, the quality of "cold" or "hot" may vary during the life of a plant, or even according to the part of the plant concerned. Thus, a grass which is "cold" at the start of its life becomes "hot" towards the end and its consumption becomes dangerous to livestock, and the buds of *Ficus* are always considered cold although not the entire tree.

The notion of "cold" is relative, therefore, and the use of *kabokeq* as a sprinkler is connected to a group of characteristics. In particular, these appear in the position occupied by the plant in the classification. To start with, this *Ficus* belongs to the category *hotel$_1$ il$_2$ bul$_3$*, "tree$_1$ foundation (of the)$_2$ water$_3$", that is to say, trees which are considered to store water. Also in this category are other *Ficus* designated by the basic term *pur* (to which are added different qualifiers), which are the banyans or "stranglers". It is easy to appreciate the use of the latter term, given that they finally kill the host trees on which they live. This phenomenon is observed perfectly by the Bunaq. Understandably, the banyans cannot be used as fertility symbols. On the other hand, *Ficus septica* (*kabokeq*), which grows independently and remains a brilliant green throughout the dry season when other vegetation in the neighbourhood is brownish, may seem more appropriate for the ritual. Furthermore, as cuttings root easily it can be planted close to the ritual places where it will be used and, more importantly, near the village communal altar where collective rituals take place.

Kabokeq belongs also to the category *hotel$_1$ susuqil$_2$* "latex$_2$ tree$_1$", and within this to the sub-category *pur-kabokeq*. This is designated, as often happens in the Bunaq botanical classification, by the names of the two most significant plants of the group (illustrating again, as in the mythical texts, association by pairs). In this last category (which contains all the arboreal *Ficus* of the region) *kabokeq* belongs to the group of trees without *purel*, the aerial roots of the *pur*, and hence is not epiphytic, but it enjoys no special classificatory status.

In the mythical texts *kabokeq* is associated, in a metaphorical formula indicating that the rains are coming, with a plant which may be regarded as even colder, *ili goru, Podocarpus imbricatus* Bl. The latter is found only on high summits bathed in mist and is rarely seen by Bunaq in Lamaknen. But *ili goru* is never indicated as being used in the cooling rituals. This is certainly partly because of its rarity, but also because it is said that, unlike the *kabokeq*, it cannot tolerate heat. In contrast, the *lal gomo*, "masters of speech", say that it is possible to use *moruk*, *Gendarussa vulgaris* Nees, for these rituals. This is mentioned in mythical texts,[7] but I have never seen it used myself. The species is quite rare in Lamaknen and it is difficult to say if its occurrence there is spontaneous or subspontaneous. However, it is never intentionally planted by an altar as is the case among the Ema, neighbours of the Bunaq, in the territory where (according to myths) the ancestors of certain Bunaq lineages lived. Whatever the case may be, the Bunaq *moruk* is also considered as "cold" because it resists the drought. Nevertheless, in their botanical classification it is very distant from *kabokeq* and is found in an unnamed category of plants with nodes (*lepu*$_1$ *guk*$_2$, "inter-nodes$_1$ nodes$_2$"), which are neither bamboos (*ma*) nor grasses (*an*), and in which are found other Acanthaceae. The plant considered closest to *moruk*, despite having thorns, is *Barleria prionitis* L.

Plants used for expelling all that is harmful to man

Among the Bunaq there exists a ritual called *heruk wa*, "to throw thorns". The purpose of this is to expel superfluous speech, either good or bad, pronounced in connection with the person for whom the ritual is performed, and to reject all harmful elements, including sickness, which may accumulate around him or her. For this ritual they kill a goat, an animal considered as "hot" and "armed" because of its horns, on which the harmful elements are believed to be carried away. In an old basket are placed the ears of the animal, coins which symbolically support the action and a thorny branch, the thorns performing the role of a foil. After a ritual recitation, the basket is placed in the fork of a tree towards the setting sun which carries it away beyond visibility.

A similar ritual called *hala pos*, "rubbish scraps", takes place after rebuilding a house or making repairs to a roof, and involves clearing the dwellings of all dirt which has accumulated during the work, the debris of the materials used and also abandoned smudges from betel quids. In this ritual, too, thorny branches are used for what may be considered as a symbolic sweeping of the house.

To what species do these branches belong?

Generally, the Bunaq conform to a model provided by myth. In one of the journeys of the ancestors, those coming from the south clean the soil with *tilon* and *bau berek*, two species which, in Bunaq eyes, symbolize all thorny plants. There are two kinds of *tilon*: *tilon asa* (*tilon* designating the canines of a dog, *asa* being a name for a man), *Caesalpina purpurea* (Prain) Hattinck, is that of myth according to informants; but it is the rarer of the two and is found only in woods far from the villages, and, therefore, is usually replaced, by *tilon lotu* (*lotu* means "short"), *Caesalpina decapetala* (Roth) Alston, which often grows around dwellings and is sometimes planted in quickest hedges. *Bau berek*, *Capparis sepiaria* L., a name also given to a human being, is a species particularly common to the lowlands and dry areas. Theoretically it would be possible to use any thorny plant in place of *tilon* and *bau berek* in these rituals. In practice, the only plant that I have seen used in the rare cases when they did not have *tilon* to hand, is *aq zon*, "wild aubergine", *Solanum ferox* L. Nevertheless, there are many other thorny species in Lamaknen, including big trees such as *lawal loi, Erythrina orientalis* (L.) Merr. or *heruk nuek, Zanthoxylum armatum* D.C.

Why have *Caesalpina purpurea* and *Capparis sepiaria* been chosen to symbolize the category of thorny plants labelled *gobuq geruk* (*gobuq* are the protuberances found on certain stems, *geruk* the thorns on the tree) and which in fact contains chiefly thorny plants?

Tilon and *bau berek* have two characteristics which group them together: they are climbing shrubs and have strong thorns curved towards the base, which explains why the term *tilon* is also applied to the canines of dogs. However, in High Lamaknen, *bau berek* is almost thornless and never reaches the size attained in the lowlands, where it can form tangled thickets. *Caesalpinia purpurea* also seems to be a species of the dry zones,[8] whereas *C. decapetala* grows more often in high places, at the level of the villages of High Lamaknen.

It is possible that the choice of *bau berek* and *tilon asa* to symbolize thorny plants dates from a period when the ancestors of the Bunaq lived in lower and drier zones. The characteristics of these two species are not so much the thorns themselves, or their shape, for there exists at least one species with the same characteristics in High Lamaknen,[9] but their capacity to form extensive, dense thickets of clinging branches from which it is difficult to disentangle oneself.

Prohibited plant species

In Lamaknen there are several types of prohibitions regarding plant species: prohibitions on planting, on use as fuel for cooking (of which the thorny trees examined above are an example) and, finally, prohibitions on consumption and contact.

Some prohibitions apply through descent; they refer to episodes of mythical history in which the species concerned performed a role and they relate, in principle, to all the descendents of the heroes that participate in these episodes. Other prohibitions, specific to each

House, are due to the fact that all the species contained in a House's war *kaluk* are forbidden to the members of that House. The term *kaluk* applies to war altars and also to a whole group of magical remedies linked with these which enable people to be both invincible and miraculously cured of their wounds. As we shall see, the distinction between the two types of prohibition is not always clear. Some prohibitions also apply to animals, but there are fewer than with plants, and they do not concern us here.

When I conducted my surveys the traditional forms of war had disappeared. Everything relating to the *kaluk* had tended to fall into disuse, except the "night" *kaluk*, that is, those used for stealing. These continued to be used by some people and therefore have kept their secret aspect. In fact, it is difficult to say to what extent the prohibitions are still respected; the young do not always know those of their own House and people do not agree on who must respect them; whether it should be all members of a House or only the couple of old persons responsible for the sacred objects and the rituals concerning them.

The punishments which threaten those who transgress prohibitions are of three types; infections of the eye, of the skin, and accidents (such as falling from a tree or breaking a limb), but I must admit that I have not discovered the system of correspondence between the types of prohibition and types of sanction.

The first example which I examine has not been found in Lamaknen, but a little further east in Bunaq territory bordering Mutul, on the western slopes of Mount Lakus.

Bon: Entada phaseolides (L.) MERR., LEGUMINACEAE

The members of the House Lep of Mutul are not allowed to touch this plant and especially the seed which is used in a game of skill. This prohibition seems to originate from the fact that the ancestors of this House are the heroes of the myth *bon gozep* (*gozep*: to cut), in which the liana uniting heaven and earth is cut. In fact, this myth is very widespread in this region of Timor and the Bunaq of Lamaknen also know it, but no members of any House, even those who also claim descent from the heroes of the myth, observe the prohibition. However, it must be mentioned that in some Houses I have come across a prohibition on *bon* attributed to its presence in the *kaluk*. Given what is said in the mythical history of the House Lep, there is no reason to think that its ancestors, more than any others, descended from the heroes of *bon gozep*. By contrast, they are supposed to be the first Bunaq to have settled on Mount Lakus and it is for this reason that the House Lep which they founded is at the top of the political hierarchy. Though their descendants claim that the territory was empty when they arrived, perhaps the House Lep borrowed the myth of *bon gazep* from the autochthonous population, using it as evidence of the anteriority of their arrival on Lakus compared with other Bunaq. Alternatively, it may be understood as evidence of what the Bunaq always refuse to admit, namely their in-breeding with the original population.

However, what concerns us here is the particular status of *bon*, *Entada phaseolides*, considered to be the liana which unites heaven and earth. Why this one and not one of the other numerous lianas which exist in Lamaknen? For the Bunaq, lianas are placed in the category *mun*, a term closer to the French "liane" than to the English "vine", in so far as it usually only refers to plants whose stem is used for binding and not to the whole group of creepers. In the category *mun*, the plants are classified according to the size of the stem, the two biggest being *bon* and *tupa* (*Derris scandens* (Roxb.) Benth.), which form a pair in the ritual texts, referring to the tether used for cattle. But what distinguishes *bon* from *tupa* is that the first possesses very characteristic, segmented fruits which can reach more than a metre in length and a no less remarkable round seed, 4 to 5 centimetres in diameter, which is a beautiful red–brown and perfectly smooth. The role that *bon* plays in mythology also relates to its form. It is the tallest known liana; it climbs to the top of trees and, in fact, one never sees its foliage, which spreads out over the vault of vegetation around water. Its presence is often only evident by the seeds which fall to its foot.

Manuk: Hiptage benghalensis (L.) KURZ., MALPIGHIACEAE

Having noted the prohibitions House by House, it became apparent that in all of the dwellings of High Lamaknen this species could not be used as fuel. The first explanation given for this prohibition is that *manuk* is part of a *kaluk* common to the entire region, the other elements of which I shall examine below. In fact the leaves of *manuk* are considered to be medicinal; they are used for reducing fever and treating bee stings. But subsequently the prohibition (which extends even to the western limits of Lamaknen) was justified on other grounds. For some people it is due to the fact that it was by means of the roots of this plant that their ancestors rose to the surface of the earth. *Manuk*, a liana also belonging to the category *mun* (within a group in which the stems are a little smaller than those of *bon* and *tupa*), is known to have very strong roots. But informants only knew of one House originating from those ancestors which arose with the help of the roots of *manuk*. Moreover, it seems that members of this House do not acknowledge it. Nevertheless this type of explanation, symmetrical with, and inverse to, that given for the *bon* prohibition, was provided by informants. This is the only occasion that the common Timorese belief in a double origin of humanity is found among the Bunaq; one part coming from heaven and the other coming out of the ground in the place concerned. The explanation was sometimes combined with the idea that certain lineages came from beyond the seas.

The impression that the prohibition on *manuk* is connected in one way or another with the autochthones is confirmed by the explanation which was given to me in a House of Abis, heir of the House of the chief *melus*. According to tradition, the ancestors of this House expelled all *melus* with the exception of two old couples who went back to live in the lineage dwelling with the newcomers. Now, one of the two old women had a dove as a protecting animal, and in the place where the bird found its food a *manuk* grew. This was why the members of this House could not use the liana as fuel. Isolated from the cultural context referred to earlier, this explanation illuminates nothing at all. Unfortunately, there exist many other prohibitions for which the only explanations we possess are narratives which are impossible to interpret.

SOME SPECIES BELONGING TO THE WAR *kaluk*
OF THE VILLAGES OF HIGH LAMAKEN

For my last example I will briefly examine some plants which belong to the *kaluk* of different Houses of High Lamaknen, beginning with those which are common to all: *hotel ewi, Mallotus philippinensis* Muell. Arg., Euphorbiaceae; *iu, Cordia* sp., Borraginaceae; and *pisul, Bridelia ovata* Decne Euphorbiaceae.

The first of these species is a little tree of the family Euphorbiaceae which is found from the Himalayas to Australia and should, therefore, be indigenous to Timor. Nevertheless its name suggests that its introduction is recent. In fact, the qualifier *ewi* is generally used to indicate that which is modern; thus *deu ewi* is a house without piles, such as those constructed nowadays. The meaning of *ewi* is possibly "white man" and this term might therefore be extended to designate things belonging to either Europeans or Chinese. However, *ewi* could also mean "pale-faced" and, in this sense, might be extended to the deceased. Thus, in Taqpoq, one of the most famous heroes of Bunaq myths is called *Mau ewi* because, as informants told me, he was resuscitated by his wives. Hence it is difficult to decide which characteristics of *Mallotus philippinensis* are alluded to by the qualifier *ewi*. It is unclear whether this tree is indigenous to Lamaknen or not, largely because the environment has been so transformed by man, and unfortunately I only possess specimens collected either in dancing places, or in the protected woods around a village, or on the road sides.

The leaves of *hotel ewi* are chewed with betel and then used as poultices for healing wounds; also Burkill (1935) mentions that it is used to treat skin diseases.

Certain informants, but specifically in villages where *hotel ewi* is not part of the *kaluk*, have told me about a category "cold *kaluk* remedy" to which this tree would belong, but the people in Abis refused to put it into any category, saying that it did not resemble any other plant.

Iu, which signifies "maggot" in Bunaq, is applied to two species of *Cordia: C. dichotoma* Forst. and *C. monoica* Roxb. The fruits of *iu* are also chewed with betel and then applied to skin diseases, being used in particular for drawing out pus. They are also used as a cure for arthritic pains. In fact, people who transgress the prohibition expose themselves to skin disease. Even those who do not have *iu* in their *kaluk* but own goats, cannot burn it, since otherwise the latter would be covered with sores and maggots.

The plant itself is considered to be the habitat of maggots, a property which it shares with *obot, Ehretia acuminata* R. Br. For this reason and also because they resemble each other, particularly in their fruits (which can be used as glue), *iu* is considered close to *obot*, which is a tree belonging to the same family of Borraginaceae. However, these trees themselves are not placed in a wider category.

Although the medicinal use of the bark of *C. dichotoma* (given by Burkill as an antifebrile (Philippines and Java) and a remedy for ulcers of the mouth (Philippines)) would lead one to believe that the plant possesses curative qualities, it is also possible that the qualities which the Bunaq claim for it are related to their belief that it is the habitat of maggots. But if so, why is it *iu* and not *obot* that is in the *kaluk*?

For *pisul*, the last *kaluk* plant common to the three villages of High Lamaknen, it seems that there is also a correlation between its assumed power to cure abscesses; its name, which curiously recalls the term *bisul*, "abscess" in Indonesian; and the fact that it is a plant with *gobuq*, "protuberances", belonging to the category *gobuk geruq*. But in this it is not alone.

However, why does there exist a *kaluk* common to all the inhabitants of the three villages of High Lamaknen, which suggests that the plants in it are efficacious for all their members? When examining the case of *manuk* we found that the prohibition relating to it seems to have had its origin in the myths of the population inhabiting the locality prior to the Bunaq. Does this also apply to the other three plants? Should we see there either the trace of a political alliance or proof that all are descended from common ancestors? This poses the problem of the transmission of the *kaluk*, masculine goods *par excellence*, in a society where goods are transmitted through women. Men, it appears, only have an effective role in the transmission of material and moral property when they establish a new House, and I should emphasize that it is the property of their matrilineage which they are able to pass on to their offspring. The contribution of the founders of a new House, men and women, is not always clearly defined in so far as the conditions of foundation are multiple. In the case of a House which spreads for reasons of demographic or territorial expansion, the new House is considered as junior, and the prohibitions of both descent and *kaluk* should be transmitted in their entirety. In the case of a move following a conflict of interests and the establishment of a new House, sometimes with people of other origins, it is very difficult to state precisely how much of the House of origin is carried over to the new one. However, when the distance between the two is great, there is often no indication of the circumstances of the move.

In the examples of transmission of *kaluk* which were given to me, there are cases where most of the elements have now been lost. It could be, therefore, that the transmission of the *kaluk* is more territorial than genealogical, the new arrivals adopting the magical remedies of the latter from the moment they become part of a village community. This is characteristic of Bunaq society: the conflict between the solidarity of the lineage, accounted for matrilineally, and the consciousness of belonging to a House itself included in a village, both of which have a territorial and political status and constitute communities of interest.

Up till now we have encountered no prohibitions on important, cultivated food plants. It seems that there are few of these and none relating to basic foods, in any case. They are found, however, for certain varieties of bananas and yams. In particular, the two *kaluk* of the two main Houses at Abis each include a prohibited yam. In one case it is a variety of the great yam (*Dioscorea alata*) called *dik bukta belis*, whose tuber is somewhat small and gourd-shaped. In the other instance it is a variety of *Dioscorea esculenta, dik zulo bule qen*, whose tuber is ovoid and not very large. Neither of these have any remarkable characteristics, and again it is difficult to think why they should be placed in the *kaluk* of these Houses. For one of the two, I have been told a story which supposedly explains the prohibition: the yam was found in the woods during a ritual hunt. This story was contested by other informants, but in any case, it explains nothing at first sight.

However, one should not forget that these *kaluk* plants were supposed to have a magical action and it is possible that the composition of the *kaluk* developed over time, increased by either newly introduced species or others which had existed for a long time in the local flora. The latter force themselves upon a member of a House when they are found in special circumstances. For example, in Lamaknen certain individuals learn in dreams how to use particular plants as medicines and then become healers. It is through an individual experience, then, that the relation between the way in which a plant is used and its place in Bunaq culture as a whole must be interpreted. If the experience is not memorized an interpretation becomes impossible. However, it is possible to imagine that some of the plants which were only "good for thinking" become useful for some purpose.

Conclusion

Here I end my examination of the different examples of socially significant plants among the Bunaq, as the range of cases considered now seems sufficient to attempt an answer to the question which I posed at the beginning: is it fruitful to compare the role which a plant may perform and the place which it occupies in the classification?

The first example examined, that of betel and areca, provided a perfect correspondence between the position occupied by these two plants in the classification and their morphological and physiological characteristics. The areca belongs to the category *hotel upan gutu* and the betel to that of the plants which are unable to live without something to climb on. Let us add that this last point enables us to refine the image of betel in the Bunaq system of symbolic representations, where this species represents the soft in opposition to the hard. But neither *pu*, the areca, nor *molo*, the betel, occupy significant positions in their respective categories.

Of those plants used in the cooling rituals, the situation is not at all the same for *kabokeq* or *moruk*. For the first of these plants the position within the category of *hotel susuqil*, "latex trees", is hardly enlightening, except in that it indicates that *kabokeq* has no aerial roots. On the other hand, its belonging to the category *hotel il bul*, "trees foundation of water", and the position which it occupies there, explains how it can appear as the symbol of "cold" and, therefore, of fertility. But the place occupied by *moruk*, next to a thorny Acanthaceae in the category of noded plants, gives no clue to the characteristics which have led to it being regarded as a fertility symbol.

As far as the thorny *tilon* and *bau berek* are concerned, if they had not been compared with all the members of the category *gobuq geruk*, it would not have been possible to grasp exactly what they represent. It would also have been impossible to understand that their symbolic significance could not have originated in an environment corresponding to that of High Lamaknen, but in lower and drier zones which were probably the habitat of the ancestors of the Bunaq.

Generally speaking, the problems of interpreting the prohibitions on the consumption and utilization of certain species are more complex than those raised by ritual plants, and seem to be inseparable from the history of the Houses which uphold them.

For *bon* and *manuk*, whose significance goes beyond the limits of a single House, their belonging to the category *mun* and their characteristics within this category are essential for understanding their role in myth.

Iu and *pisul* are plants whose roles are directly connected to their appearance; but in both cases the comparison with plants close to them in the classification raises one question: why have they been chosen when others present the same characteristics: *obot* for *iu*, and for *pisul* other *gobuq* plants (for example *akantai*, *Woodfordia frutescens* (L.) Kurz.).

Perhaps for these plant remedies the choice is based on a genuine efficaciousness. For other *kaluk* plants, as the type of efficaciousness expected of them is not always stated precisely, it is difficult to establish a link between use and classification. Thus one may wonder whether or not the fact that the best "plants for thinking" were used by the community meant that Houses chose species with more discrete characteristics for their magical remedies or their descent-based prohibitions, especially as they had to remain secret in the case of the *kaluk*.

In the case of a network classification like that of the Bunaq, it is necessary not only to find the category to which a plant belongs, in order to attempt to understand the role attributed to it, but also to place it in relation to the plants considered closest to it. We have noticed that the qualities which distinguish a particular species are not defined in the abstract, but in relation to the characteristics of the plants either classified in the same category or situated closely in the links of the network. The location of a plant within the classification is not sufficient to explain the role attributed to it by a given population; it must also be placed in the wider cultural context. However, the comparison of a species, not with all the rest of the plant world, but with plants belonging to a certain category within the classification of a community and adapted to the flora surrounding it, seems to be the safest way to understand the mechanism of attribution of a particular role devolving on the plant and, therefore, to engage in fruitful comparison.

Thus, to understand what *bon* represents among the Bunaq it has been necessary to refer to myth. But the fact that this liana, *Entada phaseolides*, is designated as the bond linking heaven and earth must lead us to ask ourselves about the role performed by this same species wherever it is found in the local flora, whether or not it is the biggest or the highest and whether or not its fruits might be considered extraordinary. At the same time we might ask if, in certain cultures, the mythical tie between heaven and earth could not be entrusted to a very tall tree with a particularly straight trunk. In the same way, one would have to find what the *Capparis sepiaria* and the *Caesalpinia purpurea* represent for populations living in a dry and hot environment. As for the Lamaknen Bunaq's choice of *Ficus septica* as a plant bringing coldness and, therefore, fertility, it is not significant in itself but because it rules out other species of the same category on the one hand, like the banyan, which nevertheless in other cultures symbolizes life and, on the other, *Gendarussa vulgaris* used by their neighbours.

While it is interesting to analyse classificatory processes in themselves, it is important to use the results characteristic of particular communities to clarify certain other aspects of the culture in which they obtain. What is discovered thus goes beyond the problematic of perception towards a perspective from which we can hope to obtain information on how these communities have developed in time and space.

Notes

1. The hierarchical order of taxa in scientific botany is: kingdom, phylum, class, order, family, genus, species.
2. This research appears particularly in Bulmer (1978, and this volume).
3. The *q* indicates a glottal stop; for the rest the transcription of Bunaq terms conforms to international conventions.
4. The term *deu* designates both a dwelling and a descent group. I distinguish the two meanings by using an initial capital letter to indicate the second.
5. Two collections of myths published with the Bunaq text opposite the French translation are given in the bibliography: Berthe (1972) and Friedberg (1978).
6. The identification of the specimens was carried out mainly in the Leiden herbarium in Holland, with the aid of botanists engaged on the *Flora Malesiana* under the direction of C. G. G. J. van Steenis. Certain identifications were made by R. C. Bakhuizen van den Brink, others required the assistance of specialists in the genus or family: T. A. Hattink for the Caesalpiniae, R. Geesink for the remaining Leguminacea, M. Jacobs for the Capparidacae and Malpighiaceae, J. H. Kern for the Cyperaceae, J. F. Veldkamp for the Graminaceae, and, finally, I am indebted to Airy Shaw of the herbarium of the Royal Botanic Garden at Kew, in London, for the Euphorbiaceae.
7. See, for example, verse 3511 in *Bei Gua* (Berthe, 1972).
8. Personal communication from T. A. Hattink of the Leiden Herbarium.
9. *Acacia pennata* Willd., *busa kuku*. *Busa* is "cat" and *kuku* has nothing to do with the austronesian term for "claw", but is the Bunaq term for "cover". The term *kuku lihut* (*lihut* = dense) means "thickets".

References

BERLIN, B. (1972). Speculations on the growth of botanical nomenclature. *Language in Society*, **1**, 51–86.
BERLIN, B. (1973). Folk systematics in relation to biological classification and nomenclature. *In* "Annual Review of Ecology and Systematics" Vol. 4, pp. 259–71.
BERLIN, B., BREEDLOVE, D. E. and RAVEN, P. H. (1968). Covert categories and folk taxonomies. *Am. Anthrop.*, **70**, 290–9.

BERLIN, B., BREEDLOVE, D. E. and RAVEN, P. H. (1973). General principles of classification and nomenclature in folk biology. *Am. Anthrop.*, **75**, 214–42.

BERTHE, L. (1972). "Bei Gua, Itineraire des Ancêtres, Mythes des Bunaq de Timor" CNRS, Paris.

BUFFON, G. L. L. (1752). "Histoire Naturelle Générale et Particulière avec la Description du Cabinet du Roi" (5th edition), Vol. I. Imprimerie Royale, Paris.

BULMER, R. N. H. (1967). Why is the cassowary not a bird? *Man (N.S.)*, **2**, 5–25.

BULMER, R. N. H. (1970). Which came first, the chicken or the egg-head? *In* "Échanges et Communications" (Eds J. Pouillon and P. Maranda), pp. 1069–91. Mouton, The Hague, Paris.

BULMER, R. N. H. (1972–3). Karam classifications of marsupials and rodents. *J. Polynesian Soc.*, **81**, 472–99; **82**, 86–107.

BULMER, R. N. H. (1974). Folk biology in the New Guinea Highlands. *Soc. Sci. Inform.*, **13**, 9–28.

BULMER, R. N. H. (1978). Totems and taxonomy. *In* "Australian Aboriginal Concepts" (Ed. L. R. Hiatt), pp. 1–19. Australian Institute of Aboriginal Studies, Canberra.

BULMER, R. N. H. and TYLER, M. J. (1968). Karam classification of frogs. *J. Polynesian Soc.*, **77**, 333–385.

BURKILL, I. H. (1935). "A Dictionary of the Economic Products of the Malay Peninsula". Crown Agents for the Colonies, London.

CONKLIN, H. C. (1954). The relation of Hanunoo culture to the plant world. Unpublished Ph.D. dissertation, Yale University, New Haven.

DOUGLAS, M. (1966). "Purity and Danger". Routledge and Kegan Paul, London. (Translated into French (1971) as "De la Souillure". Maspéro, Paris.)

DOURNES, J. (1968). Bois-bambou (köyau-ale): Aspect végétal de l'univers Jörai. *J. d'Agric. trop. Bot. appl.*, **15**, 89–156, 369–498.

FERRY, M. P. (1974). A quels critères de classification répondent les classes nominales des végétaux basari. *J. d'Agric. trop. Bot. appl.*, **21**, 101–9.

FRIEDBERG, C. (1968). Les méthods d'enquête en ethnobotanique. Comment mettre en évidence les taxonomies indigènes? *J. d'Agric. Trop. Bot. appl.*, **15**, 297–324.

FRIEDBERG, C. (1970). Analyse de quelques groupements de végétaux comme introduction à l'étude de la classification botanique bunaq. *In* ("Échanges et Communications, Mélanges offerts à Claude Lévi-Strauss" (Eds J. Pouillon and P. Maranda), Vol. 2, pp. 1092–131. Mouton, The Hague, Paris.

FRIEDBERG, C. (1971). Aperçu sur la classification botanique bunaq (Timor central). *Bull. Soc. Bot. Fr.*, **118**, 255–62.

FRIEDBERG, C. (1972). Eléments de botanique Bunaq. *In* "Langues et Techniques, Nature et Société" (Eds J. Thomas and L. Bernot), 2 Vols. Klincksieck, Paris.

FRIEDBERG, C. (1974). Les processus classificatoires appliqués aux objets naturels et leur mise en évidence. Quelques principes méthodologiques. *J. d'Agric. trop. Bot. appl.*, **21**, 313–43.

FRIEDBERG, C. (1978). "Comment fut tranchée la liane céleste et autres textes de littérature orale bunaq (Timor, Indonésie)". Société d'études linguistiques et anthropologiques de France, Paris.

KEESING, R. M. (1972). Paradigms lost: the new ethnography and the new linguistics. *S. West J. Anthrop.*, **28**, 299–332.

LÉVI-STRAUSS, C. (1966). "The Savage Mind". Weidenfeld and Nicolson, London.

MACDONALD, CH. and MACDONALD, N. (1974). Perspectives d'enquête à partir des catégories du repas palawan. *Soc. Sci. Inform.*, **13**, 29–42.

MARTIN, M. A. (1974). Essai d'ethnophytogéographie khmère. *J. d'Agric. trop. Bot. appl.*, **21**, 219–238.

REVEL-MACDONALD, N. (1975). Le vocabulaire des oiseaux en palawan. Quelques réflexions sur le problème des taxonomies idigènes. *In* "L'Homme et L'Animal, Premier Colloque d'Ethnozoologie" (Ed. R. Pujol). Institut International d'Ethnosciences, Paris.

SPERBER, D. (1975). Pourquoi les animaux, les hybrides et les monstres sont-ils bons a penser symboliquement. *L'Homme*, **15**, 5–34.

STURTEVANT, W. C. (1964). Studies in ethnoscience. *In* "Transcultural Studies in Cognition" (Eds A. Kimball Romney and Roy G. D'Andrade). *Am. Anthrop.*, **66**, Part 2 (special publication).

TORNAY, S. (1973). Langage et perception, La dénomination des couleurs chez les Myanyatom de Sud-Ouest éthiopien. *L'Homme*, **13**, 66–94.

5

The Abominations of Leviticus Revisited

A Commentary on Anomaly in Symbolic Anthropology[1]

Eugene Hunn

Marvin Harris's materialist critique of theories of culture sees little significant difference between the perspectives of cognitive anthropologists, students of folk classification in the ethnoscience tradition, and symbolic anthropologists in the French structuralist tradition (Harris, 1968, pp. 598–600). Both schools are concerned with language data and see the conceptual realities of native speakers as objects worthy of study in their own right. Thus, from the materialist perspective cited, cognitive and symbolic anthropology are but two manifestations of one idealist fallacy.

Despite the commonalities, there has been little or no theoretical effort common to these two "idealist" approaches. Even when the research focus is restricted to the domains of folk biology—the classification of plants and animals—the two schools fail to interact productively. We have penetrating analyses of totemism by Lévi-Strauss and of ritually salient animals by Leach and Douglas. On the other hand, Conklin and Berlin have stimulated a body of research and theoretical speculation concerning the particular and the universal in how people organize their understanding of plants and animals.

Though Bulmer's work contributes to both approaches and Lévi-Strauss used Conklin's and Frake's data in his *Savage Mind* (Lévi-Strauss, 1966), there is no synthesis of symbolic and cognitive anthropology.

The present essay grew out of my attempt to understand why no synthesis has occurred.[2] In lieu of proposing a synthetic programme, I will look at a classic case of symbolic analysis from an ethnoscientific perspective. The case is that of the biblical abominations of Leviticus and Deuteronomy, which raises the more general issue of the significance of anomalous categories in systems of sacred symbols. The contrast in the two approaches is instructive. In passing, I hope to show that the differences between symbolic and cognitive anthropology reflect significant differences in the role ascribed to material "reality".

Briefly, the point at issue is: why are certain species of animals ascribed special ritual potency by a given culture? Why are certain species promoted to totemic status, others treated matter-of-factly? Why are some edible, others inedible; some clean, others defiling; one permitted, another taboo? (see Ellen, 1972; Tambiah, 1969; Wijewardene, 1968). Symbolic anthropologists rightly reject piecemeal explanations which seek to explain each animal's role by reference either to "etic" properties of the particular animal or its material impact on the human society involved. A different explanatory principle might need to be invoked for each animal. The assertion that pigs are prohibited as food because they may pose a threat of trichinosis is a familiar example. Not only are such approaches logically inelegant, they fail to provide an explanation for cultural variation, since immutable characteristics of the organism are cited by way of explanation. They explain too little and they explain too much; too little in their restricted application to only one, or a small set, among the species prohibited, too much in their implied universal applicability. By contrast, symbolic anthropologists have sought a consistent and comprehensive explanation in the *systemic* properties of particular cultures. In Mary Douglas's words, "The only way in which pollution ideas make sense is in reference to a total structure of thought . . ." (1966, p. 41). In particular, the mediating role of structurally ambiguous concepts within the particular cultural framework is stressed as an explanatory principle.

It is noteworthy that in pursuing the laudable goal of consistent and comprehensive explanations, it may be necessary to reject the native rationale, the "emic" theory. For example, Lele women must take elaborate ritual precautions in handling fish. Douglas notes that if we

interpret this behavior by saying that they wish to avoid any confusion of the dry and
the water elements, . . . this would not be a translation of any Lele explanation. If asked
why they do it, they reply: "To prevent an outbreak of coughing and illness".

(1957, p. 52)

Douglas avers that

from the point of view of religious symbolism it is not relevant to ask how accurate is
Lele observation of natural phenomena. . . . A symbol based on mistaken information
can be fully effective as a symbol. . . .

(1957, p. 56)

In short, the explanatory strategy of symbolic anthropology leads to the definition of the material context as beside the point.

Leach illustrates this viewpoint in an extreme fashion in his classic study of "Animal categories and verbal abuse" (1964). For Leach,

The physical and social environment of a young child is perceived as a continuum . . .
The child . . . is taught to *impose* upon his environment a . . . grid which serves to
distinguish the world as being composed of a large number of separate things, each
labelled with a name.

(1964, p. 34)

Thus material reality is a cultural construct and, as such, cannot serve to explain cultural facts. The power of ambiguity resides in the threat it poses to the constructed cultural order: cultural order is at war with natural disorder.

This contrast between human Culture and Nature is very striking. Visible, wild Nature
is a jumble of random curves; it contains no straight lines and few regular geometrical
shapes of any kind. But the tamed, man-made world of Culture is full of straight lines,
rectangles, triangles, circles and so on.

(Leach, 1972, p. 51)

Anyone who has marvelled at the order of a beehive will perceive the ethnocentrism in this characterization of nature. Yet Douglas's renowned analysis of the biblical abominations detailed in Leviticus and Deuteronomy is inspired by just such an extreme dichotomy between ideal culture and material nature. Douglas and Leach have served us well by bringing the power of anomaly to the fore and by demanding consistent explanations of, and intellectual respect for, the ideas of non-Western peoples. However their lack of concern for the material context of the symbolic systems they analyse limits the significance of their arguments.

Though few would dispute the relevance of the empirical reality for a people's economic life, the relevance of that reality for our understand-

TABLE 1
The edible "beasts" (Deuteronomy 14:4–5)

Driver (1903)	Revised standard	King James	Scientific name
Ox	Ox	Ox	*Bos taurus*
Sheep	Sheep	Sheep	*Ovis aries*
Goat	Goat	Goat	*Capra hircus*
Hart (ᴐhind)	Hart	Hart	*Cervus elephas*
Gazelle	Gazelle		*Gazella* spp.
Roebuck	Roebuck	Roebuck	*Capreolus capreolus*
		Fallow deer[a]	
Wild goat	Wild goat Ibex[a]	Wild goat	*Capra ibex*
Addax		Pygarg	*Addax nasomaculatus*
Antelope	Antelope		*Oryx leucoryx*
		Wild ox[a]	
Mountain-sheep	Mountain-sheep		*Ovis ammon*
		Chamois[a]	

[a]See Driver (1903, pp. 159–60).

ing of religious symbolism may not be granted so readily. However, consider the eminently edible animals of the biblical texts of Douglas's well known analysis (Table 1). The biblical list is as follows: ox, goat, sheep, wild goat, mountain-sheep, hart, roebuck, gazelle, addax and the antelope or oryx.[3] These ten folk species constitute an exclusive and exhaustive listing of the species of the artiodactyl sub-order Ruminantia known from the home range of the Hebrews (Table 2). In modern folk biology the list constitutes a covert intermediate taxon—unnamed yet corresponding closely to a supra-specific scientific taxon (for definitions, see Berlin, 1973; for a discussion of the correspondence of

TABLE 2
Mammals of the Middle East[a]

Orders/ sub-orders	Families	Genera/species
Insectivora (5/7)[b]	Erinaceidae Soricidae	3/3[b] (hedgehogs) 2/4 (shrews)
Chiroptera (15/28)	eight families	(bats)
Primates (1/1)	Hominidae	*Homo sapiens*

Table 2 *continued*

Carnivora[c] (17/23)		
⎰ Arctopoidea	⎰ Mustelidae	6/6 (marten, polecat, weasel, badger, honey badger, otter)
⎪	⎩ Ursidae	*Ursus arctos* (bear)
⎨ Herpestoidea	⎰ Viverridae	2/2 (mongoose, genet)
⎪	⎩ Hyaenidae	*Hyaena hyaena* (hyena)
⎩ Cynofeloidea	Canidae	*Canis*/3 (dog, wolf, jackal)
		Fennecus zerda (fennec fox)
		Vulpes/2 (foxes)
	Felidae	*Acinonyx jubatus* (cheetah)
		Caracal caracal (caracal)
		Felis/3 (cats)
		Panthera/2 (lion, leopard)
Hyracoidea (1/1)	Procaviidae	*Procavia capensis* (hyrax)
Perissodactyla (1/3)	Equidae	*Equus*/3 (ass, horse, onager)
Artiodactyla (11/16)		
⎰ Nonruminantia	Suidae	*Sus scrofa* (pig)
⎨ Tylopoda	Camelidae	*Camelus dromedarius* (dromedary)
⎩ Ruminantia	Cervidae	3/3 (red deer [hart, hind], roe deer, fallow deer)
	Bovidae	*Addax nasomaculatus* (antelope)
		Bos taurus (cattle)
		Capra/3 (goat, ibex, wild goat)[d]
		Gazella/3 (gazelles)
		Oryx leucoryx (oryx)
		Ovis/2 (sheep, mouflon)
Lagomorpha (1/1)	Leporidae	*Lepus capensis* (hare)
Rodentia (20/35)		
⎰ Sciuromorpha	Sciuridae	*Sciurus anomalus* (squirrel)
⎨ Hystrichomorpha	Hystrichidae	*Hystrix indica* (porcupine)
⎩ Myomorpha	Dipodidae	2/3 (jerboas)
	Muscardinidae	2/2 (dormice)
	Spalacidae	*Spalax leucodon* (mole rat)
	Muridae	5/9 (true rats, mice, etc.)
	Cricetidae	8/18 (hamsters, gerbils, jirds, voles)
TOTAL 9 orders	30 families	100 + species

[a]From Harrison (1972).

[b]The numbers separated by obliques summarize the number of genera and species in the region included in the taxon cited.

[c]Fissiped carnivore superfamilies follow the phylogeny of E. Thenius (Dathe, 1975, p. 23).

[d]The wild goat (*Capra aegagrus*) is native to Kurdistan and N.E. Iraq, thus probably unknown to the Hebrews.

TABLE 3
The unclean "beasts" (Leviticus 11:4–7; Deuteronomy 14:7–8)

Revised standard	King James	Scientific name
Camel	Camel	*Camelus dromedarius* (dromedary)
Hare	Hare	*Lepus capensis*
Rock badger		*Procavia capensis* (hyrax)
	Coney (sic.)	
Swine	Swine	*Sus scrofa* (pig)

folk to scientific taxonomic systems, see Hunn, 1975). Note also that in this case the folk theory needs no qualification. The edible beasts include "every animal that . . . has the hoof cloven in two, and chews the cud" (Deut. 14:6); in short, all ruminant artiodactyls, neatly matching a scientific taxon of presumed phylogenetic relevance.

Consider next the abominations; the pig, camel, hare and rock badger (Table 3). They are alleged to have either cloven hooves or to chew the cud, but not both characteristics. The bulk of the mammals not cited specifically are presumed to exhibit neither character. Many of these are later excluded from edibility by the "paws" criterion (Lev. 11:27). A two-by-two table may be used to illustrate the options (Table 4). Animals which are + cloven hoof, + cud chewing are edible; those which are negative on both criteria are (presumably) inedible as a matter of course. However, the pig is explicitly proscribed due to the "anomalous" character combination, + cloven hoof, − cud chewing. It is interesting to note that scientists likewise classify pigs as "non-

TABLE 4
Anomaly as the off-diagonal cells of a two-by-two table of character co-occurrences

	+ Chew cud		− Chew cud
+ Cloven hoof	Ox Sheep Goat Hart Gazelle	Roebuck Wild goat Addax Antelope (oryx) Mountain- sheep	Swine (pig)
− Cloven hoof	Camel Hare Rock-badger (hyrax)		Remaining mammals

ruminant" artiodactyls (Table 2). The camel, hare and hyrax are similarly proscribed; they are − cloven hoof, + cud chewing. Here the precise meanings of the Hebrew terms translated as "hoof" and "chew cud" appear to differ from lay English and scientific usages. There is semantic overlap clearly, but not semantic equivalence. Though we might debate whether or not hares chew their cud (cf. Lockley, 1964), or if a camel's hooves are cloven, the logical pattern is clear.

Yet a consideration of the scientific classification of mammals may suggest a different sense in which the primary abominations are "anomalous". The hyraxes are placed in a family and order of their own, the Procaviidae of the Hyracoidea, and there is but one species of hyrax in the Middle East (Harrison, 1972). The hare leaves behind its cousins, the rabbits, in Europe and is the sole exemplar of the order Lagomorpha occurring in the region in question. The camel and the pig are even-toed ungulates, sharing this status with the edible ruminants of Table 1. However, the camel and the pig are isolated in sub-orders of their own within the Artiodactyla; the camel in the Tylopoda, the pig in the Nonruminantia. Both have relatives elsewhere, but are unique examples of these sub-ordinal taxa in the Middle East. A review of Table 2 shows that no other species of mammal, with the exception of *Homo sapiens*, is as singular as hare and hyrax in the scientific scheme, and none but the squirrel and porcupine are locally monotypic at the sub-ordinal level.[4] From the scientific perspective these animals are not so much anomalous, i.e. "deviating from the regular arrangement, general rule", as they are *singular*. I will return to this contrast in conclusion.

In short, the scientifically defined relationships of the animals cited predict the boundaries of the distinctions drawn in Deuteronomy (14:3–9), as well as the priestly author/Mary Douglas rationale does. Can we go further, extending this argument where they fail to provide a reasonable explanation? Douglas demurs: "Birds I can say nothing about because, . . . they are *named and not described* and the translation of the name is open to doubt" (my emphasis, Douglas, 1966, p. 55). She offers the hope that,

If the list of unclean birds could be retranslated . . . , it might well turn out that they are anomalous because they swim and dive as well as fly, or in some other way they are not fully birdlike.

(1966, pp. 56–7)

First, translation problems are hardly unique to the birds; they are no less certainly translated than are the other animals cited on the average.[5] Nor are the prohibited birds anomalous in terms of either their mode of locomotion or habitat, Douglas's strategy for explaining restrictions placed on fish, reptiles and invertebrates.

Secondly, a retranslation of the prohibited birds has been prepared by the biblical scholar G. R. Driver, in consultation with the noted ornithologist David Lack (Driver, 1955, summarized in Parmalee, 1959). Driver found the list to be carefully organized. The birds listed fall into several groups and within each group the birds are listed in order of decreasing size (Table 5).

TABLE 5
The unclean "birds" (Leviticus 11:13–19, Deuteronomy 14:12–18)[a]

Hebrew name translated (as in Young's *analytical concordance*)	Dr. G. R. Driver's suggestions	Approximate length (in/mm)	Revised standard version	Authorized version
1) *Nesher*	Griffin-vulture (sometimes the golden eagle)	45/1143	Eagle	Eagle
2) *Peres*	Bearded vulture	45/1143	Ossifrage	Ossifrage
3) *Ozniyyah*	Short-toed eagle	27/686	Osprey	Osprey
4) *Daah*	(black) kite	23/584	Kite	Vulture
5) *Ayyah* "after its kind"	{ Saker falcon / Common buzzard	22/559 / 17/432	Falcon	Kite
6) *Oreb* "after its kind"	{ Raven / Rook	22/559 / 18/457	Raven	Raven
7) *Bath yaanah*	Eagle owl	18/457	Ostrich	Owl
8) *Tachmas*	Short-eared owl	14/356	Nighthawk	Nighthawk
9) *Shachaph*	Long-eared owl	14/356	Seagull	Cuckoo
10) *Nets* "after its kind"	{ Kestrel / Sparrow hawk	14/356 / 12/305	Hawk	Hawk
11) *Kos*	Tawny owl	16/406	Owl	Little owl
12) *Shalak*	Fisher owl		Cormorant	Cormorant
13) *Vanshuph*	Screech owl	13/330	Ibis	Great owl
14) *Tishemeth*	Little owl	10/254	Water hen	Swan
15) *Qaath*	Scops owl	8/203	Pelican	Pelican
16) *Racham*	Osprey	33/838	Vulture	Gier eagle
17) *Chasidah*	{ Stork / Heron	40/1016 / 38/965	Stork	Stork
18) *Anaphah*	Cormorant	33/338	Heron	Heron
19) *Dukiphath*	Hoopoe	12/305	Hoopoe	Lapwing
20) *Atalleph*	Bat		Bat	Bat

[a]From Parmalee (1959, p. 106).

First listed is the griffin-vulture, which may stand for all the large, broad-winged falconiform birds of the region, a total of three vultures and five large eagles. Next is the lammergeier or bearded vulture, unique among birds of its size in its graceful, tapering outline and solitary mien. It is called "the smasher" in Hebrew after its habit of dropping prey from a height in order to shatter its bones. Then the short-toed eagle; it is also called "watcher", a most apt typification (Parmalee, 1959, p. 108). The black kite follows; then a category which seems to have a residual character (see Hunn, 1976, p. 511) as it includes such dissimilar medium-sized raptors as the saker falcon and the buzzard. It seems probable that seven smaller falcons, two other buzzard-like hawks and two small "eagles" were also implicated here. The smallest falconiform species, the kestrels and accipiters, are noted later in the midst of the owls listed. Among the Falconiformes, only the harriers are not provided for explicitly in this listing.

The raven tribe is cited next, the phrase "after its kind" presumably including all six species of the genus *Corvus* known to frequent the region (Heinzel *et al.*, 1972). Then come, species by species, each of Palestine's eight owls, from the huge eagle owl, called "daughter of wilderness", misconstrued as the ostrich in earlier versions, to the tiny scops owl. Somehow, earlier translations had come up with ibises, water hens, swans, seagulls and cuckoos, for one or another of these owls.

The list of inedible birds concludes with three water birds; the osprey or fish hawk, the cormorant and a catch-all category of herons and storks, probably including all the well-known species of the ciconiiform order of the region. Tagged on at the end are the hoopoe and the bat.

Fifteen of the 20 folk categories just enumerated refer to birds of prey, probably barring from the table every known species of the falconiform and strigiform orders. Three additional categories eliminate the genus *Corvus*, all birds of scavenging propensities, and the fish-eating storks, herons and cormorants. Thus 18 of 20 birds cited are meat and fish eaters. The few carnivorous species not cited are relatively small and/or primarily dependent on invertebrate food items, scarcely worthy of the name carnivorous. This food preference is clearly the dominant principle underlying the avian prohibitions. Yet this is not an anomalous trait among birds; carnivorous birds are not less typical of birds than are carnivorous mammals, reptiles and fish of their classes.[6]

The avoidance of carnivorous species as food sources might be explained as marginally increasing the efficiency of human exploitation of the natural environment (i.e. allowing local human groups to live in the region at an increased population density) by lowering *Homo sapiens* a fraction of a rung on the food chain, an exemplary materialist explanation.[7] In this connection we might note, too, that carnivorous mammals are by implication also considered inedible. Moreover, the acceptable insects, the locusts and their kin, are classic examples of herbivorous insects, sharing with the ruminant ungulates the property of concentrating protein with exceptional efficiency, converting plant tissues otherwise unavailable to humans into a highly digestible form. Locust swarms are analogous to ungulate herds. Their widespread use as food by humans beings accords with their demonstrated value as exceptional sources of animal fats and protein (see Ruddle, 1973).

Our consideration of the material context brings us part way to a solution, at least as close as the symbolic analysts' approximation. However, the goal of a comprehensive and consistent solution still eludes us. Old world bats are not carnivorous in the sense of preying upon vertebrate flesh; and, of course, the bat is not a bird at all, or perhaps it is safer to say that it is the only furred "bird" which bears live young. It is clearly anomalous in Douglas's sense. But what of the hoopoe? R. Meinertzhagen (1964), in his *Birds of Arabia*, provides an answer when he refers to a most notable hoopoe habit of "fouling its nest": it is literally "unclean".[8]

We have now accounted for the birds of the biblical texts, but only by recourse to three distinct principles of explanation. Perhaps the symbolic anthropologists demand too much in requiring logical perfection of any cultural expression. I believe they are led to seek such perfection by virture of their failure to recognize that animal categories are conditioned simultaneously by cognitive processes and by the structure of the world perceived.

In summary, I would suggest that strict reliance on either idealist or materialist principles of cultural explanation is likely to lead to limited understanding. The strict idealist rejects out of hand, for example, the potential relevance of ecological principles relating to trophic levels, stressing the radical independence of human ideas from external constraint. The strict materialist chooses to ignore the significance of pressures for logical consistency in symbolic systems and, I believe, fails to appreciate the creativity of the human response to material patterns. The value of a dialectical perspective—stressing the intimate interaction of empirical realities and mental processes in the generation of cultural patterns—may be illustrated by considering the contrast between anomaly and singularity touched on earlier.

Again, the two-by-two table provides a simplified representation (see Tables 6, 7 and 8). The on-diagonal cells are the typical cases, those off-diagonal are "anomalous", as in the case of cloven hooves and cud chewing (Table 6). They may be anomalous *by definition*, by cultural fiat, as the Douglas argument implies. Or, more likely, they may be seen as anomalous by virtue of the fact that they represent empiri-

TABLE 6

Co-occurrence probabilities of cloven hooves and cud-chewing
(Reference population: species of Middle Eastern mammals.)

	+ Chew cud	− Chew cud
+ Cloven hoof	10	1
− Cloven hoof	3	90

Guttman's coefficient of predictability (symmetrical), $\lambda = 0.67$.

TABLE 7

The co-occurrence of feathers and flying

	+ Flying	− Flying
+ Feathers	Most birds	Cassowaries
− Feathers	Bats	Most land verbebrates

TABLE 8

The co-occurrence of external scales and aquatic habitat

	+ Scales	− Scales
+ Aquatic	Most fish	Cetaceans Eels Otters
− Aquatic	Lizards Snakes Pangolins	Most birds Mammals

cally infrequent trait complexes. If animals with cloven hooves were equally likely to either chew or not to chew their cud, it seems unlikely that one combination of characters would be seen as exceptional and the other normal, by the human observer. It is precisely this quality of surprise, associated with the empirically determined improbability of occurrence of a given combination of characters, that the familiar statistical measures of association are meant to quantify. I assert that the animal anomalies are not independent creations of a cultural system imposed upon natural chaos, but rather reflect creative human reactions to the perception of empirical correlations in the natural environment.[9] We might even employ a measure such as Guttman's coefficient of predictability to estimate the empirically determined factor (Freeman, 1965, pp. 71–8), as is done in Table 6.

It is no accident that animals which chew their cud also have hooves—both characteristics favour adaptation to open grassland habitats, which in turn is associated frequently with herding behaviour. Bats and cassowaries are empirically unexpected (Table 7); feathers and flight evolved together as parts of an ancient adaptive system. Thus flightless birds and flying mammals are widely noted among ritually singular animals. Likewise pangolins, snakes, eels, otters and cetaceans are particularly likely to receive special ritual note (cf. Douglas, 1957; Bulmer, 1967; Tambiah, 1969; Anderson, 1969) as exceptions to the dominant, aquatic vertebrate pattern exemplified by the vast majority of fish (Table 8). The selection of these types of animals for special ritual service supports Douglas's emphasis on anomaly as a key to understanding symbol systems. Their widespread and repeated selection in independent cultural systems suggests that symbol systems do not exist in an empirical vacuum. Rather symbol systems must be understood as creative syntheses of material and mental regularities. The logical anomalies are at the same time empirical rarities, and idealist and materialist explanations flank the truth.

Notes

1. An earlier version of this paper was presented at the symposium "Cognitive Systems in their Material and Behavioral Contexts: Examples from Ethnobiology", at the 75th Annual Meeting of the American Anthropological Association, Washington D.C., November 20, 1976. I would like to thank my colleagues at the Language–Behavior Research Laboratory, University of California, Berkeley, and

at the Department of Anthropology, University of Washington, Seattle, for the questions they raised at earlier informal presentations of the present arguments, and Roy Ellen and Ralph Bulmer for helpful criticisms at a later stage.

2. I suspect the lack of synthesis may be primarily due to the fact that ethnoscientific-ally oriented scholars have tended to emphasize the "technical" as opposed to the "expressive" aspects of human behaviour (cf. Leach, 1972, pp. 9ff.), while since Durkheim, structuralists have focussed almost exclusively on expressive culture.

3. I follow Driver (1903) here. See Table 1 for a comparison of his list with that of the Revised Standard and King James versions.

4. I cite the scientific classification scheme as an independent operational definition of the singularity of animal categories. It might be argued that the scientific classification scheme is not historically independent of the biblical scheme. This argument is not persuasive in light of the intense critical attention paid to scientific biological classification since Linnaeus's time.

5. This may be demonstrated by counting the number of times the Revised Standard and King James version are in agreement as to the translation of the Hebrew animal terms. They agree on 12 of the 20 birds (60%) and 16 of 26 of the remainder (62%).

6. In her recent book of essays, *Implicit Meanings*, Douglas comments on the Mishnaic contention that the inedible birds are predators. She suggests that the bird list can thus be explained as reflecting the Hebrew injunction that "the eating of blood defiles" (Douglas, 1975, p. 270). This explanation is still short of the mark in that fish eaters such as the osprey, fisher owl, stork, heron and cormorant, as well as the hoopoe and the bat, are not implicated by the injunction against eating blood.

7. I do not find this rationale particularly compelling because the alleged adaptive edge to be gained by specializing in herbivores is so slight. Given the approximate 90% energy loss between herbivores and first-order carnivores, we should expect carnivores to constitute no more than 10% of the faunal biomass. Thus the energetic advantage of specializing in the remaining 90% seems hardly worth the ideological effort of a prohibition. However, *prescribing* grass-eating, herding herbi-vores such as the ruminant artiodactyls and the locust tribe might very well pay off energetically.

8. The hoopoe is also notably catholic in its tastes and will eat small animals such as frogs and lizards. It might thus be classed with the first 18 as a flesh eater.

9. Roy Ellen brings a similar point home in his analysis of "The Marsupial in Nuaulu Ritual Behaviour". "To make a symbol meaningful . . . it has to possess certain intrinsic emblematic qualities. This is what makes the cuscus [the marsupial in question] a good symbol". (Ellen, 1972, p. 234.)

References

ANDERSON, E. N. (1969). Sacred fish. *Man (N.S.)*, **4**, 443–9.

BERLIN, B. (1973). Folk systematics in relation to biological classification and no-menclature. *Ann. Rev. Ecol. Sys.*, **4**, 259–71.

BULMER, R. N. H. (1967). Why is the cassowary not a bird? *Man (N.S.)*, **2**, 5–25.

BULMER, R. N. H. (1978). Totems and taxonomy. *In* "Australian Aboriginal Con-cepts" (Ed. L. R. Hiatt), pp. 1–19. Australian Institute of Aboriginal Concepts, Canberra.

DATHE, H. (1975). Carnivora. *In* "Grzimek's Animal Life Encyclopedia" (Chief Ed. B. Grzimek), Vol. 12 (thirteen vols). Van Nostrand-Reinhold, New York.

DOUGLAS, M. (1957). Animals in Lele religious symbolism. *Africa*, **27**, 46–58.

DOUGLAS, M. (1966). "Purity and Danger: An Analysis of Concepts of Pollution and Taboo". Routledge and Kegan Paul, London.

DOUGLAS, M. (1975). "Implicit Meanings: Essays in Anthropology". Routledge and Kegan Paul, London.

DRIVER, G. R. (1955). Birds in the Old Testament. *Palestine exploration fund quarterly*, **87**, 5–20.

DRIVER, S. R. (1903). A critical and exegetical commentary on Deuteronomy. *In* "The International Critical Commentary". Charles Scribner's Sons, New York.

ELLEN, R. F. (1972). The marsupial in Nuaulu ritual behaviour. *Man (N.S.)*, **7**, 223–38.

FREEMAN, L. C. (1965). "Elementary Applied Statistics: For Students in Behavioural Science". John Wiley and Sons, New York.

HARRIS, M. (1968). "The Rise of Anthropological Theory: A History of Theories of Culture". Thomas Y. Crowell, New York.

HARRISON, D. L. (1972). "The Mammals of Arabia" (three vols). Ernest Benn, London.

HEINZEL, H., FITTER, R. and PARSLOW, J. (1972). "The Birds of Britain and Europe with North Africa and the Middle East". J. B. Lippincott, Philadelphia.

HUNN, E. (1975). A measure of the degree of correspondence of folk to scientific biological classification. *Am. Ethnol.*, **2**, 309–27.

HUNN, E. (1976). Toward a perceptual model of folk biological classification. *Am. Ethnol.*, **3**, 508–24.

LEACH, E. R. (1964). Anthropological aspects of language: animal categories and verbal abuse. *In* "New Directions in the Study of Language" (Ed. E. H. Lenneberg). MIT Press, Cambridge, Mass.

LEACH, E. R. (1972). "Culture and Communication: The Logic by which Symbols are Connected". Cambridge University Press, Cambridge.

LÉVI-STRAUSS, C. (1966). "The Savage Mind". University of Chicago Press, Chicago.

LOCKLEY, R. M. (1964). "The Private Life of the Rabbit: An Account of the Life History and Social Behavior of the Wild Rabbit". MacMillan Publishing Company, New York.

MEINERTZHAGEN, R. (1954). "Birds of Arabia". Oliver and Boyd, Edinburgh.

PARMALEE, A. (1959). "All the Birds of the Bible; Their Stories, Identification and Meaning". Harper and Brothers, New York.

RUDDLE, K. (1973). The human use of insects: examples from the Yukpa. *Biotropica*, **5**, 94–101.

TAMBIAH, S. J. (1969). Animals are good to think and good to prohibit. *Ethnology*, **7**, 423–59.

WIJEWARDENE, G. (1968). Address, abuse and animal categories in northern Thailand. *Man (N.S.)*, **3**, 76–93.

6

Symbolism as Ideology

Thoughts Around Navaho Taxonomy and Symbolism

Brian Morris

Introduction[1]

Lévi-Strauss's seminal writings on "social structure", written more than a quarter of a century ago, were more than just digs at Radcliffe-Brown's empiricism; they were the beginnings of an attempt (later abandoned) to integrate anthropological knowledge into the Marxian tradition. For the essence of this discussion was to make a distinction between the "ideological" and the actual forms of the social order, between the "model" of the social structure and the "reality". The basic problem, he suggested, was to discern the relationship between how a "society conceives its orders and their ordering" and the "real situation" (Lévi-Strauss, 1963, p. 312). There is a suggestion here of an approach that is both critical and realist,[2] and uncontaminated by a psychologism that was to later permeate his work.

When we consider the subject of folk classifications and symbolism few contemporary anthropologists seem to have followed this particular theoretical trail. Significantly, one writer who did (Godelier, 1977) has treated religious synbolism as an ideological system.[3] But most writers on symbolism, although acknowledging the influence of Lévi-

Strauss, have moved in other directions, and have seen their task primarily in terms of delineating the *meaning* of symbolic phenomena (cf. Willis, 1975). Often treating all ideation as ideological, and thus doing something Marx (and implicitly Lévi-Strauss) never did—namely conflating social consciousness and ideology—such writers have tended to concentrate their analyses at the phenomenal level and to be over concerned with meaning in an endeavour to present the conceptual schemes of alien cultures in terms of their own construction of reality. These are valid exercises, but are none the less indicative not only of a parochial and uncritical approach towards social phenomena, but a virtual denial that symbolic schemes in themselves have any ideological or "screening" significance and, indeed, that they have any function, either social or political. When Fox (1975, p. 100) writes that students of symbolism are divided into those who seek "universals" and those who attempt to record the conceptual richness of symbolic structures, he seems to evade such issues altogether. So too, do writers like Sperber (1975) who, in a worthy attempt to get away from this "concern for meaning" (which as Pocock (1961) intimated, has recently filled the anthropological stage) have linked "symbolic knowledge" with specific modes of cognition . . . largely leaving aside the purposes to which such knowledge is put.[4] Malinowski's suggestion that myth was a charter for social action has occasionally been treated with derision, and few seem interested in linking conceptual schemes with the "real situation" (however that may be grasped conceptually[5]).

In his discussion of Malinowski, Sperber poses the question why "a long, complicated and obscure discourse" (the myth) should be necessary in order to establish clan privileges (1975, p. 6)—but never gets around to answering this question, only suggesting that such discourses exemplify a particular mode of cognition. The purpose of this present paper is to point out where I think an answer to Sperber's question lies, by suggesting that we return to the early concerns of Lévi-Strauss. I want then to plead that symbolic classifications can best be understood if put in an historical and comparative context, and seen as an ideological system that serves, as Lévi-Strauss suggested, to obfuscate or cover up reality; that symbolism, in fact, is inextricably linked with religion and power, and the maintenance of normative structures. I have no set analysis to support my contention—nor can I point to any satisfactory exemplification of my theme:[6] I make a plea rather than present a thesis. However, I shall give my thoughts some semblance of order by hinging the discussion around a specific ethnographic case—that of the

Navaho. I have chosen this particular community for the singular reason that there is a wealth of published material on their religious symbolism and folk classifications; indeed, few communities have been researched in such depth.[7] The quip that every Navaho family has at least one member who is an anthopologist may well have been true.

Navaho taxonomy: two problems

Let me begin by examining Navaho folk taxonomies, for there are two problems that initially need to be posed and clarified.

The first is the relationship between folk taxonomies and biological classification. Bulmer (1965), in a review of Wyman and Bailey, remarked that their analysis of Navaho insect classification convincingly showed a lack of "tidy correspondence" between Navaho categories and biological taxa of any level. I wish to argue that though this relationship may not be a "tidy" one, there is, in fact, a fairly close correspondence between Navaho technical classification and biological nomenclature. Why anthropologists ever assumed it might be otherwise, or, conversely, felt the need to stress that other cultures have a wealth of classificatory knowledge about the natural world, has always puzzled me.

The second problem relates to the question of what aspects of the total culture constitute the ideological, or the ritual or symbolic dimension. By looking specifically at the folk taxonomy I wish to argue for the need to dismantle the notion of culture. I would prefer to differentiate not between culture and social structure as many empiricists would do (for social structure itself is an ideological or ritual system), but between those aspects of the total culture which form part of a fairly unified symbolic system and the remainder of the socio-cultural order. In the context of folk taxonomies this means differentiating clearly between folk taxonomies that order a particular domain and the symbolic classifications of a religious nature. Earlier writers have confused the issues either by treating culture itself as a symbolic system or, and it amounts to the same thing, by equating "custom" with symbolism and ideology. In the terms of Douglas (1966), what I am suggesting is that no community has a culture which is "unified" or "undifferentiated", but rather that *some* communities have either ritual or symbolic systems that form a whole by uniting *aspects* of the total social process. As Bloch

(1977) has recently argued, it is erroneous to equate either social structure with society, or ritual communication or myth with the total culture. This misleading emphasis is only too apparent in Lévi-Strauss's discussion of folk taxonomies, where he suggests that ethnobiological taxonomies often form an integral part of an all-embracing taxonomy (Lévi-Strauss, 1966, p. 139). Such conceptual harmony is never found (except perhaps in the mind of some religious specialist), for as I shall later show, only specific elements are drawn into the symbolic classifications. Lévi-Strauss's discussion is equally marred by his refusal to follow Durkheim and Mauss in distinguishing between technological and religious classifications. Let me begin with the first problem.

NAVAHO TAXONOMY AND BIOLOGICAL NOMENCLATURE

The Navaho, it must be said, seem to be ideal subjects for anyone interested in folk classifications, for they love to categorize and are ready and willing to argue about hair-splitting taxonomic distinctions. They also never fail to give a name to any specimen shown them, even if it means inventing a new variety.[8] Kluckhohn (1960) even suggests that the formal structure of Navaho language itself introduces elaborate classifications, many verbs, for instance, referring to particular classes.

The fundamental category in Navaho thought is represented by the concept *diyin* which is usually translated as sacred or holy. The term is applied to all individuals, things or events which are charged with a special kind of power. Thus "people" are of two kinds, *diyin dinee*, the supernaturals or holy people, and *nihokaa dinee*, earth-surface people. This categorization agrees in a sense with our natural/supernatural division, though it should be noted that there is no general concept embracing everything of ordinary experience and, as we shall note, certain plants, animals and natural phenomena are either equated, or associated, with the holy people. As in our own folk taxonomy, the plant and animal domains are ordered by several overlapping hierarchies, the main primary taxa among the latter indicating divisions between earth and water, and day and night travellers, and between flying, walking and crawling *dinee*. It will be noted, as in other cultures, that movement is the pervasive theme in their taxonomic ordering. There is some disagreement between writers regarding the taxonomic

TABLE 1

Navaho classification of insects[a]

Order	Common name	Species	Navaho taxa	Number
Thysanurae	Bristletails	4	*le'esoli*, soil blower	2
Odonatae	Dragon-flies	11	*tani'l'ai*, spread on water	9
Blattariae	Cockroaches	1	*celca*, rock beaver	
Orthopterae	Grasshopper	38	*nahak'izi*, which move in crevices	9
			nahacagi, it hops here and there	19
Isopterae	Termites	1	*ciny'ani*, wood-eater	
Homopterae	Winged bugs	31	*wonescidi* (cicada)	
			nahacagi	
Heteropterae	Bugs	66	*yo deelci'hi*, red-horned insect	7
			talka dilyohi, water-surface runner	
Anoplurae	Lice	1	*ya*, louse	
Neuropterae	Lacewings	19	*tani'l'ani*	
			anlt'ani, ripener	
Trichopterae	Caddis-flies	1	*icai*, moth	
			c'i'i, gnat	
Lepidopterae	Butterflies	92	*icai*, moth	32
			ka'logi, butterfly	12
Dipterae	Flies	105	*ce'edqi*, fly	17
			c'i'i, gnat	
			dezi, horse fly	6
Siphonapterae	Fleas	1	*le'cai biya*, dog's flea	
Coleopterae	Beetles	201	*yon'zi*, hard insect	
			k'ini'si, urine squirter	21
			je'iya'h, ear traveller	4
			nada bicos, corn bug	
			nlcago, rain beetle	5
			le'soli, soil blower	
			celca, rock beaver	6
			yo bicos, water bug	
Hymenopterae	Ants, wasps, bees	188	*cisn'a*, bee	10
			ce'edqi, fly	
			wo'lazini, black ant	14
			woloci, red ant	8
			na'azqi, stinger	
			ja'dneis'di, leg dragger	4

[a]Besides these intermediate or generic taxa the Navaho recognize several loose taxa which embrace several terminal taxa, examples being *c'os* (small crawling insects or worms) and *wo* or *yo* (insect).

status of the insects; Perchonock and Werner (1969) regard the insects as forming a distinct class, *ch'osh*, whereas Wyman and Bailey (1964) indicate that the insects may fall under any of the more basic categories. Let me focus on this division of the animal kingdom, for the latter writers have published a detailed study of Navaho ethnoentomology.

TABLE 2

Biological family	Common name	Species number	*Tadidi'n iyani*, pollen eater	*Asa mayehe*, pot carrier	*Jei'iyah,*[a] ear traveller	*Kini'si,*[a] urine squirter	*ceyo ali*, stone carrier	*nlcago,*[a] rain beetle	*ca'nilma'si*, dung roller	*celca,*[a] rock beaver
Anobiidae	Furniture beetles	1								
Anthicidae		1	1							
Buprestidae	Wood borers	6								
Carabidae	Ground beetles	28			21	4				
Cerambycidae	Longhorns	11				1		8		3
Chrysomelidae	Leaf-eating beetles	17	7							
Cicindelidae	Tiger beetles	4								
Cleridae	Roman beetles	3								
Coccinellidae	Ladybirds	15	1							
Curculionidae	Weevils	15					12			
Dermestidae	Carpet beetles	2								
Dysticidae	Diving beetles	9								
Elateridae	Click beetles	5								
Erotylidae		1								
Histeridae	Steel beetles	5							3	
Hydrophilidae	Water beetles	5								
Lampyridae	Fireflies	1								
Lucanidae	Stag beetles	1				1				1
Meloidae	Blister beetles	11		2						
Mylabridae		1								
Scarabaeidae	Scarabs	18				1			4	14
Scolytidae	Bark beetles	1								
Silphidae	Dung beetles	3				1			2	
Staphylinidae	Rove beetles	1								
Tenebrionida	Darkling beetles	26				21			2	
Total number of species		197	9	2	21	29	12	8	11	18
Species of other orders					9					1

[a]Includes several terminal taxa.

In fact, it is a particularly useful class to examine for insects are not usually given cultural significance and there are no specialists in insect lore. Table 1 gives a summary analysis of the main biological insect orders and the equivalent Navaho taxa.

Now, although there are some Navaho generic taxa which embrace

Navaho classification of the order Coleoptera (beetles)

le'elsoli, soil blower	yon'izi, hard insect	lin cos, wood louse	tobi cos, water bug	na'da bicos, corn bug	ndiyili bicus, sunflower bug	ndisci bicos, pine bug	cos lizini, black bug	Nayizi bicus, squash bug	cos alcozi, eater bug	cos icqsi, sucking bug	cos bic'in lizinigi, black-skulled bug	cos dilyo'igi, fast-running bug	cos nodqzigi, striped bug	cos bici licigi, red-headed bug	Number of taxa
	1														1
1					1										3
	5								1					1	4
						1	7								3
													2		4
			2	2				3					7		5
												4			1
				2		1									2
			11										1		3
11	1									4					4
									2						1
		9													1
	5														1
											1				1
		5													1
															2
					3								1	4	4
	1														1
	2														4
	1														1
									1						3
									1						1
	3														3
12	16	3	14	13	8	2	7	3	5	4	1	4	11	5	
	1	1											4		

species from more than one order (e.g. *le'esoli* and *nahacagi*), it will be evident from an examination of this list that there is a fairly clear correspondence between biological nomenclature and Navaho taxonomy. The order Orthoptera, for instance, closely matches the two Navaho taxa *nahacagi* (it hops here and there—our grasshopper) and *nahak'izi* (which moves in crevices—our cricket). Of the 38 species comprising the order, 25 species (mostly of the family Acrididae) are placed in the first taxa (which in addition contains a number of bugs which resemble immature grasshoppers), while *nahak'izi* embraces the remainder. If we focus on a specific order—take, for example, the largest and most complex, the Coleoptera (beetles)—we again find a close correspondence between Navaho and biological classifications. Table 2 gives a summary analysis of the various biological families of the order Coleoptera, indicating their placement within Navaho taxa. Leaving aside the fact that there are possible synonyms relating to the taxon *cos*, it will be noted that all members of this order are placed within about 15 Navaho categories—what Wyman and Bailey refer to as Navaho species. Interestingly, although 218 biological species of the order are classified under these Navaho taxa, such taxa embrace only a further 17 species outside the order. Of these anomalies over half (9) refer to the taxon "pot carrier", while the others belong to such descriptive taxa as "striped bug". A close fit between biological and Navaho taxa also pertains at the level of the biological family, for a fair degree of equivalence is found between the two:

Navaho category	Zoological family
Ear Traveller	Ground beetles
Stone carrier	Weevils
Urine squirter	Darkling beetles
Rock beaver	Scarabs

Thus I think it is valid to conclude that there is a general correspondence between biological and Navaho categories. But significantly the two taxonomic systems articulate only at the "generic" level of Navaho taxonomy (Berlin *et al.*, 1974), Navaho species corresponding roughly (even if not tidily) to biological families and sub-orders. At the level of primary and terminal taxa (Berlin's "life-forms" and specifics) there seems to be little, if any, correspondence. The Navaho taxa *na't'agi dinee* (flying people) and *na'nagi dinee* (crawling people) have no biological equivalents, and their terminal taxa, as Table 3 denotes, also shows little parity with biological categories.

TABLE 3
Taxonomic status of *celca* (rock beaver)

| Species | Celca | | | | | | |
	big	little	wavy-horned	striped	yellow	grey	red
Order: Blattaria							
Periplaneta americana	×						
Order: Coleoptera							
Prionus heroicus			×				
P. integer						×	×
P. palparis							
Pseudolucanus mazama	×						
Aphodius colaradensis		×					
Cheiroplaiys pyriformis	×						×
Coenonycha socialis	×						
Cotalpa consorbrine	×				×		
Cyclocephale hirta	×	×			×	×	×
Diplotaxus conformis		×					×
D. levicoxa	×	×					×
Ligyrus gibbosus	×	×			×		×
Phyllophaga opacicollis	×	×			×	×	
Polyphylla decemlineata	×			×		×	
P. (?) diffracta	×			×		×	
Xloryctes jamaicensis	×						

The sub-species of the taxa *Celca*, as shown in the above table, seem typical of the subdivisions evident in other Navaho taxa, colour and size being the main distinguishing criteria within the taxon, and the relationship between biological species and Navaho taxa being rather loose. With the larger vertebrates there seems to be a closer correspondence between Navaho taxa and specific biological species, but with the insects there are few, if any, Navaho equivalents.

On the question of the relationship between folk taxonomies and biological categories, I find little in the above analysis to support any ultra-relativist stance; but equally, universal categories at the species level are not in evidence either.

TAXONOMY AND SYMBOLISM

Let us now move on to the second problem, namely the relationship between Navaho folk taxonomies and their symbolic and ritual systems.

To a naturalist like myself there were two Navaho taxa whose taxonomic ordering seemed to make no sense in terms of morphological criteria. It was easy to understand why, for instance, the lace-wing species had been grouped with the dragon-flies under the taxon *tani'l'ai*, but the combination of a diverse number of orders by such taxa as "ripener" and "pot carrier" seemed to me rather strange. The taxon *asa nayehe* (pot carrier) was a term given to two species of blister beetle as well as to the robber flies, while *anlt'ani* (ripener) included a tree cricket, several species of the order Neuroptera (lace-wings and ant-lions) and occasionally was even applied to the cicada and certain bugs. The anomalous status, however, becomes clear when we realize that both taxa have ritual significance, and that their taxonomic status is based on metaphorical rather than morphological criteria. Pot carriers are all black insects with harmful connotations—blister beetles cause skin irritation if handled, while robber flies are carnivorous—and black to the Navaho is a sinister colour associated with death and witchcraft. The "ripener" (the familiar cornbeetle of the general literature), even more important in Navaho ritual and myth, is the symbol of female generative power. These insects are all yellow and associated with corn and pollen. As with the epiphytic orchids among the Ilongots (Rosaldo, 1972), so with the Navaho, the "ripener" taxon has a primarily metaphorical significance. Most of the "species" referred to as "ripener" have synonyms that refer to morphological categories; and for this reason the term may be considered a ritual category. Of course not all insects which have mythological or symbolic significance have this anomalous taxonomic status; normally the referent is simply a generic taxon—*dq'coh* (big fly), *tani'l'ai* (dragon-fly), *woloci* (red ant), *yo'se'ki'di* (hornworm), *ka'logi* (butterfly) and *wonescidi* (cicada) are among the more important insects in this respect.

Now what is the relation between the Navaho classification of insects and their symbolic classifications? Do their natural taxonomies form part of an all-embracing symbolic taxonomy that unites all aspects of Navaho experience into a totality? The answer to this question must be negative. In fact, what is evident is that only certain elements (and relatively few) are drawn into the "master plan", the "classification of classifications". Thus the suggestions of Lévi-Strauss (1966) and Douglas (1966) that, among pre-literate people, there is no sharp division between the various classificatory domains and that their natural and social universes are grasped as an "organized whole" (and personalized), are valid only in the sense that such statements and the ideas they reflect apply only to the ritual context. There is no vast system of correspondences; only a religious schema that unites aspects of the Navaho conceptual universe. But, of course, most of the insects and other natural phenomena recognized by the Navaho have no symbolic relevance and, therefore, find no place in their mythology, symbolic classifications and ritual patterns.

Much has been written on Navaho religious symbolism (cf. Reichard, 1974). From this material it is clear that the Navaho had a complex and structured classificatory schema based, as with many other Amerindian communities, on a spatial configuration.[9] Table 4 gives the focal structure of this cosmological system. The symbolism is by no means straightforward since the symbolic values of the various elements vary according to the ritual context, and within the schema there is a pervasive sexual dualism. Many elements are thus paired; indeed, this sexual dualism extends even to their folk taxonomies, particularly to the classification of plants. Other symbolic elements are only loosely linked to this ideologic, but in sandpaintings, myth and ritual this cosmological schema is prominent and has a certain logical consistency. The system, then, is based on myth and becomes evident in the ritual context. This structured symbolism has a limited number of elements drawn from other classificatory domains. The "cosmization", to use a phrase of Eliade (1959, p. 10), is by no means total, for there is little explicit body symbolism and social categories are only loosely linked to this cosmological schema. The matrilineal clans refer primarily to localities and though a group of clans may be associated with specific animal species they are not explicitly totemic. The relationship of these animal species—bear, mountain lion, big snake, mountain sheep and porcupine—to the symbolic classification is not clear, but evidently such animals had symbolic significance. In harmony with the symbolic schema, the hogan is always built facing east and its occupants have stipulated places: men usually sit to the south, women to the north.

The various elements that make up this "interlocking system of

TABLE 4
Navaho symbolic classification[a]

Direction	East	South	West	North
Colour	white	blue	yellow	black
Sex	M	F	F	M
Inner forms	dawn man	horizontal blue man	horizontal yellow man	darkness
Human wind soul	white good	blue happy	yellow mean	dark bad
Sacred mountains	Mt Blanca Jemez, NM	Mt Taylor San Mateo, NM	San Francisco Peaks, Ariz.	La Plata Peaks, Co.
Holy people	sun	changing woman (earth)	child of the water	monster slayer
Time	dawn light sunrise	sunlit midday	sunset twilight	night darkness
Space	sky	earth	water	mountain
Jewel	white shell	turquoise	abalone	jet
Sacred plants	beans	squash	tobacco	corn (?)
Birds	pigeon	bluebird woodpecker	yellow warbler, rock wren	blackbird night hawk
Mammals	bear	mountain lion	big snake	porcupine (?)
Insects	big fly	spider woman	ripener	pot carrier

[a]From: Lamphere (1969), Wheelwright (1946) and Reichard (1974).

associations" (Reichard, 1974, p. xxxiv), which it may be noted are largely natural phenomena, are characterized and thus demarcated by two features, apart from their symbolic role in sandpaintings, myth and ritual. Firstly, the elements take on a supernatural guise, in possessing an "inner form" (*bi'yisti'n*) that gives them life and sentience. Thus each of the four sacred mountains have an inner form and are treated as supernaturals. Other elements—animals, plants, winds, colours—are likewise personalized and treated as divinities and sacred entities. As such they are either male or female (or denote a collectivity, e.g. buffalo people) and have an important part to play in the mythological accounts, interacting with various other holy people.[10] However, the fact that many natural phenomena and species are treated as super-natural beings must not lead one to assume—as do many writers on the Navaho—that for the Navaho the whole universe is sacred and per-sonalized. This is the case only in a ritual context, and then only in the sense of being focussed on specific beings—with respect to the insects on such supernaturals as big fly, ripener, cicada and dragonfly.

Secondly, the symbolic elements are frequently associated with disease, as causative agents. Coyotes, bears, snakes and certain kinds of birds, for instance, must never be killed or harmed, and any transgression of these norms leads to misfortune. Various curing ceremonials are performed to deal with specific troubles. Mountain way, for example, is designed to treat illnesses believed to have arisen from contact with bears. Thus in the Navaho context (and, I suspect, cross culturally) religion, symbolic classifications and the problem of theodicy cannot be separated.

The interpretation of symbolism

In a paper on the philosophy of the Navaho, Kluckhohn (1959, p. 428) summed up the tacit premises underlying their world view under the following headings:

> the universe is orderly, and all events are inter-related;
> knowledge is power;
> the basic quest is for harmony;
> the price for disorder, in human terms, is illness.

Given these premises the ritual ceremonials of the Navaho, through which the symbolic classificatory schema is made manifest, are essentially means of restoring the universal harmony.[11] Thus to seek, from within the symbol system, the meaning of specific symbols, or the implicit structure of the conceptual ideologic, or even the basis of the symbolic system, is to be side-tracked. Writers who have followed such trails have spent a lot of energy theoretically getting nowhere—which is in no way meant to demean the contributions of such symbolists as Leach and Turner. An indication that this is so is borne out since contemporary writers on symbolism have largely abandoned these theoretical interests and have been content to offer descriptive accounts of specific symbol systems. The search for semantic networks or the meaning of key symbols are certainly valid exercises,[12] but these are largely uncritical stances and positively misleading when it is implied that such collective (religious) representations constitute the whole of social life.

The classic "symbolist" interpretation of symbolic classifications derives from Durkheim, of course, and, following such an approach, many writers in recent years have attempted to delineate symbolic correlations between various levels of experience (Tambiah, 1969; Douglas, 1970). Sure enough, they have indentified structural homologies (which are often implicit) between various classificatory domains and the social structure, the latter being taken as the basis of the symbolism.[13] Other writers have been equally terse in denying that there is any necessary symbolic correspondence between religious classifications (or animal taxonomies) and social structure, and like Lévi-Strauss (but for different reasons) have questioned the idea that the social structure is the basis (Needham, 1963).[14] But of course the approaches of both Douglas and Needham are not necessarily contradictory for, as Lévi-Strauss argued long ago, the relationship between social structure and other symbolic configurations is variable. In some societies, body or spatial symbolism is a virtual "mirror image" of the social structure, while in others it would be extremely difficult to discover any such relationship. The crucial point, though, as Lévi-Strauss foresaw, was that social structure was itself often part of the "model"; an aspect of the ritual or symbolic system.[15] The demonstration of homologies between various aspects of culture is to a large degree, therefore, a descriptive exercise. In a sense, as Bloch (1977) has intimated,[16] people's perception of their social structure is a quasi-religious idea.

The empiricist approach of Turner (1965), which views symbolic classifications as being derived from bodily experiences (re colour categories) is no more enlightening, nor is the alternative interpretation of Lamphere (1969), who, in an interesting discussion of Navaho symbolism, counters Turner's thesis by suggesting that the meaning of their symbols derives from their cosmological system. This idea simply replicates Navaho religious thought and is no explanation at all.

Clearly then there is no underlying basis or meaning of symbolic classifications. Although different cultures, as Douglas (1975, p. 126) noted, may highlight or give prominence to specific levels of classification in their "conceptual schemas"—colour symbolism in the Ndembu; spatial categories as with the Navaho—these are only part of a totality and cannot be adjudged as being the "basis" of the symbolism, let alone having a universal significance. The attempt to give any particular classificatory or cultural domain—myth, colour, natural species, social categories—universal primacy as the basis of ideologic systems is, I think, misleading, and can be easily refuted by reference to cross-cultural data. However, to simply describe such symbol systems or to consider them simply as the product of a particular mode of cognition, innately derived, seems to me equally unsatisfying. So what do we make of religious symbolism?

SYMBOLISM AND POWER

Let me first put the issue of symbolic classifications into a clearer historical and cross-cultural perspective.

It was the seminal writings of Lévi-Strauss and Douglas which initially stressed the structural significance of conceptual systems. Indeed the main polemical thrust of both *The Savage Mind* (Lévi-Strauss, 1966) and *Purity and Danger* (Douglas, 1966) are remarkably alike, in that both writers sought to argue that so-called "primitive" cultures were integrated at a conceptual level. Lévi-Strauss indicated that the classificatory systems of such people were not separated from but formed a part of an all-embracing taxonomy (Lévi-Strauss, 1966, pp. 138–9), while Douglas expressed a similar viewpoint suggesting that the primitive world view is "undifferentiated" and integrated into a single symbolic whole. While Douglas is concerned with interpreting pollution rules and taboos by reference to a society's total structure of thought, Lévi-Strauss is concerned to desacralize totemism. None the less, the perspectives of both writers are remarkably similar, and both are misleading by the degree to which they focus on the "global primitive"[17] and assume that all pre-literate people have integrated cosmological systems. Of course, cultures vary enormously not only in respect to what elements or levels are drawn into the symbolic system, but also in the degree to which such symbolic classifications are elaborated and systematized. Some have elaborate cosmological ideas—so complex that it becomes, as Bloch (1977, p. 288) noted of Javanese and Indian social structure, a "positive embarrassment". Some, like the Navaho, have fairly explicit classificatory systems that structure the symbol system, but others do not, and many anthropologists rack their brains to tease out the semantic associations. In this task they often outshine local magicians! However, the all-embracing ideologic is ill-understood by attempting to place it within the framework of Durkheimian sociology. Just as the primitive–modern typology—which sees change in terms of structural differentiation—has proved debilitating in trying to understand economic change (cf. Frank, 1971), so it is equally stultifying in trying to understand symbolic systems, for it is misleading to assume that societies with a low division of labour— primitive culture—have *ipso facto* integrated and homogenous conceptual systems. What is of interest is that it is not hunter–gatherers that are characterized by complex symbolic systems; many like the Hadza have a dearth of symbolism. In fact I have discussed elsewhere (Morris, 1976) the natural taxonomies of one hunter–gatherer community, the Malapantaram, and noted their relative lack of symbolism. My conclusions may be the outcome of inadequate ethnography, but this is doubtful, for, notwithstanding Hicks's (1973) important re-assessment of the Aweikoma material, there seems to be a whole class of hunter– gatherers and many marginal cultures, who place very little stress on ritual symbolism. Note in particular that Lévi-Strauss (1948) found little material of a symbolic nature among the Nambicuara. Nor indeed can we say that religious symbolism finds its most ornate and structured form among tribal cultures generally;[18] rather such symbolism finds its apotheosis among early theocratic states. It is when considering the Aztec, Mesopotamian and early Asiatic states that one finds the most complex and integrated ideological schemas; symbol systems clearly have political functions.

As there is variability in the degree to which religious symbolism is elaborated and structured by underlying classificatory schemata, so there is variability in the degree to which the ideologic itself is conceptually demarcated. But of course, it is frequently the case that ritual contexts (the sacred domain) are unambiguously delineated. Schemes of legitimation are, as it were, demarcated within the system of ideation.[19] But though this symbolic or ritual context may be contrasted with "everyday" life, it is misleading to assume that this contrast is simply one of binary opposition (e.g. Turner, 1974). For, as Douglas indicated (1966), there is "power" both in and between structures. The ritual domain thus expresses both ideal form and formlessness, rhetoric (chants) and speaking in tongues, abstinence and licence, purity and dirt, ritual and trance. Often, as many have noted, these two ritual emphases are institutionalized in the form of two separate politico-religious specialists, the one dealing with public, the other with private, curing rites (cf. Faron, 1964, on the Mapuche). In the Navaho context it is the singer who is concerned with public ceremonials, while divination is undertaken privately by the "hand-trembler". In focussing our attention on "symbolic classifications" we are concerned essentially with those aspects of a culture which, during public rites, reaffirm the structure of cosmological ideas. The symbolic system enacted is always charged with spiritual power; indeed, one writer (Berger, 1973, p. 34) has defined religion as an enterprise by which the "sacred cosmos" (ideologic) is established. Such classifications may give meaning to life and indicate the organizing proclivities of the human "mind", but they also have important social functions, as ideological forms, in maintaining normative structures. Put in its simplest form; human institutions are hinged to, or even a part of, a symbolic order; this ideologic is permeated with the spirit; confounding this order leads to misfortune.[20] As Hertz (1973, p. 3) put it, every social hierarchy "accords itself eternity" and it does so through symbolism.

Most writers on symbolic classifications have, by omission, ignored the political implications of cosmological ideas and ritual. In Turner's concept of communities we have, in fact, the virtual inversion of the idea that symbol action is ideological. For communitas (apparently exemplified in the liminal period of ritual) is seen as anti-structure,[21] linked with equality and transition, and the absence of rank and status. However, his conclusions are rather surprising for he mentions that what the ritual process does (through the association of ritual symbols with physiological referents) is to energize the "normative order" making the Durkheimian "obligatory" desirable (Turner, 1974, p. 49). Significantly, Turner never explores the implications of Goffman's discussion of total institutions, preferring instead to link "communitas" with Buber and hippie cults. But what one gets in a Navaho curing ceremonial is not anti-structure, but a spiritual wash that invokes recognition of their total cosmological structure. Ritual, in the Ndembu meaning of the term, is "obligation", and what such rituals reveal is not anti-structure but the "primary values" of the group, their "essential constitution", in a word, their ideologic.

Unfortunately, the only writer who has explicitly acknowledged the intimate connection between symbolism and power has tended to take a rather pluralist view of power (cf. Lukes, 1974). Cohen's (1974) discussion of symbolism has tended to focus on power struggles and on the "manipulation" of symbols by specific groups. In so doing the ideological nature of the symbolic system becomes questionable, since the primary purpose of ideological systems is to obscure the fact that specific social relationships are exploitative. If symbols were seen explicitly as manipulative devices, or if they are viewed only in relation to open power struggles, they would cease to fulfil their primary function, which Cohen is indeed at pains to stress, namely that of "mystification". As an ideological system the "symbolic order" serves to obscure, or, as Lévi-Strauss suggested, even to invert the "real situation".

It is not the purpose of this present paper to suggest how we may conceptualize the latter—here I plead only that symbolic classifications are not everything, and that we ought not to forget that they have socio-political functions. In abstracting "power relations" from the social structure Cohen has made a step in the right direction, and Godelier's (1977) discussion of the function of religious ideology in pre-capitalist societies are equally germane, but whatever the nature of the trail we seek to blaze in the future, it will have to steer clear of both the mechanics and the mystics.

Notes

1. The present essay is a re-draft of an article I wrote two years ago after reading Willis (1975) and Firth (1973).
2. There is a fundamental ambiguity in Lévi-Strauss's work which leads writers like Keat and Urry (1975) to have doubts about his realism and about the epistemological status of the underlying structures.
3. See also Feuchtwang (1975).
4. There are affinities between Sperber's approach and those writers who have expressed, in one way or another, the distinctive nature of symbolic thought. The latter has been put under various headings: pre-logical, mythopoeic, primitive thought, savage mind. Though there are disputes over the nature of this cognitive mode the real issue relates to its function in social life.

5. On the whole (with the exception of Turner and Cohen) those writers who have attempted to conceptualize relations or structures that were distinct from the institutional model (network and action theory, situational analysis, generative models, structure/organization) have been largely uninterested in ritual symbolism. However, such analyses have tended to have an unsatisfactory ego-centred bias, the abstract individual being the agent of change.

6. Between Godelier's promise of such a Marxist perspective on religion and his analysis of the Mbuti pygmies there is a wide gulf which is filled, as Wolf (1975, p. 103) intimates, with phrases and echoes of Durkheimian functionalism.

7. There is a good general account of the Navaho by Kluckhohn and Leighton (1962). Also relevant here were Wyman (1970) and Witherspoon (1975). For the purpose of this essay I have merely dipped into this extensive literature.

8. How different all this seems from my own experience among the Malapantaram, who showed a general disinterest in taxonomic concerns. This contrast in itself is of theoretical interest.

9. The spatial symbolism, though variable, was extremely widespread among Amerindian communities, and may be noted in such diverse contexts as Neihardt's (1974) *Black Elk Speaks* and Reichel-Dolmatoff's (1967) analysis of funeral rituals among the Kogi of Columbia. Considering the current interest in Amerindian religion I am surprised that no comparative analysis has been made of this symbolism. Although Wheelwright (1946, p. 209) suggests that "everything goes by four in ceremonies and myths, cardinal points always being mentioned", it is clear from other accounts of their symbolism that the classification was often extended to include, like the Zuni, a vertical axis with zenith and nadir dimensions. There is, of course, an interesting contrast (which correlates with their political integration) between the Navaho and both the nomadic Apache and the settled Pueblo Indians in the degree of elaboration and systematization of their ritual symbolism.

10. The more important of these supernaturals are changing woman, the sun, the hero twins, monster slayer and the child of the water.

11. The Navaho concept of *hozhq* refers to the state of affairs where everything is in its proper place and in harmony.

12. Whether the emphasis is on the exploration of key symbols (Willis, 1974, has taken this approach to the extreme) or on semantic configurations seems to depend largely on whether the writer has taken his or her bearings from either Evans-Pritchard or Lévi-Strauss.

13. Frequently the attempt to establish homologies leads to an extreme manipulation of the empirical data, e.g. Tambiah's (1969) interpretation of the metaphorical relationship between social categories and animal categories (with respect to their edibility) among the Thai.

14. Fox (1975) interprets Needham as suggesting that only certain societies—those with prescriptive alliance—are characterized by a pervasive symbolic dualism. This is not my reading of Needham (cf. 1972, p. 156), who wants, indeed, to argue the contrary. The stress on dualism is apt to obscure the fact that more complex symbolic structuring (and value hierarchies) are often found. The Mapuche Indians, for instance, have a complex spatial symbolism like many other Amerindian communities, which Faron's (1973) discussion ignores.

15. The importance of Leach in this changing orientation towards the concept of "social structure" is often overlooked. His work is full of ambiguity. On the one hand, Leach saw the relation between ritual and social structure as unproblematic,

for "ritual makes explicit the social structure" (Leach, 1970, p. 15). At the same time he was clearly aware that the social structure itself was an ideal model. Unfortunately his methodological individualism and his idealism did not allow him to develop these insights. His latest text (1976) takes us no further and is less illuminating than an ethnography he seems to think people find so dull.

16. In the same sense that Harris's (1964, 1969) materialism was perhaps a necessary corrective to idealist writers like Feyre and Boas, yet at the same time was extremely limiting as an alternative approach (cf. Genovese, 1968; Friedman, 1974), so Bloch's criticisms of Geertz, Lévi-Strauss and Douglas falls into the same pattern, in being necessary and yet equally empiricist and ahistorical. With his two modes of cognition, one seemingly universal (and concerned with politics, economics and folk classifications), the other particularistic and variable (and concerned with ritual communication and symbolism) he neatly sidesteps rather than solves many complex issues. Using his phraseology we may, in this context, pose two questions. Firstly; is the non-ritual aspect of the long communication unchanging? Clearly not. Yet Bloch seems to view "truth" as being unaffected by historical circumstances; reality (as opposed to all the ritual nonsense) being directly amenable to perception? "Touch the Earth" for Bloch is not a mystical experience, but the veritable key for exposing the nature of ritual symbolism. Yet one of the interesting points to come out of Berlin and Kay's (1969) study (which was prompted by a reaction against ultra-relativism) was that, in a sense, there were no universal categories, but rather that there had been an evolutionary process in the degree of elaboration of colours. The great virtue of Marx was that he tried to steer clear of both empiricism and idealism in his approach and, with his stress on the sociality of man, to avoid the pitfalls of both universalism and relativism. Secondly, what is the exact relationship between the "other system" of communication and the infra-structures? Bloch clearly sees the "static model" manifested in ritual as a form of mystification that is linked with exploitation but, like me, merely asserts it. Such a position will demand some radical re-thinking on the part of Marxists with respect to the nature of tribal society—something which some Marxists (e.g. Hindess and Hirst, 1975) seem very reluctant to do.

17. The phrase comes from Douglas (1975, p. 80). Her important suggestions may well be taken as a corrective to the general tenor of *Purity and Danger*. Her later work attempts to develop a typology of cosmological systems (Douglas, 1970).

18. Goody (1968) in his introduction, even hints that Dogon symbolism is derived from Islamic sources. From the evidence we have of the Australian tribes (Durkheim and Mauss, 1963) and many other tribal cultures it is clear that such communities had complex cosmological systems. Equally important, however, is that with the emergence of a literate theocracy such symbolism was greatly elaborated and systematized as astrological systems etc.

19. In this connection, Lévi-Strauss's suggestion that "taboos" have a "denoting" significance in a system of classification has been dismissed too readily by other writers. What easier way is there to indicate that cultural elements have symbolic import than by denying them pragmatic significance?

20. Beidelman's (1973) interesting discussion of the Nuer material succinctly illustrates the relation between religion (spirit) and structural separations.

21. There is a wide disparity between Turner's magnificent empirical work (Turner, 1957, 1968) and his theoretical announcements. Whereas the former indicate the political dimension of ritual symbolism (even though the over-all emphasis is on the meaning of specific symbols) the latter (Turner, 1974) is little more than an apology for religion.

References

BEIDELMAN, T. O. (Ed.) (1973). "The Translation of Culture". Tavistock, London.

BERGER, P. L. (1973). "The Social Reality of Religion". Penguin, Harmondsworth.

BERLIN, B., BREEDLOVE, D. E. and RAVEN, P. H. (1974). "Principles of Tzeltal Plant Classification". Academic Press, New York and London.

BERLIN, B. and KAY, P. (1969). "Basic Color Terms". California University Press, California.

BLOCH, M. (1977). The past and the present in the present. *Man (N.S.)*, **12**, 278–92.

BULMER, R. (1965). Review of Wyman and Bailey. *Am. Anthrop.*, **67**.

COHEN, A. (1974). "Two dimensional Man". Routledge and Kegan Paul, London.

DOUGLAS, M. (1966). "Purity and Danger". Penguin, Harmondsworth.

DOUGLAS, M. (1970). "Natural Symbols". Barrie and Rockcliffe, London.

DOUGLAS, M. (1975). "Implicit Meanings". Routledge and Kegan Paul, London.

DURKHEIM, E. and MAUSS, M. (1963). "Primitive Classification". Routledge and Kegan Paul, London.

ELIADE, M. (1959). "Cosmos and History". Harper, New York.

FARON, L. (1964). "Hawks of the Sun". Pittsburgh University Press, Pittsburgh.

FARON, L. (1973). Symbolic values and the integration of society among the Mapuche. *In* "Right and Left" (Ed. R. Needham), pp. 187–203. Chicago University Press, Chicago.

FEUCHTWANG, S. (1975). Investigating religion. *In* "Marxist Analyses and Social Anthropology (Ed. M. Bloch). Malaby Press, London.

FIRTH, R. (1973). "Symbols Public and Private". Allen and Unwin, London.

FOX, J. J. (1975). On binary categories and primary symbols; some Rotinese perspectives. *In* "The Interpretation of Symbols" (Ed. R. G. Willis). Malaby Press, London.

FRANK, A. G. (1971). "Sociology of Development and Development of Sociology". Pluto Press, London.

FRIEDMAN, J. (1974). Marxism, structuralism and vulgar materialism. *Man (N.S.)*, **9**, 444–69.

GENOVESE, E. (1968). Materialism and idealism in the history of slavery. *In* "Red and Black". Vintage Books, New York.

GODELIER, M. (1977). "Perspectives in Marxist Anthropology". Cambridge University Press, Cambridge.

GOODY, J. (1968). "Literacy in Traditional Societies". Cambridge University Press, Cambridge.

HARRIS, M. (1964). "Patterns of Race in the Americas". New York.

HARRIS, M. (1969). "The Rise of Anthropological Theory". Routledge and Kegan Paul, London.

HERTZ, R. (1973). The pre-eminence of the right hand. *In* "Right and Left" (Ed. R. Needham). Chicago University Press, Chicago.

HICKS, D. (1973). A structural model of Aweikoma society. *In* "The Translation of Culture" (Ed. T. O. Beidelman). Tavistock, London.

HINDESS, B. and HIRST, P. (1975). "Pre-Capitalist Modes of Production". Routledge and Kegan Paul, London.

KEAT, R. and URRY, J. (1975). "Social Theory as Science". Routledge and Kegan Paul, London.

KLUCKHOHN, C. (1959). The philosophy of the Navaho Indians. *In* "Readings in Anthropology" (Ed. M. Fried). Thomas Y. Crowell, New York.

KLUCKHOHN, C. (1960). Navaho categories. *In* "Culture in History". (Ed. S. Diamond). Columbia University Press, New York.

KLUCKHOHN, C. and LEIGHTON, D. (1962). "The Navaho". Doubleday Press, New York.

LAMPHERE, L. (1969). Symbolic elements in Navaho ritual. *S.W.J.A.*, **25**, 279–304.

LEACH, E. (1970). "Political Systems of Highland Burma". Athlone Press, London.

LEACH, E. (1976). "Culture and Communication". Cambridge University Press, Cambridge.

LÉVI-STRAUSS, C. (1948). Society and family of the Nambicuara Indians. *J. Soc. Americanistes*, **37**.

LÉVI-STRAUSS, C. (1963). "Structural Anthropology". Allen Lane, London.

LÉVI-STRAUSS, C. (1966). "The Savage Mind". Weidenfield and Nicolson, London.

LUKES, S. (1974). "Power: A Radical View". Macmillan, London.

MORRIS, B. (1976). Whither the savage mind. *Man (N.S.)*, **11**, 542–57.

NEEDHAM, R. (1972). "Belief, Language and Experience". Blackwell, Oxford.

NEEDHAM, R. (Ed.) (1973). "Right and Left". Chicago University Press, Chicago.

PERCHONOCK, N. and WERNER, O. (1969). Navaho systems of classification. *Ethnology*, **8**, 229–42.

POCOCK, D. F. (1961). "Social Anthropology". Sheed and Ward, London.

REICHARD, G. (1974). "Navaho Religion". Princeton University Press, Princeton.

REICHEL-DOLMATOFF, G. (1967). Funerary customs and religious symbolism among the Kogi. *In* "Native South Americans" (Ed. P. J. Lyon). Little Brown, Boston.

ROSALDO, M. Z. (1972). Metaphors and folk classification. *S.W.J.A.*, **28**, 83–99.

SPERBER, D. (1975). "Re-Thinking Symbolism". Cambridge University Press, Cambridge.

TAMBIAH, S. (1969). Animals are good to think and good to prohibit. *Ethnology*, **8**, 424–59.

TURNER, V. (1957). "Schism and Continuity in an African Society". Manchester University Press, Manchester.

TURNER, V. (1965). Colour classification in Ndembu ritual. *In* "Forest of Symbols". Cornell University Press, Ithaca.

TURNER, V. (1968). "Drums of Affliction". Manchester University Press, Manchester.

TURNER, V. (1974). "The Ritual Process". Penguin, Harmondsworth.

WHEELWRIGHT, M. C. (1946). "Hail Chant and Water Chant". Museum of Naval Art, New Mexico.

WILLIS, R. G. (1974). "Man and Beast". Paladin, London.

WILLIS, R. G. (Ed.) (1975). "The Interpretation of Symbols". Malaby Press, London.

WITHERSPOON, G. (1975). "Navaho Kinship and Marriage". Chicago University Press, Chicago.

WOLF, E. (1975). Review of Godelier. *Dial. Anthrop.*, **1**, 99–104.

WYMAN, L. C. (1970). "Blessingway". Arizona University Press, Arizona.

WYMAN, L. C. and BAILEY, F. (1964). Navaho Indian ethnoentomology. *Univ. N.M. Publ. Anthrop.*, **12**.

7

Coping with Exotic Plants in Folk Taxonomies

Jacques Barrau

I have the feeling sometimes that research on folk classification systems so far has paid much more attention to the formal structure of such systems than to the way in which they work. This often results in the presentation of a somewhat curdled picture of taxonomy and nomenclature which does not always account for the dynamics involved: the stock of natural objects organized within such a system is obviously not static. One way of elucidating how this system functions may be to see how it copes with hitherto unknown objects.

I must confess that I have not had much experience of such situations. At most, I have made some timid explorations into the problem of folk classification of introduced plants, particularly those so actively exchanged between the various parts of the tropics in colonial days. Some of these were more or less readily adopted by the indigenous populations, and the ways in which these exotics have been classified and named seems to me to be of interest to an anthropology of knowledge.

Of course, there is no need to go to some exotic elsewhere to find examples of introduced plants being included in folk classifications. Let us remain for a while in old Europe where, in pre-Columbian days, no starchy tuber producing plants were grown and, therefore, where the introduction of the American *Solanum* potato provides a good example of what may happen when a folk cognitive system is confronted with a new object.

It is said (Rhind, 1872, p. 272) that in Youghall, in the county of Cork, while looking after the first *Solanum tuberosum* grown there, the gardener of Sir Walter Raleigh expected the plant to bear "apples" and never thought of looking into the ground for tubers. *Se no e vero, e bene trovato!* Indeed, the French still call the "Irish" potato *pomme de terre* (lit. "ground apple"). Similarly, another American Solanacea, the tomato or *Lycopersicon esculentum* (lately *Solanum lycopersicum*), was first called "love apple", *liebesapfel, pomme d'amour, poumo d'amour, pomo d'oro*. . . . The Italians classified and named the potato by reference to the fungus truffle, calling it *tartufo*, tartufi.[1]

In these examples we can see a simple process of accommodating new plants within a taxonomic and nomenclatural folk system by referring them to commonly accepted standards: "apple" for fruits in general ("apple" in such case being more or less for fruits what "corn" is for grain) and "truffle" for tubers. Such standards can be of morphological significance, either relating to a category of use, part of the plant of economic significance, or to other criteria. Sometimes they may combine several different criteria.

We could easily add many similar examples. "Corn" (akin to the Latin *granum*?; cf. the German *Korn*, the Gothic *Kaurn*, the Icelandic *Koren* . . . *)* is used for exotic cereals, such as in "Indian corn" for maize. In French, *Fagopyrum esculentum*, a Polygonacea, or buckwheat,[2] is called *ble noir* (lit. black wheat) and maize was originally known as *ble de Turquie* (lit. Turkish wheat) or *ble d'Espagne* (Spanish wheat) or *ble de l'Inde* (Indian wheat), *ble* or "wheat" being also common standards for grain crops.

It is perhaps possible to discover for a given folk botanical system those vegetable species, plant organs or plant produce which are standards of reference in taxonomic and nomenclatural processes, and why they play that part. "Apple", "corn" and "wheat" are vegetable standards corresponding to economic plants in the complex of domesticates linked to the Middle Eastern agricultural neolithic, in which Occidental cultures have their main roots. As for "truffle", when one knows how this curious natural object impressed many European minds (see e.g. Malencon, 1938), it is not surprising to find that it became a standard for "tuber".

These examples indicate that folk classificatory treatment of introduced plants can be a fertile field of research in understanding the functioning of plant taxonomic and nomenclatural systems. But it is also worth looking at the methods used by migrant peoples of a given culture in classifying and naming the components of an exotic natural environment. Thus, when French settlers came to New Caledonia in the second half of the last century, they verbalized their perception of the new environment by calling local trees *pommier* (apple tree), *chene* (oak), *hetre* (beech), *sapin* (fir) etc.; and the freshwater fishes *carpes* (carp)! Polyethnic societies in the West Indies also provide striking examples of such interpretation and organization of new environments.

Similar observations can be made elsewhere in the world, in other cultures. In the Malayo-Oceanian area it is common to find that yams, particularly the greater yam or *Dioscorea alata*, the taro or *Colocasia esculenta* and the coconut palm or *Cocos nucifera*, to give only a few examples, are frequently used as standards in the classification and naming of introduced plants. Thus, when the American sweet potato was introduced to Indonesia in the fifteenth century it was classified with the greater yams, *ubi*, and called *ubi-kastela* or Spanish yam. In Oceania, the neo-tropical *Xanthosoma sagittifolium* was classified either with the *Colocasia* taro, as in the case of Samoa, where it is known as *talopapalagi* or "taro of the Europeans", or with another domestic Aracea, *Alocasia macrorrhiza*, as in the case of the Micronesian Carolines. In Palau, for instance, it is known as *bisech la ruk* or "Trukese" *Alocasia*. One could also cite examples of exotic palm-trees referred to the coconut palm, such as in the case of a *Metroxylon* called in Samoa *niu rotuma* or "coconut from Rotuma".

For mainland south-east Asia, Dournes (1972) has described how the introduced maize has been accommodated within local plant taxonomies and nomenclatures, so that for the Jorai of Vietnam, the American *Zea mays* and the old-timer *Coix lacryma-jobi* are alike and therefore share the name *kotor*.

It is also interesting to consider how people dealt with maize with no previous experience of any grain crop. In New Guinea, for instance, maize has often been placed in the same category as *Saccharum edule*. This is a cane grown for its aborted inflorescences which are eaten as a vegetable. The introduced maize is used very much in the same way. The immature corn-cob is considered as being similar to the unopened panicle of the *pit-pit*, the New Guinean pidgin name of this *Saccharum*, and it is processed for human consumption in the same way as *Saccharum* inflorescences.

On the interpretation of new plant environments by Oceanian

peoples in the course of their migrations across the Pacific, Chowning (1962) has shown how plant taxonomies and nomenclatures have been carried by these ancient voyagers and applied to components of the vegetable environment in the islands they discovered and where they settled.

While working in Melanesia some years ago I found in subsistence gardens, both in the New Hebrides and New Caledonia, a yam which did not fit with the old established group of domesticated *Dioscorea* and was treated horticulturally apart from these "noble" yams. The species was difficult to identify because I had tended to limit my investigations to those species known to be long established in these islands.

Nevertheless, I learnt that this curious and somewhat marginal yam had been introduced into New Caledonia by New Hebridean labourers who considered it as "wild", hence the name *"wael"* in pidgin. This point of view was obviously shared by New Caledonian gardeners who called it, in Houailou or Canala for instance, *yovayi*, i.e. wild. Later my friend and colleague Dominique Bourret (1973) identified this yam as the Australian *Dioscorea transversa*, which was likely to have been brought back to the New Hebrides from Queensland by Melanesians who had been forcibly moved there as labourers for the white settlers and survived this harsh experience. Deprived from their traditional staple food, they had noticed this local wild yam in the Australian bush, used it and in fact began to domesticate it, finally bringing it to their islands, from where it came to New Caledonia. Here we have an interesting case of a plant of very recent domestication which is still treated as "uncivilized". It is nevertheless considered as akin to well known and respected domesticates, but from which it is separated in the gardens and in the folk taxonomy as undeserving of the highly ritualized and respectful treatment afforded the old timers so deeply integrated into the social and cultural life of Melanesians. Dominique Bourret has noted that New Caledonian gardeners justify this qualification of *Dioscorea transversa* as "wild" because, they say, it does not behave as the noble traditional yams; it remains in vegetation if not harvested; it does not "know the seasons". In short, it does not respect the order of both nature and culture. It yields an edible tuber, but it could not be of the same rank of the older respected yams: it is cultivated but not considered to be a true "domesticate". Interesting remarks could also be made concerning the yam species recently introduced into New Caledonia from the West Indies: *Dioscorea cayenensis, D.*

rotundata, D. trifida and so on. Some have been classified by the Melanesians with the "wild" *D. transversa,* some related to *Smilax,* a Liliacea vine.

The preceding remarks are those of a naturalist without much knowledge of either anthropology or linguistics. I may be stating the obvious, but it seems that little is known of how folk taxonomic systems deal with the new, the unknown, the monstrous and the abnormal. The particular value of the work of Dournes, Chowning and Bourret, to which I have referred, is that in examining how people cope with new species and plant environments they have shown how systems of classification actully operate. Here we are confronted with the very principles of classification and nomenclature used by a given culture. To quote an unscientific example borrowed from a French humourist joking about natural history, we may well discover the reasoning behind the statement *"the ass is just an overgrown rabbit"*, but we then have to think about the peculiar significance of the rabbit and about the particular importance given to ear length as a pertinent criterion.

Notes

1. It was called *trufa* in Provencal, sometimes *tartifla,* cf. the old french *tartaufle* or *tartoufle* and the German *kartoffel* for potato. Some indication of the origin of these words is found in the Vaudois *trufla,* the Umbrian *tufer* and the latin *tuber.* It would seem that the European concept of "tuber" is linked historically to the fungus truffle.
2. "Buck" by reference to beechnuts, which its seeds resemble; cf. *boc, boek, buch,* as in the German *buchweisen,* the Dutch *boekweit.*

References

BOURRET, D. (1973). "Etude ethnobotanique des Dioscoreacées alimentaires—*ignames de Nouvelle Calédonie".* Thèse de Doctorat du 3è cycle en biologie végétale (botanique tropicale), Université de Paris VI, 131 pp., Paris.

CHOWNING, A. (1963). Proto-Melanesian plant names. *In* "Plants and the Migrations of Pacific Peoples" (Ed. J. Barrau), pp. 39–44. Bishop Museum Press, Honolulu.

DOURNES, J. (1972). Larmes de Job et tourments d'ethnobotaniste. *J. d'Agric. trop. Bot. appl.,* **19,** 208–21.

MALENCON, M. G. (1938). Les truffes européennes, historique, morphogénie, classification, culture, *Revue de Mycologie III (N.S.),* mémoire hors série No. 1, 92 pp., Paris.

RHIND, W. (1872). "A History of the Vegetable Kingdom, embracing Comprehensive Descriptions of the Plants most Interesting for Their Uses to Man and the Lower Animals; Their Application in the Arts, Manufactures, Medicine, and Domestic Economy; and for Their Beauty or Peculiarities: Together with the Physiology, Geographical Distribution, and Classification of Plants". Blackie and Son, London.

8

Nomenclature and Classification in Rumphius's *Herbarium Amboinense*

Alice Peeters

C'est renoncer volontairement au plus grand nombre des avantages que la Nature nous offre pour la connoître, que de refuser de se servir de toutes les parties des objets que nous considérons; et quand même on seroit assuré de trouver dans quelques parties prises séparément, des caractères constans et invariables, il ne faudroit pas pour cela réduire la connoissance des productions naturelles à celle de ces parties constantes qui ne donnent que des idées particulières et très-imparfaites du tout, et il me paraît que le seul moyen de faire une méthode instructive et naturelle, c'est de mettre ensemble les choses qui se ressemblent, et de séparer celles qui diffèrent les unes des autres.

Buffon, 1749, p. 29

When dealing with the large field of folk taxonomy, it is of some interest to consider our own natural history and its sequence of classification systems in order to understand the methods and criteria used in organizing nature. For this purpose, the works of pre-Linnaean naturalists are particularly valuable, yet poorly exploited until now. Indeed, modern botanists, even those interested in the history and the development of their own science, have almost completely neglected the classification of plants as conceived before Linnaeus devised his system of classification. When dealing at all with this question, they are mostly concerned with identifying and naming plants described by earlier naturalists in terms of binomial modern nomenclature. Most of them agree that both folk and pre-Linnaean classifications are not scientifically based and are, therefore, beyond their scope of interest. This paper comments on nomenclature and classification as they are to be seen in the *Herbarium Amboinense*, a major work first published between 1741 and 1750, but written much earlier, between 1662 and 1701, by a Dutch naturalist, Georgius Everhardus Rumphius. The *Herbarium* has been the object of numerous references and papers on the part of botanists, Merrill's authoritative *Interpretation of Rumphius's Herbarium Amboinense* (1917) being among the better known. But the interest of these botanists has been limited to identifying plants found in the *Herbarium* in terms of modern taxonomy.

Rumphius's *Herbarium Amboinense* is without doubt the most extensive exotic flora written in pre-Linnaean times. It is an unparalleled source both for naturalists and for anthropologists working in the Malayan and Indonesian areas, for, despite the restrictive title, Rumphius dealt not merely with amboinese plants but with those growing over the entire region. He describes in detailed terms some 1200 plants, many of them hitherto entirely unknown to westerners.

Main features of Rumphius's life and work

Georg Everhard Rumpf was born in or near Hanau, probably in 1627, in a Dutch Evangelist refugee family. After studies at the local *Gymnasium*, he entered the service of the Dutch West India Company at the age of eighteen. While sailing to Brazil he was captured by the Portuguese and brought back to Portugal. During his three-year stay in that country his curiosity about the Orient was awakened through conversations with sailors. His interest in nature was also aroused at that time and frequent references to things seen during his stay in Portugal can be found in his writings. Back in Hanau, in 1648 or 1649, he entered the service of the Dutch East India Company; he landed in Batavia in 1653 and, at the end of the year, he reached Amboina. Until his death in 1702, he lived and worked in Amboina, despite the fact that he was struck blind in 1670. His field observations were made largely during the years 1653–70, but even after he lost his sight, he continued his work with the aid of assistants, asking the Dutch Company to send him scientific books, and studying and writing his "magnum opus", *Herbarium Amboinense*, which was finished by 1696. In 1697, he ended the *Amboinsche Rariteitkamer*, six volumes dealing with amboinese animals and minerals. In 1701, he completed the *Auctuarium*, a supplement to the *Herbarium*, before his death on the 15th June 1702. Unfortunately, the manuscript of his Malay dictionary has been lost and there is nothing left of his herbarium. The original drawings for the *Herbárium* were destroyed by fire in 1687 and were replaced by new illustrations drawn mainly by his son, Paul August, and Philip Van Eyck. Rumphius's work was legally the property of the Dutch East India Company, which granted permission to Dr Johannes Burman, professor of Botany at the University of Amsterdam, to publish the *Herbarium Amboinense*. Burman translated the Dutch text[1] into Latin and added notes and commentaries. The *Herbarium Amboinense* was first published in six volumes between 1741 and 1750. The *Auctuarium*, constituting a seventh volume, was published in 1755.[2]

This necessarily short summary of Rumphius's biography gives but a poor account of the extraordinary personality, the breadth of the ideas, the capacity for work and, above all, the insatiable curiosity of that uncommon man. His deep knowledge and respect of local culture is immediately obvious from his writings. The *Herbarium Amboinense* can be considered as a work of ethnobotany, to the extent that Rumphius noted not only vernacular names, local uses and beliefs, but also presented many of the plant categories distinguished by his informants. We shall see later how Rumphius was influenced by his Indonesian surroundings in naming new species and in adopting, often consciously, a certain number of folk categories, and how, when he disagreed with the latter, he explicitly stated his reasons.

Introduction to the *Herbarium Amboinense*

Rumphius's work is divided into twelve books (in six volumes),[3] each one subdivided into numerous chapters. The internal structure of each chapter is the same throughout the *Herbarium*: first there is a detailed description of the plant and, when appropriate, of the variants of the main type; this is followed by the names of the plant in several languages: Latin, Dutch, Malay, and several languages of Indonesia; sometimes, Indian, Chinese, Arabic, Portuguese and other terms are mentioned too. Moreover, each chapter contains paragraphs on the distribution of the plant and its uses, accompanied by a full-page illustration. According to Du Petit-Thouars (1825, p. 321), this uniform outline adopted by Rumphius is borrowed from Leonhard Fuchs (1501–66).

An analysis of the division into twelve books yields the broader categories used by Rumphius in the classification of the vegetable world: trees, shrubs, woody vines, herbs/grasses and herbaceous vines, and corals or Lithophytes. These are set out in Table 1.

TABLE 1
Broad categories used by Rumphius in the classification of the vegetable world

	I. "containing trees whose fruits are edible and which require to be cultivated by man"
	II. "containing aromatic trees bearing aromatic fruits or barks or some fragrant woods"
Trees	III. ". . . trees producing resin, huge flowers or a toxic milk"
	IV. ". . . wild trees used as building-timber"
	V. ". . . all remaining wild trees"
Shrubs	VI. "shrubs standing upright"
Woody vines	VII. ". . . shrubs which cannot stand upright, but creep with a long stem and tendrils and grow upon trees"[a]
	VIII. ". . . garden herbs used as food, drugs or ornaments"
Herbs/grasses	IX. ". . . convolvulaceae and climbing herbs"
and	X. ". . . other wild herbs"
herbaceous vines	XI. ". . . remaining wild herbs"[b]
Corals	XII. ". . . shrubs and stony sea-plants looking like plants"[c]

[a]This book covers the Malay category *tali utan*.
[b]Books X and XI also deal with some algae and mushrooms.
[c]Corals, called Lithophytes and Lithodendra by Rumphius, are considered by him as having a mixed nature of wood and stone, which was probably the Indonesian conception of coral. On the other hand, it must be recalled that in Rumphius's time, western naturalists classed corals within the mineral kingdom. They were transferred by Marsigli, in 1706, into the vegetable kingdom. In 1727 Jean-André Peysonnel demonstrated the animal nature of these organisms (Leroy, 1969, pp. 3–4).

Though we can agree with Merrill's statement that Rumphius's ". . . classification is primarily the ancient one of trees, shrubs, and herbs", we cannot concur when he asserts that subdivisions are made only "according to habitats and uses", and that "there is no system based on other than the most evident, gross characters." (Merrill,

1917, p. 11). Likewise, the judgement of the botanist Robinson on Rumphius's classification is quite puzzling:

> I think more and more that the Herbarium Amboinense was not at all a complete flora of Amboina as Rumphius found it and that he selected on four bases: economic plants and others that resembled them; plants that were very different from those he had seen in Europe; plants that greatly resembled those of Europe; plants regarding which there was some superstition or legend. A fifth heading might be made for the very showy plants, but I think that this really belongs under the second group.
>
> (Letter written to Merrill in November 1913, quoted by Merrill, 1917, p. 12)

Let us leave to this otherwise eminent botanist the privilege of this assumption. Rumphius's work is rich and complex enough to sustain a variety of interpretations. None the less it deserves more than this schematical reduction. Let us just suggest that a study should be made on the manner in which post-Linnaean botanists interpret classifications (inasmuch as they recognize any) built by pre-Linnaean botanists. More positive are the remarks of De Wit:

> Rumphius was to a fair degree aware of natural affinities but not above all a systematist . . . An appreciation of Rumphius as a systematist is immediately formed if it is realized that nearly all taxa he described prove to fit into our present taxonomy, being species or, rarely, smaller taxa.
>
> (1960, p. 14)

The present paper aims to demonstrate that Rumphius's classification is never based on utilitarian criteria alone and that other attributes, mainly morphological, prevail. Although in the foreword to the *Herbarium* Rumphius insisted on the utilitarian aspect of his work, his statement must not be taken at face value: he had to justify his work in the eyes of the Dutch East India Company. In fact, his minute observations on the morphology and habitat of plants, and the detailed reports he provides on local uses, names and beliefs go far beyond a merely practical guide for travellers and Europeans settled in the archipelago. Environmental or, as we would now say, ecological factors are also important as attributes in his classification of plants, above all of wild plants, mostly herbs and grasses. Rumphius's approach can be exemplified by his own presentation of his outline which precedes the description of wild herbs:

> For the description of wild herbs, we shall proceed in the following order: the one in which these plants occur in Amboina from one coast to the other. For example, if we start from home, first we find the grasses and herbs that grow around human dwellings, in the gardens, along roads, and around cultivated fields. Then we shall meet those growing in fields and hills; we shall climb the top of mountains and from there we shall go into valleys whose wildness is unknown to the Amboinese. Afterwards, in Book XI,

F

going down abruptly to the other shore, we shall come to the mouth of a large river and we shall see herbs growing in humid and swampy places and even in the river water and the river mouth itself; we shall then proceed to the sea where we shall move away from land-herbs and plants and take leave of them and, in the following book, we shall enter the sea itself where we shall see what sort of plants of another kind dwell in the bay.

(Vol. 6, Book X, p. 1)

The terminology of classification

It is useful to study the vocabulary used by Rumphius to express differences between taxonomic levels when trying to understand his approach to plant categories. For this purpose it is necessary to refer to the Dutch text rather than to the Latin translation done by Burman more than fifty years later. Indeed, when terms such as *varietas, species* and *genus* are used by Burman, they connote much more precise taxonomic levels (though not yet exactly Linnaean ones) than the Dutch terms used by Rumphius.[4] As can be seen from Table 2, these latter terms are general ones and most have no precise botanical meaning. Moreover, the descriptions of the plants themselves are very clear and vivid, and practically devoid of technical terms.

This list shows that most of the classificatory terms used by Rumphius may indicate both a taxonomic level (often defined only by the context of its use) and a relationship of likeness or similarity. Another term, *gelykenisse* (= resemblance) is also found frequently in the text.

Rumphius's approach to the classification of plants

Even though the terms used by Rumphius to compare plants and to form categories are often drawn from common usage, they reflect faithfully a process of dividing the plant world into taxonomic units. As will be shown more concretely with rattan and *Ficus* examples, Rumphius's classification combines two rather distinct approaches: that of creating taxonomic levels ranked hierarchically, and an agglomerative approach, based on degrees of similarity. Two complementary aspects can be seen in this latter approach:

1) each plant is described in relation to one described previously. In this perspective, the sequence of chapters in each book is not arbitrary.

TABLE 2
Rumphius's main classification terms

Rumphius's term	Burman translation	English translation	Examples and comments
zoort[4] (modern Dutch: soort)	Species or genus	Kind, type, sort	
slag	-id-	Sort, kind	Used as a synonym of *zoort*
orden	Order	Order	Marks a higher taxonomic level than *zoort* "De Indiaansche Palm-boom dan wort gevoeglyk in drie ordens verdeelt . . ." (The Indian Palm-tree is most conveniently divided into three orders.)
Classis (pl.: classen)	Classis, order	Class	Can be considered as a syn. of *orden*; but a more scholarly term, often written with a capital letter. "Zoo resteert nu nog de derde Classis of orden . . ." (Now, there remains the third Class or order . . .)
verandering	Species or varietas	Variant, variation	"De Indiaansche Palma . . . heeft veel zoorten, waar onder ook slegts eenige veranderingen van de hooft-zoorten zyn." (The Indian Palma occurs in many types, each of which contain several variants of the main type.)

continued over

TABLE 2

Rumphius's main classification terms (*continued*)

Rumphius's term	Burman translation	English translation	Examples and comments
maagschap	Affinitas	Family, kindred	"Deze boom is wel geenzints uit het maagschap van the I. palma". (This tree is not at all in the I. palm-tree family.)
geslagt (modern Dutch: geslacht)	Genus or species	Kind, species, kindred, house, race, strain	"Van de Sattul heeft men twee geslagten, als Tamme en Wilde . . ." (We have two kinds of Sattul, the cultivated and the wild . . .)
fatzoen (modern Dutch: fatsoen)	Forma	Form, feature, characteristic, attribute	Used to express the idea that a plant shows a resemblance to some other one. "een gemengde fatzoen van de Indische Palma" (a mixed form of the Indian Palm-tree).

Indeed, Rumphius is guided by the morphological characters of plants as well as by their habitat; often, he points out particularities of a plant by comparison with one he described previously. When doing this, he is frequently led to the idea of mixed forms (*gemengde fatzoen*). Relative morphological distance is thus an important notion. For example, three plants, A, B and C, will be described in the same chapter either if Rumphius considered them to be very closely related or if B and/or C are just variants of A. For example: "I have observed three kinds of Dryopteris . . . , all three described in this chapter." (Vol. 6, Book X, p. 73). On the other hand, plants A, B and C will be described in three distinct chapters if, though belonging to the same group—named or not—they exhibit a sufficient degree of remoteness or dissimilarity. In this case, Rumphius starts the chapter dealing with A, by saying something like: "A, B and C belong to the same group. I shall describe A in this chapter, and B and C in the next chapters." Thus ". . . the Macuerus are of two kinds, the male and the female, but they are so different that I must attribute a chapter to each one." (Vol. 6, Book XI, p. 132). One can ask whether the difference between the first and the second case reflects distinctions between taxonomic levels under consideration; or, in other words, whether Rumphius deals merely with "varieties" when grouping several plants in the same chapter, and distinguishes between "species" when describing plants in separate chapters. In my opinion, such an interpretation does not fit with Rumphius's practice. His emphasis on greater or lesser proximity between plants does not necessarily include an idea of hierarchical ranking or the inclusion of smaller categories in larger ones. At least, this notion of relative morphological proximity can function at any taxonomic level between plants that may belong to widely different and distant groups. This leads us to a second aspect.

2) Cross-cutting the more obvious dendritic classification, a "network" arrangement is apparent in many cases and may be seen as a key factor in understanding Rumphius's conception of plant relationships. Thus, a plant or a group of plants, at any intermediate, lower or terminal level, may occupy more than one place in the classification according to (a) a "vertical", hierarchical axis, and (b) a "horizontal" axis, which brings plants together on yet another basis. While trying to assign a place to each plant according to a dendritic model, Rumphius often encountered difficulties and, as a result, was unable to design an

overall framework which is coherent at all levels of inclusiveness from higher to lower or terminal taxa. This situation arises mainly because, either successively or simultaneously, criteria of different kinds are employed in the classification process without a definite ranking of their relative importance. This problem was not solved satisfactorily until Linnaeus and Jussieu designed their systems of classification. However, the use of multiple criteria or attributes is not a handicap in a network arrangement based on logical principles of association and relative distance: each plant can be given its place on the basis of several morphological, ecological or utilitarian attributes. As a result, no plant remains completely unaffiliated or placed in a separate remote "box"; its position is always known along one axis at least. An important aspect of such a system is that links can exist between plants or group of plants that belong to widely different domains; also these links are not necessarily of the same kind. When a plant is placed on the basis of two or more attributes, it can either belong to two or more categories or be a link between two other plants or two different categories. The following example may help to make this clearer (Table 3).

TABLE 3
The position of rattans in the Rumphius classification

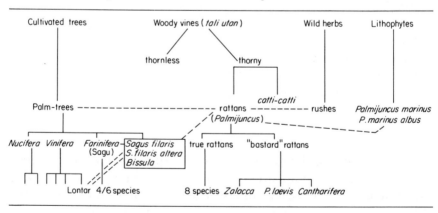

——— Hierarchical relationships
– – – – Network relationships

In this example, which centres on rattan, this group of plants has relations with other taxa in two different ways.

a) On a vertical axis, it shares the same taxonomic level as the *catti-catti* (called by Rumphius *Indica genista aculeata* or thorny-broom), both included within the thorny sub-category of the Malay *tali utan* or woody vines. In this instance, the classification based on a hierarchical model is a complex one, including several intermediate taxa. At the same time, it presents certain obstacles to the inclusion of three forms among rattans, which he consequently calls "bastard".

b) If we consider rattan as the centre of a network, we observe that it is linked to such larger groups as the palms and the rushes which, on other grounds, belong to widely divergent higher taxa: the trees and the wild herbs. From Rumphius's standpoint, rattans are "a mixed form between palms and rushes" or a "degenerate form of palm". It must be noted that, for him, a number of shrubs and climbing plants are degenerate trees.

The somewhat isolated position of the "bastard rattans" is interesting as an example of Rumphius's hesitation between an Indonesian model of classification and his own system. To solve the problem of the *rottang utan* or *Palmijuncus laevis* (*Flagellaria indica* L.),[5] he explains: "This plant is not akin to rattan, except in that it is a vine, though not woody; it looks like a rush and is green; however, in accordance with common usage, we shall describe it with rattans." (Vol. 5, Book VI, p. 120). Obviously, notwithstanding his controversial opinion, Rumphius preferred to adopt the Malay point of view. However, in other cases he suggests different groupings which do not agree with native categorization.

At first sight, the presence of *Cantharifera* or *daun gundi* (*Nepenthes mirabilis* (Lour.) Druce) within the "bastard" group of rattans might seem surprising. Rumphius explains it in this way:

I say that it is in the family of the previous Rottang Oëtan because it has the same leaves and growth. However, it has not the length of a thick woody vine, and does not stand taller than a climbing herb. . . . Said nerve widely protrudes beyond the end of the leaf and coils itself repeatedly like in the preceding plant, but it changes on this occasion into a long stiff thread . . .

(Vol. 5, p. 121)

The link between the rattans and *Palmijuncus marinus* or *rottang laut*, belonging to the Lithophytes, is probably not of the same kind as for previous plants. The Latin name is the exact translation of the Malay term and is explained by Rumphius "because of the form of the plant called rottang". We are led to conclude that Rumphius made the analogy for the purpose of nomenclature and not for taxonomical reasons. Moreover, the text does not indicate clearly whether or not the Malay peoples classify *rottang laut* among the rattans.

Sagus filaris, *Sagus filaris altera* and *Bissula* are classed among palms, though not within the three main sub-groups: *Nucifera*, *Vinifera* and *Farinifera*. The first three taxa are thus considered as intermediate or mixed forms of sago and rattan for the first plant, of *lontar* (Vinifera) and rattan for the two other plants. The fact that all three plants are used for their textile fibres may explain why Rumphius does not include them within one of the three main sub-categories of palms. However, Rumphius's choice rests explicitly on morphological criteria: "it (*Sagus filaris*) is indeed a mixed form of Sagu-calappa and Rottang, though closer to the first one. First, it grows into a shrub like a Sagu-tree or rather like a Rottang from which grows one stem alone." (Vol. 1, p. 84). In adult forms, the leaves rise up like a half-opened book, as do those of the sago tree.

Botanical nomenclature

Except in the case of exotic plants that are well known and named either in antiquity or in previous exotic floras, Rumphius is often in the position of a pioneer and needs to assign both a Latin and a Dutch name to the plants he describes. In most cases, his Latin nomenclature is built on a Malay model, either by giving a Latin form to a Malay word, by translating this word or, frequently, by combining the two operations:

> *Laharong:* Laharus (*Nauclea moluccana* Miq.)
> *caju titti:* Tittius (*Gmelina moluccana* Back.)
> *caju langit:* Arbor Coeli (*Ailanthus integrifolia* Lam.)
> *waringin daun besar:* Varinga Latifolia (*Ficus altissima* Bl.)

Some times he starts with a named category already known in Europe, and includes in that category plants that he considers as lower taxa, for example Convolvulus, Arum, Sinapi, Basilicum, Amarantus and many others. In this way, two plants, *Clematitis amboinica* and *C. Ronica*,[6] are assigned to a category which Rumphius calls *Clematitis indica*.

It must be added that, as usual in pre-Linnaean botany, Rumphius's nomenclature is mainly descriptive in type and non-binomial:

Arbor nigra parvifolia (*Polyalthia rumphii* (Bl. ex. Hensch.) Merr.)
Nugae sylvarum minimae (*Acacia concinna* (Willd.) DC).

Besides Latin labels, Rumphius also wished to give Dutch names to plants. Four main cases may be distinguished.

1) Rumphius adopts a Malay or vernacular term and gives no other name in the Dutch text: *kellor*, named *Morunga* in Latin, is *kellor-boom* in Dutch (*Moringa pterygosperma* Gaertn.) (Vol. 1, p. 185).

2) The Dutch name is, like the Latin one, a construction which is not based on the vernacular name of the plant: *Aytuy* (an Amboinese term) is called *Ichthyoctonos litorea* in Latin and *"de strandt visch-dooder boom"* in Dutch (*Sapium indicum* Willd.)

Sometimes, a plant having its own vernacular name, bears names in Latin and Dutch referring to a higher category. In the following example, this category has itself been derived from the Malay term *mangi mangi: Mangium caseolare* or *kaasvormige mangi-boom* refers to the plant called *brappat* (*Sonneratia alba* J. Smith) in Malay.

3) Both Latin and Dutch names are translations of at least some part of the Malay name: *sajor calappa = Olus calappoides = de moeskruidige calappus* (*Cycas rumphii* Miq.)

4) In addition to vernacular, Latin and Dutch names, we can find examples of what may be considered to be Dutch folk terms for plants commonly known in the Dutch colonies of the East Indies. So, the *bilimbing* (*Averrhoa carambola* L.) is called *vyfhoek* (= five corners) owing to the shape of the fruit.

It must be added that the general tendency in Rumphius's nomenclature is to give a prominent role to a Malay term when creating the Latin one. For example, about *cussambi* (*Schleichera oleosa* (Lour.) Merr.), the author says:

It could be named in Latin *Staphylodendron Indicum,* that is grape-tree (druive-boom), owing to the shape of the fruit; however we have preferred to keep its common name and we have called it *Cussambium* from Malay cussambi which is also known in Java and Bali.

(Vol. 1, p. 155)

Influences on Rumphius's classification

Common features shared by pre-Linnaean botanical classifications
and folk classifications include the use of multiple criteria which: (1)
belong to various aspects of plant morphology or to other characteristics such as smell, taste, uses and environment; and (2) are not applied
in the same order or given the same rank throughout the entire
classification. The result is not one single coherent classification but
several which, nevertheless, may be viewed as a *system* comprising some
parts which are more loosely related and determined and others which
are more tightly structured and have a higher degree of internal co-
herence. Rumphius is perhaps one of the naturalists who has stated most
explicitly the criteria underlying his attempts at classification. A full presentation of these criteria would require a lengthy and minute analysis of
the *Herbarium Amboinense*, and would lead us beyond the scope of this
paper. A few general remarks on the subject will suffice, with the understanding that they are far from exhaustive. Among the influences which
have played a major role in shaping Rumphius's way of organizing the
vegetal kingdom and which suggested the criteria he used for
classification, three main ones can be distinguished:

  1) a profound, long-standing acquaintance and intimate contact
with the Malay environment;
  2) Rumphius's own passionate interest in nature, ways of life, languages and customs, and, in addition, an outstanding capacity for
acute observation; and
  3) a vast erudition stemming from the reading of the scientific
literature available in his time.

As seen earlier, the most inclusive categories of Rumphius's
classification are no more than the well-known tree–shrub–vine–herb
categories of almost world-wide distribution. Immediately below,
criteria such as cultivation or economic use serve to subdivide those
primary or higher taxa. Rumphius's approach to plant classification is
most clearly and exactly revealed by an analysis of the intermediate
and terminal levels of his classification where the Malay influence is the
most obvious. In many cases, Rumphius consciously adopts either
large folk categories, such as *ubi, siri, waringin* (*Ficus* having aerial
roots), or certain very minute distinctions made between two or more
closely related forms of plants, particularly in the case of cultivated

plants such as areca, banana, rice and mango. On the other hand, covering terms such as *bunga* (flower), *caju* (tree), *daun* (leaf) and *sajor* (pot-herbs), which in Malay nomenclature emphasize the part of the plant which is utililized, do not lead Rumphius to derive categories from them. He uses those terms when naming plants, translating them into Latin and Dutch, but he definitely gives them no taxonomic value. In fact, he avoids the pitfall of considering those general terms as Malay categories. This is proof that, contrary to what many botanists have claimed, Rumphius does not give priority to utilitarian criteria. Deeply influenced by the local perception of plants, his observations often lead him to agree with folk categories. Yet sometimes he doubts that a plant placed in a given Malay category is in its right place. When faced with such a situation, he reacts in one of two different ways: (1) while mentioning the dissimilarities which exist between the plant in question and the remainder of the category, he prefers to conform to local tradition; (2) he presents the native classification but then argues for his own. For example, sago is subdivided into six taxa according to the shape and colouration of ripe fruits, according to local tradition, but Rumphius proposes a classification into four sub-groups based on the general appearance of the tree.

Another interesting aspect of Rumphius's process of classification is that he expands native categories, and in doing so, he uses already existing categories to include plants originally outside them. For example, *brappat*, mentioned earlier, seems to have been included in the *mangi mangi* category in this way. However, it is not always clear whether the place attributed to a plant within a given category is the one it has in the Malay system, or whether Rumphius has drawn his inspiration from the Malay model when placing a plant which is actually not included in this category according to the local system.

On the other hand, the influence of the writings of other naturalists on Rumphius's classification is hard to define precisely. The *Hortus Indicus Malabaricus*, written by Hendrick Van Rheede Van Draakenstein, is his main reference. In the foreword of his work, Rumphius states:

In many chapters, I have tried persistently to find under which name the same plants have been described by other authors, and differences in naming them that may exist; above all, I have looked for what may help to interpret the *Hortus Malabaricus* written by His Excellency the Commissary Hendrick Van Rheede, whose Malabar terms are not known in our Nation.

A glimpse at the *Hortus Malabaricus* is more than enough to conclude that, with respect to classification, that work did not influence Rumphius. Concerning nomenclature, no plants are named in Latin nor in Dutch by Van Rheede. Many other naturalists, such as Carolus Clusius, Leonhard Fuchs, Joseph de Acosta (Peru), Christobal Acosta (India), Garcias ab Orta, Jacobus Bontius, Gaspard and Jean Bauhin, are frequently quoted by Rumphius.

Widely distributed and cultivated plants, long known in the Latin, Greek and Arabic traditions, provided categories for some of the new plants. Thus, taxa such as *Solanum, Amarantus, Cucumis* and *Vitis* among others, all of which are very ancient, were used by Rumphius to name and classify local plants which, in his view, were related to European species. However, until a thorough and detailed investigation of this point is made, there will remain much uncertainty as to the actual influences of Rumphius's botanical erudition on his approach which was, first and foremost, grounded in his field work. It should be emphasized here that Rumphius began his observations, information gathering, and plant collecting long before he began a systematic study of natural science. I would be inclined to think, therefore, that a greater part of Rumphius's classificatory practice is derived from his own reflections and his intimate contacts with Malay culture than from his subsequently acquired botanical erudition.

Male and female plants

The distinction between male and female plants, frequently made in the *Herbarium Amboinense,* allows us, at least on this point, to get a clearer understanding of some of the theories which influenced Rumphius. The author separates into two forms, male and female, "species" which are actually monoecious. Yet he also describes a male and a female papaya and in this his practice agrees with the fact that this tree is dioecious. Must we conclude thereby that Rumphius had notions of sexuality in the vegetable kingdom? Such a hypothesis must be discarded immediately, as Rumphius states:

Male (papayas) bear flowers which do not turn into fruits and are hence *useless and only ornamental.*

(Vol. 1, p. 146) [Italics mine]

It must be recalled that in Rumphius's time, and even later, flowers were not recognized as having a sexual role in the formation of the fruit. Tournefort (1694, p. 107), for instance, asserts that the only role of the flowers is to prepare sap that will be the first food for fruit embryos.

Rumphius's ideas on male and female plants must be related to the Malay conception, according to which male plants are those whose flowers either do not produce fruits or produce fruits smaller than those of the other form called female, and whose leaves, flowers and overall size are smaller than in the female form.

Still, Rumphius does not always state clearly whether a "species" is subdivided into male and female on the basis of the local knowledge itself, or whether he is improving upon the existing model. For example, the two following forms are opposed:

Bancudus angustifolia et mas: Bancudu lacki lacki (male)[7]
Bancudus latifolia et femina: Bancudu daun besar (leave/large)

By Malay criteria, Rumphius is perfectly correct in ascribing a female label to the large-leaved *Bancudus*, but is there a symmetrical opposition here, and should we understand that the word *perempuan* (female) is implied? More obviously, Rumphius distinguishes two forms, *Machilus mas* and *Machilus femina* (*Litsea* sp., Lauraceae), according to the size of the leaves, where the Amboinese have just one form, *makelan*.

From modern botanical classification back to Rumphius's classification: the *Ficus* example

Thirty-five plants described in the *Herbarium* belong to the genus *Ficus* (see Table 4) and they do not constitute a single taxon for Rumphius. For several reasons, this genus has a revealing distribution in the *Herbarium Amboinense* and provides a good test as to whether or not Rumphius noticed affinities between the *Ficus* he describes. *Ficus* are distributed in three distinct books depending on whether they belong to the wild tree (Book V), shrub (Book VI) or *tali utan* (Book VII) categories.

ARBORESCENT *Ficus*

The first group of arborescent *Ficus* is the *Varinga*, a category derived from the Malay *waringin*, which are compared with, and distinguished

TABLE 4

Ficus described in the *Herbarium Amboinense*

Rumphius's name	Vernacular name	Category	Botanical name
Varinga latifolia	*Waringin daun besar*	Tree/Varinga	*Ficus altissima* Bl.
Varinga repens	*Waringin malatta*	Tree/Varinga	*F. aff. calophylla* Bl.
Varinga supa	*Supa* (Amb.)	Tree/Varinga	*F. forstenii* Miq.
Varinga pelal	*Pelal* (Amb.)	Tree/Varinga	*F. aff. forstenii* Miq.
Grossularia domestica	*Sajor nuno*	Tree/Varinga	*F. trematocarpa* Miq.
Varinga funicularis	*Nuno batali*	Tree/Varinga	*F. sp.*
Grossularia silvestris	*Nuno hauessi puti* (Amb.)	Tree/Varinga	*F. albinervia* Miq.
Varinga parvifolia alta	*Waringin daun kitjil*	Tree/Varinga	*F. benjamina* L.
Varinga parvifolia humilis	*Nuno assan* (Amb.)	Tree/Varinga	*F. sp.*
Arbor conciliorum	*Caju bodi*	Tree/Varinga	*F. rumphii* Bl.
Caprificus amboinensis esculenta latifolia	*Gaudal*	Tree/Caprificus	*F. racemifera* Roxb.
C.a.e. angustifolia	*Sacca* (Amb.)	Tree/Caprificus	$\begin{cases} F.\ aff.\ racemifera\ \text{Roxb.} \\ F.\ aff.\ variegata\ \text{Bl.} \end{cases}$
C.a.e. silvestris		Tree/Caprificus	*F. sp.*
C.a.e.s. hahuol altera	*Hahuol* (Amb.)	Tree/Caprificus	*F. sp.*
C.s. sycomorus chartaria (Amboinensis)	*Sakka*	Tree/Caprificus	*F. sp.*
C.s. sycomorus chartaria (Javanica)			
C. aspera latifolia	*Gohi*	Tree/Caprificus	*F. sp.*
C. aspera angustifolia	*Gohi*	Tree/Caprificus	*F. teregam* Pennant.
C. aspera tertia	*Gohi*	Tree/Caprificus	*F. teregam* Pennant.
Caprificus viridis minor	*Mussu*	Tree/Caprificus	? *F. moseleyana* King.
Caprificus viridis major	*Mussu*	Tree/Caprificus	*F. adenosperma* Miq.
Ficus septica	*Lipo, siri boppar*	Tree/*siri boppar*	*F. peru-teregam* Pennant.
Ficus septica silvestris	*Lipo, siri boppar*	Tree/*siri boppar*	*F. septica* Burm.f.
			F. septica Burm.f.

Folium politorium vulgare fruticosum	*Ampelaas*	Shrub/ampelaas	*F. ampelos* Burm.f.
Folium politorium arborescens	*Ampelaas*	Shrub/ampelaas	*F. coronata* Reinw. ex Bl.
Rudens silvatis latifolius	*Wöit laun ela* (Amb.)	Woody vines/woit	*F. aff. recurva* Bl.
Rudens silvaticus parvifolius	*Wöit laun maun* (Amb.)	Woody vines/woit	*F. recurva* Bl.
Rudens silvaticus rugosus	*Wöit kuri* (Amb.)	Woody vines/woit	*F. aff. recurva* Bl.
Rudens silvaticus IV	*Wöit ?* (Amb.)	Woody vines/woit	*F. sp.*
Crusta arborum minor	*Wöit laun maun* (Amb.)	Woody vines/woit	*F. falcata* Thunb.
Crusta arborum alba	*Wöit* (Amb.)	Woody vines/woit	*F. spp.*
Crusta arborum odorata	*Wöit haour* (Amb.)	Woody vines/woit	*F. spp.*
Crusta arborum minima	*Wöit* (Amb.)	Woody vines/woit	*F. spp.*
Solulus funicularis	*Gummi susu*	Woody vines/wild siri	*F. sp.*

from, the *mangi mangi* described at the end of the preceding book. Both "classes" are characterized by their aerial roots, but *mangi mangi* grow in the water whereas *waringin* are mainland trees. In this connection Rumphius discusses descriptions written by other naturalists and points out that they have often confused both groups of plants which, in his opinion, must be differentiated.

Waringin are subdivided into several "classes", having the following features in common:

a) they have no single, erect trunk, but several branches joined together, and hiding the trunk;

b) several shoots stand out as large boughs; these reach down to the ground and form new roots, from which grow new trunks;

c) they are full of milk, generally non-toxic;

d) they bear no flowers, but their fruits are like those of the fig-tree and all trees related to *Sycomorus*, described as *Ficus Indica* by the ancients; and

e) their leaves and particularly the lower face of their leaves have special kinds of ribs with small intertwined veinlets.

After the four "classes" of *waringin*, Rumphius goes on to describe, in the same book, the *Caprificus* group which, he says, "are not affiliated with the Varinga, except for their fruits and their milk." (Vol. 3, p. 145).

SHRUBBY *Ficus*

Two species of *Ficus* are described in the sixth book devoted to shrubs. Together they form the category *ampelaas*. Rumphius notes: "Ampelaas can be viewed as a kind of Varinga, although it is merely a shrub; moreover, it occupies a special position in the minds of the islanders, so we shall likewise attribute it a special place." (Vol. 4, p. 128).

CLIMBING *Ficus*

Several *Ficus*, classed in the seventh book dealing with the *tali utan* or woody vines, have no special Malay names, but in Amboina constitute a category called *woït*. *Woït* includes many local species, among which

Rumphius describes only the several which he knows. This group is characterized as "vines having a mixed nature between European ivy and Indian *Varinga*." (Vol. 5, p. 80). Close relationships are pointed out between *woït kuri (Woït rugosum vel pilosum* in Latin) and *Varinga funicularis*.

On the basis of this survey we may conclude that Rumphius does not see the species belonging to the genus *Ficus* as a unit. A division between trees, shrubs and vines prevails at the highest level, while native categories provide the models for the grouping of species at lower levels. Nonetheless, he is aware that some resemblance can be found in the morphology of plants belonging to this genus.

Conclusion

These few remarks on classification and nomenclature in Rumphius's *Herbarium Amboinense* have shown the potential interest of his approach in understanding the process of classification. This paper does not pretend to be an exhaustive study of Rumphius's classification of the vegetal kingdom; its purpose is merely to draw attention to some aspects of his classification, to the criteria most frequently used in it and to the logic underlying his systematization of the plant world. A more thorough analysis would doubtless reveal and render explicit a more complete picture of his plant classification and the kind of relations he sees between plants. In such an analysis particular attention would have to be given to articulations between taxonomic levels and to the precise operation of the two modes of organizing plants, one based on principles of inclusiveness, the other on an analogical approach which leads to a network type of classification. Aside from the interest this holds for a better understanding of the history of classifications in botany and the interesting parallels to be seen with folk classifications, Rumphius's *Herbarium Amboinense* remains, above all, as evidence for the ethnobotany of East India during the second part of the seventeenth century. Though it is clear that Rumphius engaged in re-interpretation of the native system, this rarely obscures actual information, and he is a scrupulous reporter. From this point of view, the *Herbarium Amboinense* is of great value to ethnobotanists working in Indonesia on folk classification systems and deserves further attention.

Notes

1. Rumphius, in the preface to the *Herbarium Amboinense*, writes that the first version of his manuscript had been in Latin but that he translated it into Dutch in order to make his work accessible to a wider audience.
2. More detailed information about Rumphius's biography can be found in Heeres (1902), Merrill (1917) and De Wit (1960).
3. In this article I refer to a copy of the second edition of the *Herbarium Amboinense*, published by Meinard Uytwerf in Amsterdam, in 1750. In this copy, the *Auctuarium* is bound with the sixth volume at the end of Book XII. For bibliographic remarks, see Rouffaer and Muller (1902). The English translations of Rumphius's quotations are mine, apart from the second part of the quotation dealing with the *Nepenthes mirabilis* (p. 155) which has been drawn from De Wit (1959 p. 18).
4. Rumphius's spelling has been followed in Dutch, Latin and Malay.
5. All botanical identifications of Rumphius's plants cited in this paper are either from Merrill (1917) or De Wit's (1959) revision.
6. *Aristolochia rumphii* Kostel. and *A. tagala* Cham.
7. *Morinda bracteata* Roxb. var. *celebica* Miq. and *Morinda citrifolia* L.

References

Buffon, G. L. (1749). "Histoire Naturelle", Vol. I, 451 pp. Paris.
De Wit, H. C. D. (1959). A checklist to Rumphius's Herbarium Amboinense. *In* "Rumphius Memorial Volume" (Ed. H. C. D. De Wit), pp. 339–462. The Royal Tropical Institute, Amsterdam.
De Wit, H. C. D. (1960). Georgius Everhardus Rumphius, "Belmontia Miscellaneous publications in Botany; IV Incidental", Fasc. 4, pp. 1–26. Wageningen.
Du Petit-Thouars and L. A. Aubert (1825). Article "Rumft". *In* "Biographie Universelle Ancienne et Moderne . . . rédigé par une Société de gens de lettres et de savants", Vol. XXXIX, pp. 317–22. L. G. Michaud, Paris.
Heeres, J. E. (1902). Rumphius' Levensloop. *In* "Rumphius Gedenkboek, 1702–1902", pp. 1–16. Koloniaal Museum, Haarlem.
Leroy, J. F. (1969). La notion de vie dans la botanique du XVIII. siecle. *"Histoire et Biologie"*, Fasc. 2, pp. 1–9. Paris.
Merrill, E. D. (1917). An interpretation of Rumphius's Herbarium Amboinense. Department of Agriculture and Natural Resources, Bureau of Science, Publication No. 9, 595 pp. Manila.
Rouffaer, G. P. and Muller, W. C. (1902). Eerste proeve van eene Rumphius-Bibliographie. *In* "Rumphius Gedenkboek, 1702–1902", pp. 165–200. Koloniaal Museum, Haarlem.
Rumphius, G. E. (1741–50). *"Herbarium Amboinense*/Het Amboinsche Kruidboek", 6 Vols. Amsterdam.
Tournefort, J. P. de (1694). "Elemens de Botanique", Vol. I. Paris.
Van Rheede Van Draakenstein, H. (1678–1703). "Hortus Indicus Malabaricus", 12 Vols. Amsterdam.

9

Classification of the Sciences

The Nineteenth Century Tradition

R. G. A. Dolby

I

Introduction

The classification of the sciences has been a continuing concern in the philosophy of a wide range of cultures. In Europe, there has been a continuous tradition since the time of Plato and Aristotle.[1] European discussions rose to a peak during the nineteenth century, but since then the tradition has declined to a few scattered and uninfluential publications. A few writers, especially Catholics and Marxists, still argue their special philosophical interests in terms of this theme. But while the nineteenth century discussions of classification formed a cohesive tradition, modern publications often fail to cite one another and seem to be dispersed among the backwaters of intellectual thought. In some recent English-language writings on the history of philosophy, the works on classification by still-studied philosophers are systematically repressed.[2] It is historically interesting to explore the striking contrast between the nineteenth century preoccupation and the modern relative neglect. We may hope to learn the internal intellectual and external socio-cultural factors which led to the change in fortunes of this philosophical tradition.

Classification of the sciences is concerned with contrasting and relating different branches of phenomena, the intellectual activities of investigating them and the knowledge produced. It is just one of a number of classificatory activities related to science. In this paper, it must be distinguished from more abstract discussions of the theory of classification in general, usually in a logico-mathematical manner. For most of the period we will be dealing with, the theory of classification remained relatively unchanged. The classification of the sciences must also be contrasted with the classification of the objects of study within a particular science—as in biological classifications of living organisms. This is naturally an important part of scientific activity in the early stages of development of a science, and was a widespread concern in the eighteenth and nineteenth centuries. Finally, we should distinguish the philosophical traditions of classification of the sciences from related practical classifications intended for particular purposes. A relevant example is library classification, which stems from similar pre-nineteenth century sources to the classification of the sciences. However, since then the problems of arranging books on shelves have led to a quite different set of literature.[3] The practical problems of organizing knowledge for teaching at intermediate and advanced levels remained closer to the tradition we will be studying, but they have tended to be governed by the difficulties of changing established practice far more than by theoretical discussion. The practical problems of the exposition of knowledge in an encyclopaedia was of central importance in the rise of the nineteenth century tradition of classification of sciences, but this problem has declined as encyclopaedias have come to rely on alphabetical ordering, and attempts at presenting wide fields of knowledge systematically have declined in favour of specialized works. In this paper, I will deal only with other kinds of classificatory activity as they impinge on the classification of the sciences.

An important indicator of the continuity of the tradition we will be discussing is given by the custom of many of the writers classifying the sciences to preface their own ideas with a more or less extended discussion of their predecessors. This indication of the intellectual influences a writer wishes to acknowledge is useful in showing changing historical perspectives within the tradition. Although every writer has his own bias in his choice of references, one source—Flint (1904)—is especially comprehensive, and has been a useful lead into the subject. My paper is intended to complement Flint's exposition. Although Flint concentrated on writers who approach the subject through philosophy and tended to over-represent Italians and to under-represent Germans, he treated sixty-seven nineteenth-century authors, and gave details of the classificatory schemes of most of them, with critical comments. Thus, in spite of the many mistakes he made and his limitation to English, French, Italian and German sources, his book is an invaluable source. Another source covering the history of the classification of the sciences is Kedrov (1961, 1964). Kedrov adds a few names missed by Flint, and also treats large numbers of Russians.

II

Classification of the sciences until the nineteenth century

In the Aristotelian tradition, the concern to clarify concepts and to systematize knowledge through classification, was a prominent and continuing concern. Aristotle himself produced a classification based on a three-fold division of theoretical, productive and practical philosophy. This division, related to the purpose of the knowledge, was reduced by early Aristotelians to the contrast between theoretical and practical, and in this form has become one of the basic contrasts within science. Plato was identified, especially in Stoic and Epicurean philosophy, as the source of a three-fold division of knowledge into physics, ethics and logic (or dialectic). Subsequently, every coherent and systematic philosophical position has tended to involve pronouncements on the relations between the various fields of knowledge, from which a classification can be extracted. Flint, in his *History of Classifications of the Sciences*, did this with most of the major philosophers since Plato. For many of these figures, explicit concern with classification was either absent, as in Plato, or transient, as in Descartes and Kant.

Until the nineteenth century, much of the work on classification of science, particularly that stimulated by philosophical rather than practical motives, formed not a continuous tradition, but a series of by-products of philosophical positions. It was no wonder that Comte could exclaim with despair that in the two centuries before him there had been almost as many classificatory schemes as there were people proposing them (Comte, 1864, Vol. 1, p. 48).

However, it was not only changing philosophical positions which led to diversity in classification schemes. The growth in the scale and complexity of knowledge, the flowering of the arts in the Renaissance, and of the natural sciences in the seventeenth century, meant that even the best classifications inevitably became dated. The practical requirements for organizing knowledge needed currently applicable classifications. For example, the seven departments of knowledge preparatory to theology that sufficed in the Middle Ages (the Trivium and Quadrivium), could not serve the new growth of science of the sixteenth and seventeenth centuries. This encouraged Campanella and Bacon to devise more elaborate schemes in which to fit their accounts of the sciences.[4]

With the growth of knowledge, classification of science was needed not merely for pedagogy, but for the organization of libraries. Leibniz, for example, in his *Idea Leibnitiana Bibliothecae ordinandae contractior* set out his nearest approach to a classification of science (Flint, 1904, p. 125).

Although classification of the sciences depended more on external factors than on an internal logic of development up to the nineteenth century, there is some interest in looking for stages in its development, stages which should bear a close relationship to the changing complexity of scientific knowledge. B. M. Kedrov, filled with feeling for the dialectic of history, distinguishes three stages in the classification of science, each with its own problems and solutions (Kedrov, 1964). In the first stage, ancient science and most of the middle ages, the context was a single philosophy that embraced all realms of knowledge, and the concern was to *divide* it. In the second stage, from the Renaissance to the end of the eighteenth century, the concern was to *co-ordinate* a series of separate sciences. In the third stage, from the nineteenth century on, when new connections were constantly being discovered between the sciences, the concern was to *unite* sciences that had previously been separated.

This scheme is very much a first approximation. Throughout the whole tradition there have always been simultaneous trends to unification and division. In the Aristotelian tradition, claimed to be a period of unity through simplicity, the sciences were distinguished by their subject matter, each with its own method, so that it was impossible in demonstration to pass from one genus to another. The period from Bacon to Kant has been seen as one of the search for unity in the sciences, previously so strongly divided (McRae, 1957, 1961). Since the beginning of the nineteenth century there has been a trend towards the unification of scientific knowledge at the same time as an increased tendency towards specialization. Classification of the sciences is too multifaceted to be successfully encapsulated in one simplistic theory.

It is clear, however, that the conflicting tendencies of diversification and unification of knowledge provide a continuing theme, amenable to study by an historian of ideas. It will not be the object of this paper to explore the changes from the philosophical systems of the Greeks, through the sophistication of conceptual distinctions of the Middle Ages, and the opening up of new fields in the Renaissance and the seventeenth century, through the maturation of scientific ideas and organization of the nineteenth century, to the programmes for methodological unification of modern science. The abstraction from the changing intellectual environment would make such a task difficult and necessarily inconclusive. I propose to limit myself to the period when there was a self-conscious tradition of developing new classifications on the basis of criticism of previous schemes. This period was centred on the nineteenth century, spilling over at each end.

A number of factors drew attention to classification of the sciences by the late eighteenth century, and helped to make it an explicit problem. One of these was the recent success of classification schemes in botany (and, in the early nineteenth century, in zoology). Biological classification, though also going back to Aristotle, had, particularly in the eighteenth century, been closely tied to the study of the subject matter, in the search for a natural yet logical system. Both Comte and Ampère acknowledged the stimulus of the classificatory schemes of botany and zoology. On the other hand, S. T. Coleridge felt that biological classification was to be contrasted with his own progressive arrangement of the sciences. Botany of the time was "Little more than an enormous nomenclature, a huge catalogue, bien arrangé, yearly and monthly augmented, in various editions, each with its own scheme of technical memory and its own conveniences of reference!" (Coleridge, 1835).

A second factor stimulating interest in classification of the sciences was the sheer number of classification schemes available, particularly in philosophical writings. In his chapter covering the period from the Renaissance to Kant, Flint discussed Poliziano, Nizolio, Campanella, Descartes, Bacon, Alsted, Comenius, Weigel, Hobbes, Locke, Leibniz,

Vico, and Christian Wolff and his school. In the face of such diversity, Comte, for example, felt that a new approach was necessary.

A third factor stimulating the tradition was the rise in encyclopaed-ism in the eighteenth century. Works such as Buffon's *Histoire Naturelle* aspired to give an account of all the knowledge of nature that could be amassed. Encyclopaedias, in particular the *Encyclopédie* . . . (1751–65) gave systematic coverage. In Germany, Christian Wolff's philosophy claimed to include all science, and the literature of the time abounded with works either introducing or surveying particular fields.[5]

The *Encyclopédie* itself was undoubtedly a strong influence on the tradition of classifying the sciences. The article on *Encyclopédie* by Diderot, the *Discours Preliminaire* by D'Alembert, and the *Prospectus* by the two of them, set out the plan of the work. Bacon's classificatory scheme, modified only in minor ways, but added to slightly, was adopted and given new significance.[6] By this means, classification of the sciences was brought before a wide public. It was only Bacon and D'Alembert that Comte referred to by name when dismissing the classifications that preceded him (Comte, 1864, Vol. 1, p. 47); and Ampère was stongly influenced in his youth by a systematic reading of the entire *Encyclopédie* (St. Beuve, 1843, p. viii). The *Encyclopédie* stimu-lated classification of the sciences not merely by giving the matter unprecedented publicity, but also by using a system which many people considered to be out of date. Bentham, for example, began a detailed criticism of D'Alembert's scheme in this way:

Of the sketch given by *D'Alembert*, the leading principles are—as he himself has been careful to declare, taken from that given by *Lord Bacon*. Had it been entirely his own, it would have been, beyond comparison, a better one. For the age of *Bacon*, Bacon's was a precocious and precious fruit of the union of learning with genius: for the age of *D'Alembert* it will, it is believed, be found but a poor production, below the author as well as the age." (Bentham, 1843, p. 73)

Bentham, certainly, was stimulated to devise a classification of the sciences of some sophistication in 1816 because of the deficiencies of the best known scheme of the day. His original practical motivation of devising a school syllabus could have been satisfied far more simply.

We shall see that this concern to criticise in detail previous classifications of science was one of the strongest factors in creating a self-conscious tradition in the subject. It did not in itself guarantee that the tradition is worth while; indeed, my impression is that many sterile discussions were perpetuated by people who thought that they could do better than a well-publicised predecessor. Certainly Bentham's classification of the sciences never gained the acclaim which the Baconian scheme continued to receive in the nineteenth century.

Another factor stimulating classification of the sciences was a recurring one, not unique to the late eighteenth century. This is the general concern of scientists to characterize their own field, its status and relation to neighbouring subjects, and its subdivisions. The results of this concern appear in introductions to books, in lectures, and in popular writings. The classifications resulting were largely fragmentary, and of wider value only when some recurring philosophical problem is brought in. For example, classificatory questions of the relation of the physical and the life sciences could turn into debates over vitalism. Psychologists, sociologists and others striving to give their science some legitimacy often did so by arguing for its primacy in a classification of science. There was a strong tradition since Vico, particularly in Italy, to argue for the fundamental importance of history and to consolidate this in an appropriate classification. And recurring throughout the discussions of classification by the less positivistic was the question of whether or not theology should be recognized with a place in the scheme. Quite frequently in the nineteenth century, this kind of restricted interest in classification led on to more general and elaborate schemes. Ampère, for example, wrote in the preface to his work that his immediate stimulus had been to distinguish general physics from other sciences and to divide it into its branches for teaching purposes. This interest became generalized into a search for a classification scheme to cover all aspects of systematic knowledge (Ampère, 1834, pp. v–x).

Finally, a factor favouring the rise of attention to classification in general was the related rise of an inductive philosophy of science. Classification has been an essential part of inductive schemes of scientific method, particularly since Bacon. Karl Pearson in his *Grammar of Science* put this in a strong form: "The classification of facts, the recognition of their sequence and relative significance is the function of science" (Pearson, 1900, p. 9). In inductive philosophy, classification is especially important in the initial stages of development of a subject. In the decades around the beginning of the nineteenth century there was a surge of interest in reflection upon science as a whole. The philosophy of science, as an activity distinct from both philosophy and science, became a self-perpetuating tradition from about this time, and apart from the recurring question of scientific method, it was seen as an appropriate part of this activity to characterize the sciences and their relationships. Thus, along with classification *in* the sciences, the inductive philosophy tended to favour classification *of* the sciences.

III

Classification of science in the nineteenth century

We have given reasons why there should have been increased attention given to classfication at the beginning of the nineteenth century. Flint illustrated this by discussing twenty writers in the first three decades of the century. About half were German, and most were rather minor figures. The writers on Naturphilosophie were well represented, as a mystical concern with the unity of science and the interconnectedness of its parts could readily lead to classificatory schemes at a time when the prevailing culture favoured an all-embracing, somewhat encyclopaedic approach to science.[7] Schelling, Oken (1809–11) and Hegel (1817) were among the better-known German writers of the period who classified the sciences.

The leading figures in the nineteenth century tradition were, however, undoubtedly Comte and Ampère. For example, E. Goblot introduced his *Essai sur la Classification des Sciences* by saying, "It was only in this century that two great minds, Ampère and Comte, considered the entire body of science as a sort of organism and attempted to describe its structure" (Goblot, 1898, p. 1). The numerous, thinly connected discussions before them were replaced by a solid chain of work in which each writer established his position after criticism and evaluation of his predecessors. Although later classifications may have employed earlier ideas, particularly from Aristotle and Bacon, this needed to be done in a way that met the standards of contemporary discussion. Comte and Ampère did not produce completely novel schemes, but they do mark the high point in the history of the tradition.

Because of the interest aroused in his law of three stages of development, Auguste Comte is undoubtedly the best remembered writer on the classification of the sciences. In spite of his claims to originality, his scheme shows the considerable influence of his predecessors. As George Boas observed, "Perhaps the secret of Comte's charm for his successors s not so much his originality as his clever use of old materials in a new arrangement" (Boas, 1925, p. 254). Credit for Comte's law of the Three Stages is generally distributed between Turgot, Condorcet, and Saint-Simon (Boas, 1925, pp. 263–76). The earlier two writers gave a sequence of sciences, but in an historical account of the progressiveness of mankind. Saint-Simon gave the same sequence of sciences as Comte: astronomy, physics, chemistry and physiology, suggesting, as Comte did, that the order is from simple to complex, and that all depend on mathematics (Saint-Simon, 1966, pp. 36–40). But apart from those writers who accepted the Marxist dismissal of Comte and so featured Saint-Simon instead, it was Comte's formulation of the classification which subsequently gained the most attention.[8]

Comte had a wide variety of reasons for wanting to classify the sciences. He clearly wished to replace earlier schemes which gave a prominent place to religious and metaphysical thought. In this way he was representative of the many people who have tried to either gain or deny legitimacy for particular sciences. Comte was also clearly aware of the increasing tendency to specialization in the rapid growth of modern science. He saw it as an inevitable effect of the increase of knowledge. In order to encourage growth and yet retain the unity of modern science, he argued that division of labour should be perfected, and the sharply divided subjects which resulted should be co-ordinated by a new group of scientists, drawing the sciences together under the smallest number of general principles (Comte, 1864, Vol. 1, pp. 25–8).

The second lesson of the *Cours de Philosophie Positive* contains one of Comte's discussions of the classification of the sciences. In it he set out to establish a hierarchy of the sciences in the manner of the encyclopaedic tradition. Comte presupposed that this should be done by establishing a linear order of the sciences.[9] In spite of his own objections to its naturalness, he did not seem to question the importance of devising "les échelles encyclopédiques" (Comte, 1864, Vol. 1, p. 76). Comte felt that the inadequate schemes that had preceded him had been proposed by people who were unfamiliar with the subject matter of science: this, concomitant with their failure to distinguish theological, metaphysical and positive science, prevented them from establishing satisfactory schemes,[10] unlike the successful classifications of recent botanists and zoologists (Comte, 1864, Vol. 1, p. 49). What was needed was a natural classification of the sciences which reflected the real connections between phenomena. But in the *a priori* manner which so

often characterized him, Comte immediately went on to make preliminary divisions. He distinguished theoretical and practical concerns,
and insisted that theory be kept apart from practice. Within the
theoretical sciences, a further division was made between the abstract,
in which laws regulating all conceivable phenomena were sought, and
the concrete, where the laws were applied to the history of particular
existing objects. The abstract sciences, which were fundamental, were
the ones Comte dealt with fully. Because he had denied himself
metaphysical arguments, Comte could only justify these distinctions by
appeal to their practical value and their naturalness to any who have
studied the sciences. But as they preceded his own survey of the
sciences, his justification was inevitably very thin. Comte recognized
two methods of ordering the sciences: the sequence in which they
developed historically and that in which they could be developed by a
single individual rationally reconstructing all science. The former,
although important, is complicated by the fact that many branches of
science developed simultaneously and in interaction. Comte, therefore,
followed the latter, less historical method, but claimed substantial
agreement with the history of science, since the logical dependence of
the later sciences on the earlier ones implied that this must also be an
historical ordering. Comte set up his problem as the ordering of six,
theoretical, abstract, positive sciences in one of the 720 possible series.
His sequence was from the most simple and general to the most complex and least general. This was achieved by making a series of divisions.
The first was into inorganic and organic. Inorganic was divided
into astronomic and terrestrial, and terrestrial into mechanical and
chemical. Organic physics was analogously divided into physiology
proper and, founded on this, social physics. As all these divisions were
based on comparative generality and complexity, the resulting sequence
of five sciences—astronomy, physics, chemistry, physiology and social
physics—was one of decreasing generality and increasing complexity.
The subdivisions within each science could be ordered in the same way.
Each of these sciences has gone through theological, metaphysical and
positive stages, the simplest and most remote from man becoming
positive first. To these five subjects was added mathematics, which is
both a part of science and the basis of it. Abstract pure mathematics is
purely instrumental, and concrete mathematics, i.e. geometry and
rational mechanics, a natural science, based on the simplest and most
obvious phenomena.

Comte believed that this ordering could be applied in education. The student of each subject need only learn his own science and those earlier in the sequence. The series thus had practical as well as theoretical importance.

However, even these general principles generated protracted criticism in the later tradition. Many people felt that astronomy should not have come directly after mathematics, and tried to develop new principles of division to improve on Comte's.

André-Marie Ampère published his *Essai sur la Philosophie des Sciences* (1834, 1843) at about the same time as Comte, but he took a very different approach to the classification of the sciences. He, too, criticized the many classifications that had preceded him, mentioning only Bacon, and the *System figurê des connaisances humaines*, on which the *Encyclopédie* is based. He mentioned also the artificial classifications that philosophical principles provide, contrasting them with the recent success of more natural classifications in the biological sciences. But apart from these criticisms the two works are very different. Ampère was in his late fifties and a famous physicist when the first volume of his classification was published. He had not filled in the details of a grand conception of the world, but had worked on the general scheme after classificatory studies of the subject matter of physics (Ampère, 1834, pp. v–x), chemistry (Ampère, 1816) and psychology.[11] Ampère did not reject religion and metaphysics as Comte had done. His interest in mataphysics in particular, extended throughout his life. Where Comte felt he could simplify the task of classifying the sciences by setting to one side the first two stages of the development, Ampère followed a different path. He felt that Bacon's classification and those that came after it were limited by accepting the grouping of knowledge into sciences which were established by custom. They had not realized the double necessity of first grouping all truths in a rational manner, and then of giving new names to each of the groups so formed which had not yet been named (Ampère, 1834, p. 2). Ampère regrouped the truths of science in a way which was both a strength and a weakness of his system. It was a strength because the new subjects he devised were far better suited to the state of knowledge of his own time than were the traditional subject divisions which other people accepted. It was a weakness because the resulting classification had an added strangeness which made it inevitable that it would not be accepted in practice. Ampère complained that dividing the sciences by *a priori* principles tended to bring together quite unrelated subjects. In contrast, he followed a method of careful comparisons, seeking to associate those subjects which showed the greatest analogy. In addition, he thought that it was important that the sciences should be divided not only by subject matter, but also by the point of view adopted in studying them. He came to recognize four points of view and used them to characterize four levels of science. The first was the level of immediate observation, and the determination of the facts that can be ascertained directly. The second was the level of experimental and analytical investigation required to determine the hidden facts about the subject matter not directly observable. The third was the comparison of facts already obtained and the inference of general laws from them. Finally, the scientist could return to the *causes* of the facts observed in the first, analysed in the second, and reduced to general laws in the third (Ampère, 1834, pp. xviii–xix). This four-fold division occurred to Ampère in stages as he classified the sciences, and he became more convinced by it when it occurred to him that it corresponded to stages in the development of the human intellect which he had already noted.[12]

When trying to group the sciences he had arrived at, Ampère finally decided that they could most naturally be arranged in pairs, and was pleased to find that he could organize them by successive pairing within his basic division of cosmology and noology (matter and thought). Comte, too, had arrived at his sciences by applying principles of two-fold division. But Ampère claimed to have built up his table by associating the basic arts and sciences in pairs, the pairs into further pairs, and so on. The scheme had thus been *built up* as a natural classification. Once the scheme had been obtained, Ampère, following the example of Bernard de Jussieu's biological classification (Ampère, 1834, p. xii), sought a key, a unifying principle which would allow him to descend through the seven stages of bifurcation to the 128 sciences of the final stage. The key he found was to apply the four stages of human thought to the two kingdoms of cosmology and noology, thus dividing them into sub-kingdoms and, in turn, to branches. The same four stages could then be applied again, producing sub-branches and then sciences of the first order, exactly as they had been specified in the original process of building them up from below. Applying the principle a third time gave the four sciences of the third order from each of the sciences of the first order. There Ampère stopped, saying that there was no practical value in dividing each of these 128 sciences still further. A second key, more practical and simpler to follow than the first, which was philosophical and profound, was promised for an appendix (Ampère, 1834, p. xxix).[13]

As an example of the way Ampère's classification differed from prevailing practice, we may mention the case of chemistry. This was already a professional subject, recognized as such in most classifications of the time. Ampère had made a number of important contributions to chemistry and therefore might have been expected to tackle its status with some sympathy. However, he treated it as a science of the third and most specific order, a part of general elementary physics (Ampère, 1834, pp. 197–204). He argued that general physics deals with the inorganic properties always shown by bodies, while chemistry limits itself to a sub-group of these—those of homogeneous substances (whether originally derived from inorganic or organic bodies). The only problem he recognized was that chemistry had been studied more than most other sciences of the third order, so that it was harder to trace the limits separating it from other sciences.

Another deviation from established practice was Ampère's insistence that sciences and arts should be dealt with together. He reasoned that the best conception of each is identical, rejecting arguments for separating the two, such as the difficulty of modifying established practice.

Comte thought very little of Ampère's work on classification. The references to Ampère in the *Cours de Philosophie Positive* make it clear that Comte regarded Ampère as a prime example of a scientist who should have kept to his speciality (mathematical physics) and away from the generalities of philosophy of science (Comte, 1864, Vol. 2, pp. 471–2 and n, Vol. 3, pp. 65, 387).

It was inevitable, therefore, that Ampère's classification, ingeniously conceived though it was, should have had little influence on the labelling and division of sciences in practice. The influence that it did have was on the self-perpetuating tradition of theories of classification of the sciences, and it has played a small part in increasing the separation of that tradition from practical issues.

It is in France that the influence of Comte and Ampère is to be most expected. Flint discussed six French authors up to the early 1880's who all revealed this influence (Flint, 1904, pp. 191–3).

Flint did not consider the undoubtedly less original writings by

French scientists on classification of the sciences. Two chemists will serve as examples. The motivation of M. F. Chevreul's classification of the sciences was in part to set out the leading ideas of chemistry and its relations with human knowledge. His scheme was claimed to be *a posteriori* and based on evidence, rather than the result of the artifices of abstract reasoning (Chevreul, 1863). M. Berthelot in his "Science ideal et science positif", arranged facts in a pyramid, from the most general and most certain in mathematics to the least general and least certain in "les grands sentiments moraux de l'humanite" (Berthelot, 1886, p. 35). The ordering is reminiscent of Comte's

In England, two main streams of thought can be detected in writings on the classification of science during the nineteenth century. The earlier and less influential group included P. E. Dove (1850), Lord Lindsay (1846) and Neil Arnott (1828, 1861). It considered classification in the context of the theme of human progress, both mental and cultural, much as it had inspired French writers of the late eighteenth century. The second, appearing mainly in books of logic, related classification of science to discussions of the inductive method. There were also some schemes outside these two groups, such as those of S. T. Coleridge (1835), Jeremy Bentham (1843), or Sir William Hamilton's division of philosophy and the mental sciences (Hamilton, 1859–60, Lecture vii).

The nineteenth century English writing on induction naturally starts with the work of Sir John Herschel. *A Preliminary Discourse on the Study of Natural Philosophy* (Herschel, 1831) did not make an explicit issue of classifying the sciences. However, the book was inspired by Bacon's philosophy of science and, like Bacon's work, was organized around a classification. In the first two parts of the book, there was a basic division into abstract science (the knowledge of reasons and their conclusions) and natural science (knowledge of causes and their effects and of the laws of nature). In the third part, the physical sciences were subdivided into distinct branches and their mutual relations discussed. Herschel did not wish to stress the importance of the division of science, for he wanted to show how interconnected it was:

What we have all along most earnestly desired to impress on the student is, that natural philosophy is essentially united in all its departments, through all which one spirit reigns and one method of enquiry applies. In [misprint for "it"] cannot, however, be studied as a whole without subdivision into parts; and, in the remainder of this discourse, we shall therefore take a summary view of the progress which has been made in the different branches into which it may most advantageously be subdivided, and

endeavouring to give a general idea of the nature of each, and of its relations to the rest.
(Herschel, 1831, p. 219)

The second important figure in the British tradition of methodology of science in the nineteenth century was William Whewell. Whewell had a conception of induction which drew from Kant an importance for innate ideas which give form to experience. The resulting discussion made classification seem a less important problem than it was for the usual nineteenth century form of induction. In the first edition of his *Philosophy of the Inductive Sciences* he recognized the need for a classification, primarily as a guide to the discussion of a whole succession of topics connected with particular sciences. In his classificatory scheme, each science rested on a "fundamental idea". Whewell's classification of the sciences was to be a guide through his philosophy of science:

In this undertaking, inevitably somewhat long, and involving many deep and subtle discussions, I shall take, as a chart of the country before me, by which my course is to be guided, the scheme of the science which I was led to form by travelling over the history of each in order.

(Whewell, 1840, Vol. 1, p. 76)

Whewell's ordering of the science was historical rather than logical, and therefore did not tend to challenge the subject schemes in general use.

In the third edition of his philosophy of science, the *Novum Organum Renovatum*, Whewell devoted a brief chapter to the classification of the sciences, ending with a table classifying the sciences and their ideas (Whewell, 1858, pp. 136–40). This slightly more explicit presentation of classification seems to have been in response to the greater prominence classification had attained in England since his first edition. Whewell later commented briefly on Comte's classification of the sciences (Whewell, 1860, p.236). He pointed out merely that the principles by which Comte identified each science were far inferior to his own system in terms of the ideas on which each science was based. In a remark on Mill's discussion, stimulated by Comte, on classification by series (Whewell, 1860, p. 270, n), Whewell objected to the idea of a "mere linear progression in nature", judging it to be inadequate. Whewell did not wish to waste attention on Comte's philosophy, except as a negative example of philosophy.

Whewell's philosophy of science was soon overshadowed by the work of John Stuart Mill. Mill did not elaborate a new classification of the

G

sciences, although he did comment on the general *theory* of classification (Mill, 1843, Book I, Chapter vii, Book IV, Chapter vii, viii). However, Mill helped to draw English attention to Comte's work. He regarded it favourably, in the main, and commented on Comte's classification of the sciences (Mill, 1865).

Another important influence in popularizing classification of the sciences, especially as presented by Comte, was Herbert Spencer. His work had a strong influence on the English inductivist tradition of classification of the sciences. Spencer's main stimulus was undoubtedly a wish to show that his predecessors, and especially Comte, were mistaken in their classifications of science. The essay, "The genesis of science", is at first concerned with a critique of the classification schemes of Oken, Hegel and Comte (Spencer, 1858, pp. 166–85). Spencer was prepared to admit the importance of this stimulus.

It is probable that the doctrines set forth in the essay on "The Genesis of Science" might never have been reached had not my very decided dissent from M. Comte's conception, led me to work them out; and but for this, I might not have arrived at the classification of the sciences exhibited in the foregoing essay.

(Spencer, 1874, p. 79)[14]

Spencer wished to deny in particular that the sciences can be arranged rationally in a serial order, which Comte had presupposed as the task of an encyclopaedic arrangement. He was prepared to recognize only the ordering resulting from the instrumental dependence of the sciences of concrete products on more formal abstract sciences. This he expressed in terms of three levels of sciences, the abstract, the abstract–concrete, and the concrete. Comte's series of mathematics, astronomy, physics, chemistry, biology and sociology did not follow through these levels. Spencer did allow, however, that there could be an evolutionary order, at least in the concrete sciences. Thus astronomy, geology, biology, psychology and sociology are the sciences of phenomena that have appeared successively in the evolutionary sequence. Here Spencer's work bears more similarity to the classifications of Oken and Hegel he quoted. Although Comte stimulated Spencer into thinking that he could do better, it cannot be denied that Spencer's general philosophical system and, in particular, his classification of the sciences, drew much from Comte's work. As many of his critics pointed out, Spencer's knowledge of the physical sciences was inadequate for his purposes, so that he made many errors of detail. But he must certainly be recognized in the present context for popularizing classification of science, especially in England, and making it into a critical tradition. Spencer also had one follower, J. Fiske, who wrote on classification of the sciences (Fiske, 1874).

The later tradition, especially in England, was particularly involved with one issue Spencer made explicit; whether or not there can be a logical, linear ordering of the sciences. At one extreme, H. M. Stanley could quote with approval T. A. Ribot's remark:

> The philosophers of the present century have shown (and the positivist school has performed a fair proportion of the work) that the sciences are not isolated systems of doctrine, each detached from each, but that there exists among them a hierarchical subordination, so that the more complex rest upon the more simple, and presuppose them.[15]

At the other extreme, Karl Pearson concluded,

> It is clear that we have in Comte's staircase of the intellect a purely fanciful scheme, which like the rest of his *System of Positive Polity* is worthless from the standpoint of modern science.
>
> (Pearson, 1900, p. 510)

Alexander Bain, in his *Logic, Deductive and Inductive* provides a clear example of work in the critical tradition of classification of the sciences. Classification played a large part in both volumes on *Deduction* and on *Induction* in his work. In the first, there was a discussion of classification of the sciences (Bain, 1870, Vol. 1, pp. 24–9), supplemented by an appendix, where the schemes of Bacon, D'Alembert, *The Encyclopaedia Metropolitana* (S. T. Coleridge), N. Arnot and Comte were discussed briefly, and that of Spencer in some detail (Bain, 1870, Vol. 1, Appendix A). Bain's own ideas appeared mainly in the conclusions drawn in critical discussions, and in the organization of the whole work. He presented the logic of the sciences in successive chapters, revealing their order and connection through the narrative. He followed the Comtean positivist tradition of denying status to theology and metaphysics.

Other English and American writers in the same critical tradition included C. W. Shields (1822), H. M. Stanley (1884), Karl Pearson (1892), Thomas Whittaker (1903) and Robert Flint himself.

This main tradition stimulated a great deal of secondary discussion. For example, there were many English scientists, particularly around the mid-nineteenth century, who felt it worth while to expound on the classification of science and of their own science in particular. For example, Sir William Thomson, in the introductory lecture to his course on natural philosophy in Glasgow, announced that since definitions of branches of science have generally proved failures,

... I shall rather attempt to explain in general terms the relation which Natural Philosophy bears to other branches of human inquiry, observation science, and philosophy, and to divide our treatment of it in the manner which we find most convenient for our work in the Natural Philosophy Class and Laboratory of the University.

(Thomson, 1910, Vol. 1, p. 239)

Such lectures and popularized accounts of classification of the sciences were symptomatic of the public awareness of the issues involved.

One measure of the rising popular recognition of the classification of the sciences by the end of the nineteenth century is that it gained a place in successive editions of the *Encyclopaedia Britannica*. Early editions did not deal with classification of the sciences, but the ninth edition (1875–89) discussed it in the "Logic" entry, and in entries on particular people important in the tradition. The eleventh edition (1910–11) had an article on classification which included classification of the sciences, but later editions discussed classification only as a method used in descriptive sciences.

The later nineteenth century English-speaking interest in classification of the sciences was primarily stimulated by rather sterile and academic discussion. It is hardly surprising that this soon went into decline. We must, however, follow the theme further in continental Europe.

Italian classifications of science in the nineteenth century followed a different pattern from those in the rest of Europe. With the greater importance of Roman Catholic thought, theology was more often stressed as a science and scholastic Aristotelian thought persisted. The eighteenth century philosopher of history and social theorist G. Vico also played a major part in setting the Italian philosophical context. He argued that history was the most comprehensive science, since the history of human thought embraced all other sciences. He also argued that history could be divided into periods which were also stages of human intellectual development (Flint, 1904, pp. 127–9). His periodization was criticized and developed in later discussions. Flint mentions eighteen Italian writers on classification of science in the nineteenth century. They were almost all philosophers with little interest in natural science, and tended to follow the older pattern, no longer so favoured in other countries, of deriving a classification from a philosophical system. They were usually less concerned with natural classification. Theology, metaphysics and history all played a far larger part in their various schemes than elsewhere.

In the later part of the century, German philosophy tended to move away from the metaphysical system-building that had earlier dominated. This was reflected in the stress in academic teaching on the history of philosophy, followed by logic and psychology, with metaphysics and ethics gaining least attention.[16] The major historians of philosophy had descended from Hegel's school (Wundt, 1887, p. 511), and two of the best known, E. Zeller and B. Erdmann, are among those discussed in Flint's history of classification. The work of Wilhelm Wundt is, however, among the most significant. He was internationally famed as a psychologist who took an experimental and physiological approach. But his concept of psychology related it closely to philosophy, and he wrote widely in both fields. He wrote on classification of the sciences in all his chief philosophical works, developing his ideas through several stages (Wundt, 1883, 1886, 1889). His work combined the three branches of philosophy which were taught most at the time: a strong bias towards an historical treatment going back to Plato, but culminating in Comte, Spencer and Mill; a treatment of logic similar to that prevailing in England, showing a strong interest in classification and an emphasis on psychology as a legitimate field of knowledge. Wundt, besides classifying the sciences, wrote extensively on the theory of classification as in the contemporary English tradition of textbooks of logic.

Another strand of late nineteenth century German philosophical thought stressed the division between science and history. This was important for such Neo-Kantians as W. Windelband and H. Rickert. Rickert, for example, used the distinction between generalizing and individualizing thought, and that between valuing and non-valuing thought to generate four types of science forming a scale from arbitary and abstract thought as in pure natural science, to valuing and individualizing thought as in history proper (Rickert, 1896; Collingwood, 1946, pp. 165–76).

More nearly in the positivist tradition was the book by the Czech, T. G. Masaryk (1887), translated into German as *Versuch einer Concreten*

Logik, Klassifikation und Organisation der Wissenschaft. Like Wundt's, this work was based on critical discussion of the main English, French and German writers on classification (Flint, 1904, pp. 272–83). Another groupf of German writings concerned with classification from the point of view of the natural sciences was that of the energeticists. Wilhelm Ostwald, for example, followed Comte's scheme closely, ordering the sciences in terms of generality, grouped into sciences of co-ordination or function, energy and life (Ostwald, 1911, pp. 54–7).

One writer of this period who was important retrospectively in Marxist thought, was Friedrich Engels. His *Dialectics of Nature* (1927), was written between 1872 and 1882 (Haldane, 1940, p. ix). The work pronounced on many nineteenth century scientific and classificatory writings.[17] Engles treated the Hegelian dialectical laws as laws of the development of nature. He based his classification on the forms of motion in inorganic and organic phenomena. The dialectical development of these forms of motion in the evolution of nature provided a linear ordering of the sciences. Engels formed a viewpoint on classification influenced by Hegel, Saint-Simon (rather than Comte) and Spencer. It was therefore very much a product of its time.

In France, there were a number of substantial writings on classification of the sciences near the end of the nineteenth century. A. Naville wrote that his father, Ernest Naville, had told him that classification of the sciences was a natural beginning to philosophical study. So, for example, the new programme at the University of France placed it at the beginning of the course (Naville, 1888). Such an academic stress on classification stimulated a scholarly approach, in which earlier systems were reviewed and criticized, before some more or less original scheme was produced. The chief French names of the period were those of A. Naville (Flint, 1904, pp. 283–9) whose own system was fairly novel; Raoul de Grasserie (Flint, 1904, pp. 289–92) influenced mostly by Ampère, Comte, Spencer and Wundt; Paul Janet (Flint, 1904, pp. 301–7) who commented on five systems—of Aristotle, Bacon, Ampère, Comte and Spencer, before describing his own conclusions; Edmond Goblot (Flint, 1904, pp. 307–15), who reacted to and developed from Comte, but drew into his discussion the main names in the tradition; and J. P. Durand (Flint, 1904, pp. 324–6), who wrote a book primarily on the theory of classification, which saw the classification of the sciences as a minor problem to be settled only through a rational evolution of the science of taxonomy.

IV

The decline of classification of science in the twentieth century

We must explore next what happened to this thriving and varied tradition of classification of the sciences in the twentieth century. The tradition did not die out completely, but no new major figures appeared, and the secondary and tertiary figures were less often stimulated to raise their problems in terms of the tradition, so that the literature in the subject has tended to decrease even though discussion of related topics has mushroomed.

The main reason for the decline of the tradition was the increasing artificiality of the main lines of discussion. Many of the issues which had motivated early writers had originally come from a practical context, but had acquired a life of their own within the relatively autonomous tradition of classification of sciences. In the meantime, the sciences themselves had changed. Since the mid-nineteenth century, many new scientific disciplines had emerged and some older ones had undergone revolutionary transformations which sometimes affected their relations with other sciences. Furthermore, several of the original practical contexts had developed so that they no longer had so much to gain from improved classifications of the sciences. Library classification became a separate subject early in the nineteenth century, and its later development was largely restricted to pragmatic changes in the artificial classifications devised (Edwards, 1859; Sayers, 1946). Interest in encyclopaedic arrangements of knowledge declined by the beginning of the twentieth century. Encyclopaedias had come to be directed at a less scholarly audience and the only systematic ordering attempted was alphabetical. There were still practical questions about the division of science for teaching purposes, but these were so constrained by established practices that the most enlightened theory could have had little influence.

Those seeking the inclusion of a new subject or the enlargement of a growing one in university courses found that, with the decline in attention to classification of the sciences, new methods of justification were necessary. In the nineteenth century, science was regarded as an adornment to culture as a form of systematic knowledge. Classification of the branches of knowledge was thus an important aspect. In the twentieth century, in contrast, the widespread acknowledgement of the importance of science-based industries and the crucial role science could play in war served to encourage support for science because of its potential applications. Thus, support for major new developments in the academic curriculum were more likely to be based on appeal to the potential applications of the new subject rather than its place in the system of scientific knowledge.

Although classification of the objects of study *within* sciences has remained important, it had generally been separated from classification *of* the sciences in the nineteenth century, and has subsequently tended to go its own way.[18]

The problem of the unity of the sciences has also developed a separate stream of discussion. In the nineteenth century, Comte had used classification of the sciences to make points about their interconnectedness: twentieth century writers have used quite different techniques. The Vienna Circle, which has been so influential in modern philosophy of science, was very much concerned with the unification of science, but its members took the approach of reducing all the sciences to a basic language, in which scientific argument follows a common method. Different subjects are then merely a division of labour. This stress on the single level of the verifiable data of sensational experience, rather than the metaphysical differences of the real things beyond the senses, minimized the significance of classification of the sciences.

This century, those attempting to argue against the reducibility of all the sciences to a single basis, have tended to decline in numbers. Just as vitalism is now rarely defended, psychologists have increasingly identified their subject with the natural sciences. When such arguments occur, they are now very often in terms of methodology rather than the divisions of knowledge. Similarly, debates over the drawing of boundaries between neighbouring disciplines are now conducted on a different basis. Flint ended his history with a discussion of the overlap in his time of anthropology, ethnology and sociology (Flint, 1904, pp. 328–38), and showed how some figures had been stimulated by this to develop partial classifications that might justify particular divisions. There is a contemporary overlap of biochemistry, microbiology and biophysics, but now the arguments are historical, sociological and methodological.

Many issues which were brought into discussions concerning classifications of the sciences remain, but they are now either discussed in isolation, or related to other general themes. Ideas of the relation between pure and applied science are often discussed, as is the relation between science and philosophy. The classificatory methods of relating these in the nineteenth century seem to offer little satisfaction to modern philosophers. Or perhaps it is just that old solutions have been forgotten, due to lack of historical interest.

Robert Flint, writing close to the end of the tradition, declared with great vehemence his belief in its lasting value. What then is to be made of his arguments? He preceded his discussion of the history of classifications of the sciences with an essay "Philosophy as Scientia Scientiarum." This would mean that a major function of philosophy is that it should:

> show how science is related to science, where one science is in contact with another, in what way each fits into each, so that all may compose the symmetrical and glorious edifice of human knowledge, which has been built up by the labour of all past generations, and which all future generations must contribute to perfect and adorn.
>
> (Flint, 1904, p. 4)

The arguments Flint put forward for the need of such a science of science seem as pertinent and as relevant as ever, but today these arguments are turned into justifications for liberal studies and for the teaching of interdisciplinary science. Co-ordination of sciences and avoidance of the evils of overspecialization have turned into arguments that now promote quite different types of academic study.

Classification of the sciences, which, in the nineteenth century, had become the organizing theme for the discussion of a wide range of issues, was itself perpetuated mainly through a rather sterile critical tradition built on the work of Bacon, Comte, Ampère and Spencer. When the main tradition died, the live issues were still discussed but either in isolation or in the context of methodology. It must always be a problem in any cultural tradition to determine whether it continues for any reasons other than because it has become established as a self-perpetuating activity. One cannot ignore and try to eliminate branches of academic study with no immediate application, if only because the knowledge they represent may suddenly become vital. Anybody reading Flint, for example, must recognize that he *did* give good arguments for the tradition, but few people today argue that discussions of classifications of science should be resurrected in their nineteenth century form.

Notes

1. For a brief survey, which stresses how widespread has been the concern to classify knowledge, see P. Speziali (1973–4).
2. For example, the *Encyclopedia of Philosophy* (1967), which is oriented towards entries on numerous philosophically significant figures of the past and present, covers an important proportion of the writers on the classification of the sciences, but usually ignores this aspect of their work, or even, as in the entry on Ampère, finds the proportion of his philosophy of science devoted to classification a positive embarrassment.
3. See, for example, Edward Edwards (1859, Vol. 2, pp. 761–831). A brief history written in the twentieth century is in W. C. Berwick Sayers (1946, pp. 74ff.).
4. R. Flint (1904, p. 105) points out that Bacon may have seen his classification as little more than a framework on which to hang his aphorisms about each particular science.
5. Flint (1904, p. 131) points out, however, that this German work was neither deep nor profound and of no value in itself in the history of classifications of the sciences.
6. For a discussion of the relation between Bacon and Diderot, which reviews earlier accounts, see L. K. Luxembourg (1967).
7. See, for example, J. D. Morell (1856, p. 47). One excellent discussion of Naturphilosophie in English, which is itself symptomatic of its influence in England, is J. B. Stallo (1848).
8. B. M. Kedrov illustrates the Marxist category; "Comte took over and systematised the ideas of his master, but gave them an exaggerated and banal character." (Kedrov, 1964, p. 172).
9. "En effet, le but principal que l'on doit avoir en vue dans tout travail encyclopédique, c'est de disposer les sciences dans l'ordre de leur enchainement naturelle, en suivant leur dépendance mutuelle; de telle sorte qu'on puisse les exposer successivement, sans jamais être entrainé dans le moindre cercle vicieux."
   (Comte, 1864, Vol. 6, pp. 60–1)
10. Comte presented this as a reason *not* to classify the sciences (Comte, 1864, Vol. 1, p. 48), but it is clear that Comte himself took it as a challenge, just because he felt he could do better.
11. At his course in philosophy, at the Faculté des Lettres in Paris, 1819–20, where he developed his ideas on the general classification of intellectual facts, expressing the results in a "tableau psychologique" (Ampère, 1834, p. xxvi). See also the letters exchanged with Maine de Biran in Ampère's correspondence (Bertrand, 1893).
12. The first two stages correspond to the human baby before it has learned the language. First it just observes, then it actively seeks out things in the process of learning. On learning language, the child names things and makes comparisons using names. Finally it can start a deep examination of the faculties of beings and the causes of physical facts (Ampère, 1934. pp. xxi–xxii).
13. This second key does not seem to have appeared.
14. The "foregoing essay" is "The classification of the sciences".
15. T. A. Ribot (1875, p. 193), quoted by H. M. Stanley (1884, pp. 273–4).
16. See W. Wundt's numerical survey (1887, p. 495).
17. The work has acquired the status of revealed knowledge for orthodox Marxists on the subject. See for example, B. Kedrov (1964, p. 176).
18. For example Timmermans (1963) combines papers on the theory of classification with discussions of the classificatory method in general, but does not mention classification of the sciences.

References

AMPÈRE, A.-M. (1816–7). D'une classification naturelle pour les corps simples. *Annales de Chimie et de Physique*, **1**, 295–308, 373–94; **2**, 5–32, 105–29.

AMPÈRE, A.-M. (1834). "Essai sur la Philosophie des Sciences", Vol. 1. Bachelier, Paris.

AMPÈRE, A.-M. (1843). "Essai sur la Philosophie des Sciences", Vol. 2. Bachelier, Paris.

ARNOTT, N. (1828). "Elements of Physics". Longman, London.

ARNOTT, N. (1861). "A Survey of Human Progress from the Savage State to the Highest Civilization yet Attained". Longman, London.

BAIN, A. (1870). "Logic". 2 Vols. Longman, London.

BENTHAM, J. (1843). Chrestomathia. *In* "The Works of Jeremy Bentham" (Ed. J Bowring), Vol. 8, Appendix IV, Section 7. William Tait, Edinburgh.

BERTHELOT, P. E. M. (1886) (1905). "Science et Philosophie". C. Lévy, Paris.

BERTRAND, A. (1893). Lettres inédites de Maine de Biran à André-Marie Ampère. *Revue de Metaphysique* **1**, 313–23, 468–84, 553–63.

BOAS, G. (1925). "French Philosophers of the Romantic Period". Johns Hopkins Press, Baltimore.

BUFFON, G. L. L., Comte de (1749–1804). "Histoire Naturelle Générale et Particulière". De l'Imprimerie Royale, Paris.

CHEVREUL, M. E. (1863). Sur la méthode expérimentale en générale. *Comtes Rendus Hebdomadaires de l'Académie des Sciences* **57**, 409–12, 457–63.

COLERIDGE, S. T. (1835). General introduction or a preliminary treatise on method. *In* "Encyclopaedia Metropolitana", Vol.1, Section III.

COLLINGWOOD, R. G. (1946). "The Idea of History". Clarendon Press, Oxford.

COMTE, A. (1864). "Cours de Philosophie Positive", 6 Vols, 2nd edition. Bachelier, Paris.

DOVE, P. E. (1850). "Theory of Human Progression". Johnstone and Hunter, London.

EDWARDS, E. (1859). "Memoirs of Libraries", 2 Vols. Trübner, London.

"Encyclopaedia Britannica" (1875–89). 24 Vols and Index, 9th edition. A. and C. Black, Edinburgh.

"Encyclopedia of Philosophy" (1967). 8 Vols. Collier Macmillan, New York and London.

"Encyclopédie ou Dictionaire Raisonné des Sciences, Artes et Metiers" (1751–65). Par une société des gens de lettres. 17 Vols. Paris.

ENGELS, F. (1940). "Dialectics of Nature". Lawrence and Wishart, London.

FISKE, J. (1874). "Outlines of Cosmic Philosophy", 2 Vols. Houghton Mifflin, Boston and New York.

FLINT, R. (1904). "Philosophy as Scientia Scientarum and a History of Classification of the Sciences". William Blackwood and Sons, Edinburgh and London.

GOBLOT, E. (1898). "Essai sur la Classification des Sciences". F. Alcan, Paris.

HALDANE, J. B. S. (1940). Preface. *In* "Dialectics of Nature" (F. Engels). Lawrence and Wishart, London.

HAMILTON, W. (1859–60). "Lectures on Metaphysics and Philosophy". 4 Vols. William Blackwood and Sons, Edinburgh and London.

HEGEL, G. (1817). "Encyklopädie de Philosophischen Wissenschaften". Offenbach, Heidelberg. The middle part has been translated twice as "Hegel's Philosophy of Nature", by A. V. Miller, Clarendon, Oxford (1970) and by M. J. Petry, 3 Vols. Allen and Unwin, London (1970).

HERSCHEL, J. F. W. (1831). "A Preliminary Discourse on the Study of Natural Philosophy". Longman, London.

KEDROV, B. M. (1961). "Classification of the Sciences", Book I, Engels and his predecessors (in Russian, but a 21-page English summary is available). Moscow.

KEDROV, B. M. (1964). The history of classification of sciences. *Organon*, 165–85.

LINDSAY, A. W. C., 25th Earl of Crawford (1846). "Progress by Antagonism", especially appendix: "Classification of human thought according to the preceding theory", J. Murray, London.

LUXEMBOURG, L. K. (1967). "Francis Bacon and Denis Diderot: Philosophers of Science". Munksgaard, Copenhagen.

MCRAE, R. (1957). The unity of the sciences: Bacon, Descartes and Leibniz. *Journal of the History of Ideas*, **18**, 27–48.

MCRAE, R. (1961). "The Problem of the Unity of the Sciences: Bacon to Kant". University of Toronto Press, Toronto.

MASARYK, T. G. (1887). "Versuch einer Concreten Logik, Klassifikation und Organisation der Wissenschaften". Wien.

MILL, J. S. (1843). "System of Logic", 2 Vols. Longman, London.

MILL, J. S. (1865). "Auguste Comte and Positivism". (Reprinted from *Westminster Review* New Series, Number LIV, April 1865.) Trübner, London.

MORELL, J. D. (1856). Modern German philosophy. *Manchester Papers* **I**,

NAVILLE, (1888). "De la Classification des Sciences". Paris.

OKEN, L. (1809–11). "Lehrbuch der Naturphilosophie". F. Frommann, Jena. Third edition translated as "Elements of Physiophilosophy" by A. Tulk (1847). Ray Society, London.

OSTWALD, W. (1911). "Esquisse d'un Philosophie des Sciences" (Trans. M. Dorelle). F. Alcan, Paris.

PEARSON, K. (1892). (2nd edition 1900). "The Grammar of Science". Walter Scott, London.

RIBOT, T. A. (1873). (Trans. 1875). "L'Hérédité". Ladrange, Paris. (Translated as "Heredity". H. S. King, London.)

RICKERT, H. (1896). "Die Grenzen der Naturwissenschaftlichen Begriffsbildung". Freiburg iß and Leipzig.

ST. BEUVE, C. A. (1843). Biography of Ampère. *In* "Essai sur la Philosophie des Sciences" (by A.-M. Ampère). Vol. 2. Bachelier, Paris.

SAINT-SIMON, C-H. (1966). Lettres d'un habitant de Genève à ses contemporaines. "Oeuvres de Saint-Simon" (Ed. E. Dentu), Vol. 1. Editions Anthropos, Paris.

SAYERS, W. C. B. (1946). "An Introduction to Library Classification". Grafton, London.

SHIELDS, C. W. (1882). "Order of the Sciences, an Essay on the Philosophical Classification and Organisation of Knowledge". Scribners, New York.

SPENCER, H. (1858). The genesis of science. *In* "Essays: Scientific Political and Speculative", First Series. Williams and Norgate, London.

SPENCER, H. (1874). Reasons for dissenting from the philosophy of M. Comte. *In* "Essays: Scientific Political and Speculative", Vol. 3. Williams and Norgate, London.

SPEZIALI, P. (1973–4). Classification of the sciences. *In* "Dictionary of the History of Ideas" (Ed. P. P. Wiener). Vol. 1, pp. 462–7. Scribners, New York.

STALLO, J. B. (1848). "General Principles of the Philosophy of Nature". W. Crosby and H. P. Nichols, Boston.

STANLEY, H. M. (1884). On the classification of the sciences. *Mind*, **9**, 265–73.

THOMSON, W. (1910). Introductory lecture, reproduced in S. P. Thompson, "The Life of Lord Kelvin". Macmillan, London.

TIMMERMANS, J. et al. (1963). "La Classification dans les Sciences". (Publié avec le concours du Centre National de Recherches de Logique et de la Société Belge de Logique et de Philosophie des Sciences.) J. Duculot, S. A., Gembloux.

WHEWELL, W. (1840). "Philosophy of the Inductive Sciences". 2 Vols. J. W. Parker, London.

WHEWELL, W. (1858). "Novum Organum Renovatum", being the second part of the "Philosophy of the Inductive Sciences", 3rd edition. J. W. Parker, London.

WHEWELL, W. (1860). "On the Philosophy of Discovery", including the completion of the third edition of the "Philosophy of the Inductive Sciences". J. W. Parker, London.

WHITTAKER, T. (1903). A compendious classification of the sciences. Mind (new series) 12, 21–34.

WUNDT, W. (1883). "Logik", Vol. ii. F. Enke, Stuttgart.

WUNDT, W. (1886). Philosophische Studien, 5, i.

WUNDT, W. (1887). Philosophy in Germany. Mind 2, 493–518.

WUNDT, W. (1889). "System der Philosophie". W. Engelmann, Leipzig.

10

The World Seen as
a Colour Chart

John Bousfield

Epistemological chauvinism is difficult to see, especially when it is
oneself who displays it. There are no apparently disastrous consequences, no wars to be waged, and the assumption underlying it seems
as ideologically innocuous as it is true. That all people see the world in
more or less the same way and have to say about it more or less the same
sort of things seems to be a practically worthy assumption beyond
legitimate scepticism. In particular, that others perceive the world as
we do and that this is correct seems a hopeful and productive assumption to make. It is hard to see how people could lead tolerable lives if
they did not tacitly accept this; if this is to be chauvinistic then all
people are presumably chauvinists in their epistemology, at least most
of the time.

Sometimes, however, it becomes an active principle—on those occasions when we are apparently confronted with a view of the world
which either conflicts with, contradicts or just refuses to fit with ours.
Then, we may attempt to show the alternative to be wrong or misguided. And we may do this with more or less sophistication, varying
from physical violence at one extreme to the dexterous use of
methodological considerations at the other. Another, more subtle,
technique involves translating away the differences so that they become
more apparent than real. When it is not realized that this is what has
happened we have full-fledged epistemological chauvinism. It is the

harder to see just to the extent that we are all sinners—most of the time, at any rate—translating the other viewpoint into our own terms.

The process is unfortunate, if not disastrous, because it prevents understanding not only of others but also of ourselves. And while it may not do so often, this process of systematic mistranslation sometimes *can* support the assertion of a "cognitive superiority"[1] which goes hand in hand with technological and economic hegemony. The attempt to expose the illusion is often taken to be in itself a quixotic illusion relying on the revival of a discredited relativism.

At the risk of bringing such charges upon myself I want to discuss what seems to be an important case of this chauvinism which has repercussions for our understanding of a wide range of cultural phenomena. I refer to the work of B. Berlin and P. Kay on the classification of colour, *Basic Color Terms*.[2] Since its publication, the book has evoked much comment, not least from people working in parts of the world other than the San Francisco Bay area. Their research displays what seem to be obvious weaknesses, which were soon pointed out.[3]

One may doubt, for example, the validity of conclusions about colour perception and the logic of colour language drawn from the presentation of a colour chart to a relatively small number of people living, with one exception, in the San Francisco Bay area. This seems to sever artificially the logic of colour terms from their real social, cultural and economic contexts. The use of a colour chart presented to people in an urban environment seems to work against the perception of colours as symbolic, a factor which, it can be argued, is intimately connected with the classification of colour. I am sympathetic to such doubts and I will try to show what seems wrong with these conclusions from a philosophical viewpoint. The original research and the conclusions drawn have been attacked and in turn defended and modified. This has involved the accommodation of more data and also refinement of the theoretical framework in which it is placed. Given this it may seem misguided to treat *Basic Color Terms* as an almost autonomous text, as if it were a definitive and isolated statement of an *epistemological* position. Yet it does contain a powerful statement about the nature of perception and it sets a pattern for the structure of future research. In particular, it uses a set of central concepts which accords status to certain types of data and provides a way of interpreting them. It is with this conceptual structure that I am concerned and it seems appropriate to focus for this purpose on its articulation in *Basic Color Terms*. I will discuss the use of the concept of a "universal semantic category" and contrast this with the different idea of a rule of classification.

I assume the accuracy of Berlin and Kay's data.[4] I hope to show that the evidence is at least highly ambiguous and that the conclusions they draw follow largely from certain moves in translation which one is not compelled to make. I will argue that other conclusions are possible which should be taken seriously. These tend to undermine a universalist position and at the same time suggest that the complexity of the field of colour classification cannot be dealt with adequately using what can be called the colour-chart method.[5]

Berlin and Kay set out to subject to testing the "prevailing doctrine" of "extreme linguistic relativity" which they put thus:

... the doctrine ... holds that each language performs the coding of experience into sound in a unique manner. Hence, each language is semantically arbitrary relative to every other language ... the search for semantic universals is fruitless in principle. ... Proponents of this view frequently offer as a paradigm example the alleged total semantic arbitrariness of the lexical coding of color.[6]

Berlin and Kay's intuitive hypothesis was that "color words *translate too easily* among various pairs of unrelated languages for the extreme linguistic relativity thesis to be valid".[7] Their findings are not only taken to support this, but are also quite specific and startling in their refutation of linguistic relativity. They draw three main conclusions:

First, there exist universally for humans eleven basic perceptual color categories which serve as the psychological referents of the eleven or fewer basic color terms in any language. Second, in the history of a given language, encoding of perceptual categories into basic color terms follows a fixed partial order. The two possible temporal orders are:

$$\left. \begin{array}{c} \text{white} \\ \text{black} \end{array} \right] \longrightarrow \text{red} \rightarrow \text{yellow} \rightarrow \text{green} \rightarrow \text{blue} \rightarrow \text{brown} \longrightarrow \left[\begin{array}{c} \text{purple} \\ \text{pink} \\ \text{orange} \\ \text{grey} \end{array} \right.$$

and

$$\left. \begin{array}{c} \text{white} \\ \text{black} \end{array} \right] \longrightarrow \text{red} \rightarrow \text{green} \rightarrow \text{yellow} \rightarrow \text{blue} \rightarrow \text{brown} \longrightarrow \left[\begin{array}{c} \text{purple} \\ \text{pink} \\ \text{orange} \\ \text{grey} \end{array} \right.$$

Third, the overall temporal order is properly considered an evolutionary one; color lexicons with few terms tend to occur is association with relatively simple cultures and simple technologies, while color lexicons with many terms tend to occur in association with complex technologies.[8]

The second conclusion is perhaps most provocative. Not only do they find no more than eleven basic categories, but "if a language encodes fewer then eleven basic color categories, then there are strict limitations on which categories it may encode".[9] Taking the above schema, if a language contains, say, six basic colour terms then it contains terms for blue, green, yellow, red, black and white; if it contains three terms only, it contains terms for red, black and white, and so on. The thesis that this ordering of categories in any language reflects the historical, evolutionary stage it has reached is based essentially on the internal evidence of so-called internal linguistic reconstruction and the adoption of the hypothesis as the simplest explanation of the distribution found.[10]

Berlin and Kay's technique was to assemble data from two sources. The first involved asking informants representing twenty languages to map their basic colour-categories onto a chart made up of Munsell standard colour chips. The second consisted of studying evidence from other languages reported in the writings of various field-workers, in dictionaries and so on.[11] Altogether, their sample consisted of ninety-eight languages from a range of linguistic families.[12]

In the experiments, the colour terms were mapped thus: the informants were to indicate for each basic colour term, x, first, all of the chips on the chart which they "would under any conditions call x" and second "the best, most typical examples of x".[13] That is, they were asked to map the extent of a colour and also to locate its centre; I will return to the implications of this request below.

With their schema Berlin and Kay are able to place every one of the ninety-eight languages more or less in one of seven stages. The marginal cases are treated as either likely to succumb to classification after further research or as being in a transitional phase.[14]

The correlation between linguistic stages and the level of economic and technological complexity is stated as intuitively obvious and I will take it as given for the moment.[15]

What is wrong with these conclusions? I will begin with the concept of a basic colour term.

It is not obvious that the etymologically basic status these terms are supposed to have points necessarily to any equivalent semantic or logical status. The sorts of reasons given for calling them basic are: that they belong to the language and are not borrowed from elsewhere; that they are not descriptive terms; that they cannot be further analysed; and so on. In the terminology of logical atomism they are "primitive".

This means that they cannot be defined other than through "ostensive definition", through pointing to examples. It is worth remembering, however, what ostensive definition involves. The logical model in which ostensive definition plays a central role locates the foundation of the meaning of terms an intuitively obvious connection between the sign and its referent which is displayed in the unproblematic gesture of pointing. But this gesture is not all that it seems; it is actually more.

A gesture of pointing can be ostensive definition only to the extent that it is interpreted as such in the context of a more or less tacit semantic background.[16] What is being pointed to? How do I know that I am learning the name of a colour? Unless I already understand much of the language and much of the situation, no amount of pointing can focus my attention on what it is that is being pointed at. One does not gain understanding through ostensive definition so much as understanding that definition through prior understanding of either the language or the world of that language. An ostensive definition can always turn into a verbal identification: "the colour of a primrose", "the sound of bells", "the smell of fried fish", etc. The ostensive definition contains, as it were, an implicit articulation such as "the colour of x". So terms which are "primitive" are just those terms the meaning of which can be taught through the substitution of a so-called "descriptive" term or phrase. "Basic colour terms", then, do not occupy any semantically privileged position. It will be seen that this has important implications.

Indeed, it seems odd to hold that terms which are basic in the sense of being apparently non-derivable must have a similarly non-articulate meaning. If it is argued that Berlin and Kay do not hold any such doctrine then much of the force of isolating "basic" colour terms disappears. Sometimes, of course, one wants to say that a new move in the language has been made. A new expression seems to open up the semantic field and even ostensive definition cannot be guaranteed to work; or the meaning of an established term seems to get extended. We would learn much from the investigation of this *avant-garde* of language (see Barrau, Peeters, this volume).

Equally, however, if new "basic terms" in the colour lexicon cannot emerge in contexts previously covered by descriptive expressions, then an evolutionary schema such as that posited will also be impossible.

This leads to what seems to me to be a major ambiguity in the evidence. However, I confess that the interpretation sketched below is speculative and offered intuitively only as a possibly adequate alternative. Berlin and Kay posit the existence of semantic universals, irreducible perceptual categories, designated by basic irreducible terms. Yet a rather different thesis can be put forward which gives their historical schema a much more complex appearance.

The basic terms of the colour lexicon could be regarded as second-order terms, or what I will call (rather inadequately) "summary" terms.[17] They function as a sort of perceptual shorthand for discriminations which are always more complicated. They cover a wide range of discriminations where more rigorous specification is either not necessary or not possible for an individual for reasons I will discuss shortly. To illustrate what I mean let me take the small range of "basic" taste terms in the lexicon applied to wine by the (English) layman. The ordinary drinker may use no more than the following range in choosing and characterizing the wines he drinks: dry, medium dry, medium sweet, sweet, red, white, rosé. The last three function both as a simple wine colour lexicon and also as the crudest taste lexicon. Using just these terms, many people will succeed in classifying a particular wine for their own and others' future use. But if, as happens, consuming wine becomes a passion or a profession, this small, banal lexicon, while not becoming redundant, functions alongside of and in relation to a much fuller and more complex semantic field in which descriptive characterization is dominant. The small "one-dimensional" lexicon still works as a shorthand but is underpinned by "mult-dimensional" characterizations. Out of these open-textured and rich characterizations, there may arise, in turn, further summary logics. So, for example, we find introduced "smooth", "acidic", "heavy", and so on, each of these establishing an axis along which to rank and compare wines. But the validity of these taste dimensions rests ultimately on there being socially shared, agreed paradigms of what is a dry wine, a light wine, and so on. These wines will then often be identified through elaborate, descriptive expressions such as ". . . an almost freakish amount of scent . . . a really spicy blend of raspberries and dead leaves and mushrooms . . ." (I may add that the writer goes on to say "impossible to analyse but enthralling to sniff, think about, and sniff again") or "strong and clean, dry and scented, incomparably subtle and delicate and yet solid and substantial in your mouth" (i.e. "dry"!).[18] In this sort of characterization reference is made not only to "taste-paradigms" from outside the domain of wine, but to categories from other areas of experience.

I want to note here some important features of the language used. First, it is possible, using only one dimension, e.g. dry to sweet, to make a fairly comprehensive classification of the wines one may drink through a series of relative juxtapositions, e.g. "dryer than this", "sweeter than that". A simple criterion of classification of this kind is adequate both when there is neither the need for, nor the interest in, further articulation of experience and when the latter is just not possible. This second case is important. Were we all to live and breathe in a universe of wine and its discourse, such rudimentary classifications might be dropped in favour of more complex and possibly highly symbolic logics involving high degrees of description, metaphor and analogy. Most of us do not, however, and our acquaintance with such a universe is at best peripheral; in relation to us, it is the world of the specialist. I will argue that this is the situation for most of us in the "technologically complex" world in relation to colour classification.

Second, when the taste-lexicon, i.e. the set of what I am calling summary terms, expands in a (partly) ordered way, it does not do so through a further unfolding, so to speak, of discriminations within the same dimension. It is not a matter of re-articulating the *same* perceptual feature as was previously located on the dry–sweet scale, only more accurately. When "bitter", "smooth", "soft", "solid", "light", "biting", for example, are introduced new perspectives by which to characterize and classify are established. Moreover, we are using the wrong logical picture if we think of this as a matter of attaching names to discrete or at least distinguishable categories of taste perception, as if we were giving proper names to areas of a sort of taste spectrum (cp. Reason, this volume). What is actually happening is that new fields of relationships are being clarified within which a particular taste-experience can be located. The more such relationships can be established for some taste the more it can actually be characterized in its particularity. The fewer dimensions of comparison we have the less able we are to communicate the nature of the particular taste.

This leads straight to the third point, which has been noted already. The different axes of classification are established analogically or through a process of what Ernst Cassirer called "radical metaphor",[19] when terms "proper" to other sensory domains are applied, e.g. texture words such as "smooth", "rough". We also find terms like "solid", "heavy" which, to use the old language of empiricism, refer to "primary" properties of the object even though revealed through the secondary data of sense. We come across descriptions of the following kind: the wine "always seems to me to have a touch of lovely sweetness, a trace of some very generous and kindly quality, only partly concealed by the considerable power of a great and classic wine".[20] The analogies here take us into the realm of emotional response and the implicit paradigms are drawn from personal relations. One often hears sexual analogy in talk about wine; frequently ludicrous, equally sexist, I will not dwell on it here. The important point is that a classification scheme can and often does rest ultimately on a semantic field in which diverse aspects of experience are all related and the classification of taste is an example of this. It might be objected here that these connections between tastes, textures, emotions, lusts, etc. are established purely on the basis of association. Certain tastes come to be associated with certain smells, indirectly with various textures and so on. The emotional and sexual connotations arise from the reminiscence of occasions on which the wine was drunk. I cannot enter into an argument with associationism here and so I will pronounce dogmatically instead.

Associationism can only ever be a solution (not a good one, at that) to a problem which itself is the result of a false and distorting picture of our experience of the world, that which arose out of the battle between rationalism and empiricism. It was in the course of this debate that the object itself was severed from its "properties" which constituted its appearance to the senses. Of importance for the subject under consideration here, these sensory properties—colour, texture, smell, sound, taste—came to be viewed as discrete elements of experience. The consequences of this still hover malevolently over our attempts to understand how experience is ordered—and ordered differently from one culture to another. In opposition to this dominant trend to empiricist thought one must argue, I believe, for an organicism in perception which is always partially captured by these very basic analogical fields of which we have had a glimpse (cp. Reason, this volume). We need to understand the level at which analogies are experienced prior to an articulation which seeks justification in established linguistic meanings.[21]

Before ending this brief excursion into the world of wine, one final point remains to be made. Whatever may be the lexicon in established use, understanding of terms such as "dry", smooth", etc. must rest on there existing agreed upon and sufficiently shared paradigms, and on descriptive references which make sense. The validity of the lexicon, or perhaps one should say its legitimacy, is culture-based. To characterize a wine by recommending the food to which it is a perfect complement may not always work. As one wine writer says when speaking of a great wine: "game is usually suggested as the food for Hermitage and the other Rhône wines. Well-hung venison and wild-boar, however, rarely come my way, and I prefer briefly hung game-birds with a lighter wine".[22] Not the clearest reference for one of the urban poor.

Now returning to basic colour terms, many of the features of the taste discourse which we have been looking at can be seen in colour language, especially the use of terms from other domains, "soft" and "harsh" being descriptive of colours, for example. But with colours it does seem possible to regard these characterizations as secondary, cultural elaborations and to isolate a primary colour lexicon. In what follows I hope to undermine to some degree just this idea.

We can, I think, see "basic" colour terms as second-order "summary terms" either proliferating or disappearing in a dialectical relationship with what I am regarding as the primary "descriptive" expressions. Let me reverse the evolutionary schema of Berlin and Kay in the following way. At one end, we have a cultural environment in which there is a low division of labour and in which each person has a high "semantic contact", to coin an expression, with the total environment. As a result of this, descriptive references of a highly fluid nature can be shared with most if not all other members of the culture without misunderstanding or incomprehension; or conversely an active and elaborate network of colour identifications is unnecessary. The number of summary terms is low in inverse proportion to the availability *to every member* of descriptive and analogical ascriptions *or* in direct proportion to the lack of concern with any great rigour in colour identification. This contrasts, at the other end of the scale, with the position of someone in a technologically and culturally complex society with a high division of labour. The "normal" member of such a culture has a very low "semantic contact" with the possible total environment, which is mirrored in the proliferation of universes of discourse within the culture. Each member is likely to participate in only a very small sub-set of these universes, but at the same time may have contact with others from any of these realms in areas of common concern and participation. A shared, richly descriptive language fails just to the extent that the crucial paradigmatic references cannot be picked up. As a simple example, think of how few people living in an urban environment can distinguish species of tree and hence could use a lexicon of bark and leaf colour. So what we find is a much higher number of summary terms, crude in their classificatory power, in inverse proportion to the decrease in semantic contact of any one individual and in direct proportion to the impossibility of keeping up with proliferating new domains of discourse. Thus one of Berlin and Kay's "eleven-term" systems *would* reflect a high level of complexity but not a development of classificatory power more advanced than, say, a two-term system. Moreover, such a "system" must still rest on a more basic descriptive and paradigmatic logic. To this I will return.

This interpretation seems to accord more with a feature of colour perception which Berlin and Kay themselves point out and it is that there seems to be no important variation in the perception of the spectrum between different cultures.[23] Now this could be expressed by saying that someone from a "few-term" culture can learn to use the language of a "many-term" culture. It would not only be philosophically interesting but humanly distressing if this were not so. We would have important reasons for accepting a pernicious relativism if we were forced to accept that at *this* perceptual level, different people saw the world in radically different ways. (I will not examine here the argument about whether or not such a position can be held coherently.) What we get is not so much a picture of either evolving perception or evolving language of perception, but of language changing, expanding and contracting with changes of interest and of problem, and changes in the distribution of knowledge and so on.

Yet even if this interpretation is plausible it can be argued that it is just too significant that Berlin and Kay find such an apparently ordered and limited field of basic colour terms, that they find sub-sets of one set of eleven terms only, rather than an indeterminate number of sets which refuse to map onto each other. However, this is exactly what makes me suspicious. Let us isolate another key feature of the schema.

Each stage is presented as probably an historical development. A three-term system appears as a two-term system with a third term added, a four-term system as a three-term with a fourth added, etc. The evidence at the lower end of the schema especially is speculative. But the problem I have can be posed thus: is each additional term in the systems after the initial two-term system deemed to be later on internal evidence, e.g. that it *has* a descriptive derivation or is borrowed? Or are these terms deemed to be etymologically basic but also *later*, having developed more recently in the language, as a result of extrapolating evidence from languages for which we have some history? If the former is argued then we must accept that so-called basic terms are not all of a piece but that only the "original" two-term systems, the "black–white" systems, are truly basic, all of the others being derived.[24] If the latter is accepted we lose a major reason for the historical ranking of these lexicons. All we can say is that at one time and place we find one system, at another time and another place, a different system. Even if we had unshakable evidence that the English language as it is now spoken developed from a two-term system to an eleven-term system, each term being *strictly* basic, this would not offer a good enough reason for generalizing to other languages; and I am not sure that even if we can *strictly* identify a set of eleven-term systems we can go beyond identifying their common features within that set of languages. We would need similar lexical histories of languages from cultures which had not followed those technologically advanced in their development but which nevertheless displayed a similar lexical history. The evidence as it stands seems equally to incline us to an alternative interpretation of the sort proffered here. We see descriptive expressions becoming in their logical behaviour summary terms, removed more and more from their immediate and specific context of reference.[25]

We lose the neat historical appearance of the schema and what begins to emerge is an array of "systems" which falls into rank only when the ethnocentric vantage point of highly industrialized society is adopted. The latter is most advanced and so other societies must occupy a position on an evolutionary scale established by placing it at the top. Without this scale we simply find cases with such and such a lexicon but no good reason for placing them, other than alongside each other. Of course I have not argued here for *not* accepting *some* scale of evolution.

What I have said, however, seems to ignore the link which Berlin and Kay find between the number of basic terms in any one set and the meaning of those terms; e.g. if there are four terms they must have the same meaning as the English terms "black", "white", "red" and either "green" or "yellow". *This* correlation surely supports so strongly both an evolutionary hypothesis and the notion of some universal semantic set that the particular interpretation of the correlation is less important than its discovery as such.

However, this does not stand up. We assume that people from all

cultures perceive the same spectrum as we do and we leave the unravel-
ling of this statement aside. Denying it, as I have said, opens up a
veritable bag of epistemological bombs. What is at issue is how this
spectrum is cut up and classified, how it is encoded into the language.
Now, once again, the remarkably neat ordering displayed in the
schema collapses if we abandon as our point of reference the eleven
"basic" terms of the speaker of English. This can be brought out by
asking which of the two following theses Berlin and Kay hold:

a) in a low number system, e.g. two-term, the native speaker when
confronted with the colour chart assigns the chips which we designate
as black and white to the two categories named by their two "basic"
terms while all other chips can only be classified through the expression, "the colour of . . .";

b) all chips have somehow to be placed, *if at all*, in one of these two
basic categories which divide up the whole spectrum.

If we are to hold (a) then while such a pattern for the emergence of
this sort of colour term would be interesting and would raise various
important questions it would certainly not be as dramatic as the
evolutionary schema proposed by Berlin and Kay. But it seems clear
that it is the second hypothesis Berlin and Kay present[26] and this gives
a completely different complexion to the schema, as can be seen from
their diagrammatical presentation of the two-term Jalé system. All
"dark" colours are *siŋ* and "light" colours *hóló*; in relation to the
colour-chart chips in the top half are *hóló* and in the bottom half *siŋ*.[27]
Now, while it is easy for us to translate these terms as "black" and
"white", it is quite clear that the two terms do not mean the *same* as our
terms "black" and "white". Such terms as "dark brown", "deep
purple", "dark red" do not mean for us as native speakers of English
the same as "black"; nor does "pale blue" mean the same as "white".

Now we can, of course, avoid this appearance of mistranslation by
making it clear that these are used as second-order terms and not with
their *original*, i.e. English (or American–English) meanings. (This
would actually make them *third-order* terms, following the idea of summary terms.) Then, dropping the original colour terms we introduce
new expressions to fit the different contexts more accurately, e.g. using
the light–warm/dark–cool distinction instead of black/white and
"grue" when a term seems to cover the areas designated by English
"green" and "blue".[28]

But there are two important points here. First, the new two-term classification itself illustrates exactly the argument against the notion of a basic term as such, a term which simply designates a perceptually given (more or less), demarcated category. The need to introduce the tactile terms "cool"/"warm", indicates that we seek not to *name*, give proper names to categories, but rather to relate, establish comparisons, characterize, describe. Second, while such modifications may result in a set of terms which for each stage in the schema can be adequately substituted for the native term, it does emerge that it is *not* a cumulative series in which new terms are added, leaving the meaning of earlier terms unchanged. Yet again the danger of mistranslation creeps in. English "black" does not mean the same as either *siŋ* or "cool–dark", but the way in which Berlin and Kay rank systems does still seem to rest on the requirement of (rough) synonymy with an English eleven-term system.

If we want to avoid the thesis that different peoples have radically, fundamentally different perceptions as such, that is, literally see a different colour continuum, we have to conclude instead that their colour lexicons relate to the continuum in different ways and that these terms do have significantly different meanings. We have to postulate, without its being severe, linguistic relativity. To avoid a severe Heraclitean relativity of perception, in which our actual experiences can never be shared, we have to allow somehow that terms can "translate" without having the same meaning. This is not a reformulation of a relativist paradox but the dissolution of the problem of relativism as Berlin and Kay pose it. Relativity as a problem rather than as a solution—as I argue it to be—always arises after translation. We translate some term "*x*" as "green". Now the arbitrariness which would have to appear if linguistic relativity holds would then involve the use of this term in ways in which our term "green" cannot be used, e.g. to cover reds as well. The evidence of successful translation is invoked and the relativity hypothesis is refuted. The "evidence" of translation is misunderstood when this refutation is proposed. The original term had a different meaning to our term "green" covering, say, what we might call blue and yellow, and not covering what we might call dark green. But there was *enough* of a connection for us to bring together, to relate the two terms, theirs and ours, which *might* consist in focus placement. This process in which we have to learn a different colour category but which we can encode, so to speak, by using our term "green" in a special, extended sense is not one of simple substitution where one term can take the place of another without loss or change of meaning. We can get the impression that translation "is too easy among various pairs of unrelated languages" from a number of sources. First, it may be the case that many terms in any language can be given substitutes in any or at least some other languages with no problems. Second, we find no reason, from actual conversation in the field, to doubt the translation offered us in bilingual dictionaries, and have no competence to judge whether or not there has been "interpretation", good or bad. Third, sometimes we turn to a dictionary in our own language looking for an authoritative definition of some term with which we may or may not be familiar already. But it is equally possible and quite common to quibble with the dictionary's definition of a word which one already understands. One may do this without feeling able to get any closer in articulating the meaning of the word than the dictionary; yet this does not necessarily imply any inability nor any lack of understanding. If this phenomenon, which we might call the irrecoverability of meaning, appears *within* a language we can expect it to appear frequently between languages. But conversely, one *can* learn the meaning of a word of his own language with the *help* of a dictionary and a grasp of the contexts in which it appears. The meaning cannot be rendered in a *formula* which itself does not require further interpretation but nevertheless people can come to use the word appropriately and with understanding. This is what happens in translation; the mistake arises when the sense of the expression is treated as if fully articulated in the "equivalent" expression. "Contradictions" arise when the native expression is used in ways which our substitute would exclude.[29]

This underlying learning process whereby we, as it were, go to the others' language rather than it coming to ours is clearly seen in the area of colour terms. We can get a *sense* of how a two- or three-term "system" is used, and we can *relate* the two terms to our "black" and "white". But it is absolutely crucial to remember that we would be changing the meaning of these two English terms if we now had to assign more or less every hue and shade in the room to one category or the other. We could do so, just as the taste of wines can be located on the dry–sweet dimension, and this is why, relativity notwithstanding, we can translate. But we have lost something if we do not realize that this change has occurred in the meaning of our terms, and if we think instead that their terms "mean the same as" ours.

It becomes clear that it is not possible to rank the different sets of terms as Berlin and Kay do. The strict limitations on how the spectrum is perceived only appear to exist from the perspective of an eleven-term system (e.g. English), assuming *a priori* and surreptitiously that the meaning of these terms is universal. One cannot say, without imposing this perspective, that if a system has three terms it has terms meaning the same as "red", "black" and "white". Each system is semantically *sui generis*—though not unintelligible from other perspectives. Berlin and Kay's transitive ranking is representative of our perception of the spectrum and of how, looking back from that point of view, we can imagine it developing. But, dropping that perspective, all we can say is, "If a system has three terms it has *these* three which divide the spectrum *thus*"; we cannot say that they must be terms for red, black and white, or some super third-order category. Our mistake in concurring so readily with Berlin and Kay is in thinking that in an *ultimate* and absolute sense there exist these colours red, black and white, whether or not one has adopted a particular system of *rules* of classification. Below, I hope to clarify a little better the idea of a *rule* of classification.

Surely, though, an important and central element in Berlin and Kay's thesis remains intact. While the semantic framework in which they are expressed may be misleading, nevertheless it may be argued that they are right in presenting these stages as *the* options in elementary colour classification. Given this, codification of the spectrum is not arbitrary. This is, after all, the core of the hypothesis. There is a sense in which this may be correct but the import of it is not that which Berlin and Kay find. We cannot legitimately make the interesting claim that if there were three "basic" terms these would have the meanings of "red", "black" and "white" (as we use them ordinarily). Rather we should think of these so-called systems as alternative ways of dealing with the spectrum, as semantic options. This can be expressed by putting the question: "How could one adequately classify the spectrum using x number of categories (e.g. two, three and so on)?" Now, if one's task were to get as many items as possible in this room into two piles on the basis of something like a colour criterion[30] it can be seen why one might end up with a "lighter-than–darker-than" distinction. Indeed it can probably be shown why we would *have* to make a distinction like that apparently expressed in the Jalé "two-term systems". Any other possibility, e.g. "red/not-red", because it requires hue-discrimination, would no doubt prove too ambiguous. So, in this way, the Berlin and Kay schema expresses a number of logical possibilities—there may, of course, be more. One can imagine also turning this into a series of psychological experiments with people from widely different cultural backgrounds. As far as we know, these options are based on discriminations given physiologically. As that is not in dispute, it might be thought that this supports Berlin and Kay's thesis. But what is important is the "use" to which are put such discriminatory potentials as *criteria* of classification. Once again, this brings us back to emphasizing that no differences are postulated between members of different cultures at the physiological level, and that we have no reason for assuming that in some drastic sense they *see* a different realm of colour. Certain salient features *become* significant and come to carry a classificatory burden in relation to items in the world of daily experience. These in turn can be represented as "basic" systems in Berlin and Kay's sense.[31]

Even so, there are still serious doubts about putting the correlation like this. The first consideration has been touched on already. People allegedly operating with one of these systems of basic colour terms can make colour discriminations and articulate them through a so-called descriptive language. Now to understand more adequately the *actual* logic of their colour classification one needs to know when and how they make do with these basic/summary terms and when they use descriptive language instead; and also, when the latter occurs, how established this language is. As I have already said, while a term *may* be regarded as logically primitive it is better viewed in terms of how it would be located descriptively by native speakers if they were unable to use ostensive definition.

A further question which arises concerns the relations between different systems of the same size, for example between all of the members of the three-term set. To sustain the modified hypothesis that there are to be found only seven "basic" ways of categorizing colour we would have to engage in a rigorous comparison of as many classifications of the *same* basic nature as possible. If we look at the presentation of all the "stage-two" systems in the "Data" section of Berlin and Kay's book, it is easy to be suspicious given their *second-order* classification of the different languages. It is quite explicit that "red", "black" and "white" are inferred categories from indigenous terms which *do not* translate readily and about which workers in the field express ambivalence.[32] Among stage three languages, to take another example, there seems to be doubt sometimes about whether the fourth category should be called "green" or "yellow". The revised schema introducing "grue" not only accommodates apparent counter-examples, but also represents an attempt to sharpen, as it were, a schema which is losing its semantic grip on the data. It is as if too much of a tinge of English meaning creeps over the spectrum. The point is not to challenge the specific results of the work, but to question the relation of the general schema to each specific case found. Differences which may be significant in inter-cultural contact are hidden in an artificial system the terms of which allow mapping because they are so open.

It is necessary now to turn to an ultimately crucial issue. Whether much of what I have said raises real difficulties or is mere sophistry depends on it. It is the way in which, at least for the twenty languages in the experiment, the extensions of the basic colour terms were elicited through the Munsell colour chart. The final experimental grounds for translating basic colour terms into a universal schema represented by English terms are constituted by agreement on the location of the *foci* of up to eleven colour categories; e.g. in a four-term system the foci of the terms will always coincide sufficiently with the foci of "black", "white", "red" and "green" or "yellow". This means apparently that while the extension of a term may be greater than that of its English equivalent there is no need to maintain linguistic relativity.

What is worrying is that so much is inferred from response to a colour chart.[33] This is not a quantitative failing which can be resolved through accumulation of more data. It involves the meaning and status of the colour chart, *as such*. It is, after all, a remarkably localized cultural phenomenon. To use Berlin and Kay's terminology it goes with a culturally and technologically complex society. It would be interesting to study, as a minor indicator of changing relations to the environment, exactly when and why someone or some group first produced a colour chart.

We use colour charts in everyday life most often when selecting paints, fabrics, make-up, cars and so on. One can note, to begin with, that these charts encode much non-colorimetric information and indeed are heavily symbolic:[34] images of status, of sexuality, of power abound, often intertwined in elaborate networks. And one very important feature of these loaded charts is that the different colours are very often given an exotic name,[35] as if this is necessary for any symbolism to take root. This is connected essentially to the phenomenon of the colour chart itself. It is a feature of a cultural environment in which people have a low degree of semantic contact, as discussed above. Only a relatively few people are engaged in activities as a result of which they will use a complex colour language; these will be those who are involved in the manufacture of paint for decorating, the design of fabrics, etc. We saw that the same held for taste classification and it is no doubt the case with the classification of smells (e.g. those involved in the perfume industry). The need to provide a symbolic cipher with the colour chart goes with the unlikelihood of a sufficient number of people having sufficiently similar and established responses to the possible symbolic values of a potentially large range of reproducible colours.

Now I think we can legitimately contrast societies in which these colour charts are thus used with societies which are technologically simple, but ritually complex, like that of Ndembu.[36] In the latter one cannot see the point of a colour chart; it would be unnecessary. Members of such a society are acquainted, in the course of their everyday lives, with what we might call the colour options. Literally, they regularly perceive more or less all of the colours from which they are to select their "decorations". Moreover, any symbolism is socially disclosed and prescribed (at least in a *limiting* sense)[37] within the context of their rituals. We could say that the environment itself is the colour chart and ritual use of colours the supplier of symbolic content.[38]

Nevertheless what these contrasting worlds have in common is that certain colour categories are highly symbolic. I can only attempt to indicate what the connection here is. I will do so by examining the nature of the "neutral" Munsell colour chart.

First, let me state what seems to be the *wrong* thesis about the connection between colour categories and symbolism: basic colour categories become the bearers of symbolic value because they are basic and universal, at least in the experience of all members of a particular society.[39] I have argued already that, logically, "basic" colour terms are not so different in their status to descriptive expressions. I have also claimed that they do not stand in relation to perception of the spectrum simply as the names proper to perceptual categories which are given once and for all. Bringing this together with the problem of symbolism in colour, the mistake—and it has huge repercussions—is to use a neutral colour chart representing the spectrum itself and to ask people to relate to it their "basic" terms by locating the foci of the latter. Eliciting this response **was crucial in getting the data which** allowed the elaboration of colour-term systems as such and the ranking of these systems. Having to locate foci among options presented in the form of a two-dimensional representation of the spectrum allowed the translation necessary to preserve meaning from one set to another. As I have argued above, there is good reason to expect some sort of "agreement" here. But people just do not perceive the spectrum in their everyday lives. They do not perceive colours as such in the way that these are presented, in isolation, in the colour chart. Nor do they (usually) learn colour language by being given a colour chart.[40] To bring out to some degree the real situation I want now to focus on two aspects of classification: the notion of a *rule* of classification and as integral to that the role of paradigms.[41] First, the place of paradigms.

We learn how to use an expression like a colour term by being shown examples to which it applies which are paradigmatic. Among other things, this means that they are examples of, in this case, a certain colour and are accepted as such by all members[42] of the relevant society. If this condition were not satisfied and people did not agree about paradigms there would be no logic of colour classification in the first place. Moreover, paradigms have what could be called significance. They have some power to sustain their roles as paradigms, in the semantics of the domain.

What I want to suggest is that the question "What would be a good example of 'red'?" is misleading if it makes us think that the paradigm is selected *because* it is a good representative of a colour category which under *ideal* circumstances could be presented *in itself* through presentation of the spectrum. On the contrary, that colour *category* is established in perception and language *through* the establishment of the paradigmatic set, i.e. the colour category is established as the colour *of* such and such. The paradigm is, so to speak, the true focus of the category. This means that colour categories are not directly elicited by the presentation of a colour chart. Rather, one has to relate his colour categories *to* the chart. Given the structure of the chart and of colour vision we can expect that inter-cultural regularities of the sort found will emerge.

Now while the subject, when presented with the colour-chart, may settle for a classification which has a sort of universal structure, such a classification does not really inform us about the actual logic of colour language in any particular society. Thus if we want to know what "black" means we need to know what black is the colour of; and so on for "red", "green", "yellow", "brown", "blue", etc. It is not so impor-

H

tant from this point of view that some colour terms have etymological primacy. Their semantic "surrounds" are what interest us.[43]

This paradigmatic structure of classificatory logic does seem to be a feature of how a person, as a cultural being, perceives and relates to an environment in which *natural* properties and culturally established meanings cannot be separated.[44] This leads directly to the connection between colour categories which seem basic and their symbolic content. That there is such symbolic content can be seen in English; all of the eleven terms may have direct and immediate meaning[45] for an individual and certainly do have culturally available meanings for all members: black with its connotations of evil, death and also sexuality, primeval lifeforce; white with connotations of purity, decency, maternity and so on; red with its connotations of life and also violence; yellow, cowardice but also gaiety and fun; and so on through the lexicon. None of these connotations desplays any one symbolic connection; we are presented with a loose ragbag of meaning, the motivations of which are not all of one piece.[46]

For us, however, this symbolism does emerge and is highly charged when we view it not under our own noses but at a distance in the exotic, ritualistic other of primitive culture. Now, if we look at the three "basic" colour terms of Ndembu, those which are translated as black, white and red, we see that each has a paradigm: white as white clay and the sap of the milk tree, red as red clay and blood, black as charcoal, river mud, etc.[47] One could say that both the colours and their paradigms carry the symbolism, the paradigms representing at one and the same time the colours and the symbolic values in the rituals. It is easy to express the relationships here as follows. First, the colour terms themselves stand for perceptual categories, whiteness, blackness and redness, and that these are slices of the colour continuum as it is structured at least in part by the brain. Second, these categories "stand for", "represent" cultural values of various sorts. But, given features of classificatory logic which we have noted above, it seems that such an analysis is not only clumsy but actually distorts the way in which the language works. It is not clear that we can separate from each other the symbolic references of, e.g. "red" and "blood". It is red-as-the-colour-of-blood which carries the symbolism.

Anyway, what seems more likely is that basic colour terms do not sustain symbolic values *because* they are basic, but are sustained in their apparently basic position *because* they are located in symbolic networks.

They have a central position because of the evocative power of the paradigms and *their* cultural centrality.[48]

The other aspect of rules of classification to which I want to draw attention can be brought out by quoting Berlin and Kay on a difficulty noted in mapping category boundaries.

> Repeated mapping trials with the same informant and also across informants showed that category foci placements are highly reliable. . . . Category boundaries, however, are not reliable. . . . This is reflected in the ease with which informants designated foci, in contrast with their difficulty in placing boundaries.[49]

Not only does such difficulty seem to match our experience and be intuitively obvious, but if we adopt the notion of applying rules of classification which we have been taught in our socialization, then it is not only to be expected; it is seen as an integral feature of such rules. When a person learns the rule of application of an expression, one criterion for saying that they understand the rule is that they can "go on" in new situations.[50] However, it is also the case that one can, more often than not, state *no* general rule for telling whether this is so, i.e. whether the person *can* really "go on" as opposed to having learned by rote a series of responses. Let us take one of Wittgenstein's main examples, that of having learnt how to count. While one *general* test is that of always being able to continue the number series, i.e. answer the question "Which number comes next?", there is no ultimate, guaranteed test of whether or not the person understands continuing to count or just knows a series "by heart". In any one case, a particular judgement of competence must be made in which the details of the situation (e.g. whether or not the individual was required to count a series of objects unseen before) are brought together with others from their past in a complex of evidence.

Nevertheless, while this tacit knowledge cannot be articulated into a set of rules which themselves do not require interpretation involving just such tacit knowledge, we do succeed often enough in such judgements. Now, complementing this feature of rule-governed behaviour is another: one important way of demonstrating that one understands a rule and can apply it correctly is being able to "have a shot" in a situation where there is no established correct answer which a rote-learner could produce. There is no one fixed answer, but we can judge when an attempt to produce one "makes sense".

And this is often enough the case with colour classification. A person who understands the meaning of the word "red" may be faced with a

H*

situation in which they cannot say that x is red but have to *decide* whether it is red or not; we judge their understanding on the basis of how they handle this situation. There is a point, as it were, when interpretation is best thought of as decision. This is seen if we imagine someone who *has* been taught the meaning of colour words from a colour chart which they carry around with them as a classificatory guide. Even in this case, after they have taken their chart from its case, they must make a judgement, interpret the category established for them by the chart. Indeed, even coming to the judgement that "that is the *same* colour as this one on the chart", requires that a rule be applied. I hasten to point out that I am not using this Wittgensteinian approach to rule-governed activity as a way of attacking a physicalist account in which the semantic base of colour language is related ultimately to brain structure. I am not denying that colour perception is determined in some way by the physiological structure of perception. But I am saying that the notion of "universal semantic category" is introduced too soon and possibly unnecessarily—and certainly misleadingly.[51] The actual logical behaviour of colour language seems, at first analysis at any rate, to display a rather different structure.

If what I say about paradigms is correct then in relation to the Munsell colour chart we do not have the direct mapping of perceptual categories onto a colour continuum but rather the application of learned rules of classification to a new series of examples. Given the "individual history" of the tacit knowledge involved we can expect that disagreement over colour boundaries should occur. Moreover, it seems likely that this will occur not only between individuals but also between members of different cultures to the extent that their colour paradigms establish different networks of relations among colours; e.g. it will make a difference how one maps the boundary of Berlin and Kay's category "red" depending on whether or not one has a term covering their "yellow".

I have argued that this way of looking at colour classification is truer to experience than that which sets up "basic colour categories", these being like storage bins in the brain. If I had a series of perceptual categories into which sense-data fitted *without* my having to put them there according to rules I have learnt, then many of the problems of classification as such would not arise. We would not notice discrepancies or else we would react to them rather differently. The "hypothesis" I have proposed here is this: the rules of classification do not reflect the categories; rather the categories are sustained through the application of rules which themselves form part of complex social practices. To argue for this further would require a much more fundamental analysis not only of classification and concept formation but of the deepest epistemological issues, such as that of the status of physicalism.

These considerations lead to a negative response to the experimental work of this nature. What is necessary is that one learns how people classify in the environment in which they live; what their paradigms are and how the world is organized around them. I realise full well that this is problematic. How, it will be asked, can we ever get scientific understanding if the laboratory must always be out there in the field? To resolve this would require one of those discussions of methodology, too wide to be discussed here.

Let me stress again that I am not hostile to Berlin and Kay's work and this sort of experimental work in general for the sake of some idealism. Nor is the accusation of chauvinism meant to be insulting. I have, however, been questioning the validity of some of their basic concepts such as those of a universal semantic category, of a basic colour term and of a discrete domain of classification. Any theoretical account must deal first with the complicated, untidy logics actually found. I am sure that this is possible.

Notes

1. The phrase is Gellner's. See "The new idealism", in Gellner (1973).
2. Berlin and Kay (1969).
3. See e.g. Conklin (1973); Hickerson (1971).
4. While the initial schema, which I will keep to here for convenience, may be continually modified there is no question in this context of trying to find—or imagine—any "direct counter-example" which suggests a different schema. To the extent that I do seem to be challenging their evidence, this will be because I am questioning their interpretation. While this is not the place to engage in philosophy of science I hold that to do so does ultimately "restructure" the evidence. In particular my suggested approach to rules of sensory classification would make me less happy with the status of the schema than, e.g. Sahlins (1976). For the debate in philosophy of science see Kuhn (1973) and Feyerabend (1975).
5. Many of the following points have been made elsewhere. I hope however that the discussion is not redundant in that I dwell longer on certain points, such as translation, which while easily made need to be drawn out in their implications.
   Perhaps I should stress a feature of the genesis of this discussion. Originally I intended to present, in a primarily expository fashion, the nature and relevance of a (roughly) "Wittgensteinian" understanding of *rules*. It seemed appropriate to limit

this discussion to an area of immediate interest. That of colour classification was suggested and in particular a discussion of *Basic Colour Terms*. I studied this text from a position of great ignorance. I feel now that I am in many ways close to the position of Sahlins (1976). But my emphasis on the role of object-paradigms presents a somewhat different version of the cultural determinations, though it is not necessarily antithetical to his structuralist approach.

6. Berlin and Kay, *op. cit.* pp. 1–2.
7. *Ibid* p. 2.
8. *Ibid* p. 104. The schema has since been revised, thus:

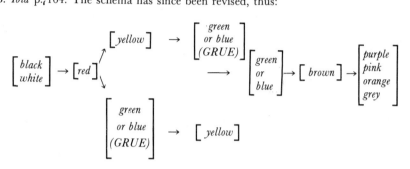

For this and reasons for modification see Berlin and Berlin (1975). See also Hage and Hawkes (1975).

9. *Op. cit.* p. 2.
10. *Ibid.* pp. 5–7.
11. *Ibid.* p. 5 and Chapter 3.
12. See Hickerson, *op. cit.,* for criticism.
13. *Op. cit.* p. 7.
14. *Ibid.* pp. 41–5.
15. *Ibid.* pp. 16–17.
16. See, e.g. Wittgenstein (1968, para. 27–37); also Sahlins *op. cit.* pp. 8–9.
17. The second-order nature of these terms has been pointed out elsewhere (Hickerson, 1971; Sahlins, 1976). In calling them "summary" terms I do not imply that there is only *one* sort of summary, one logic at work.
18. Johnson (1974, pp. 208 and 175).
19. Cassirer (1946, pp. 83–99).
20. Johnson, *op. cit.* p. 174.
21. See Merleau-Ponty (1962).
22. Johnson, *op. cit.* p. 201.
23. Berlin and Kay, *op. cit.* p. 5.
24. The two-term system is now usually characterized as "light–warm/cool–dark".
25. See Conklin, *op. cit.*
26. Berlin and Kay, *op. cit.* pp. 23–8.
27. *Ibid.* p. 24.
28. See Berlin and Berlin, *op. cit.*
29. For example, terms translated as "witchcraft", "God", "Spirit", etc. which cause so much confusion.
30. We must speak reservedly here because it is not clearly a question of *colour* as *we* normally understand it. As Sahlins points out, this is "the most comprehensive

'color' contrast the human eye can make applicable panchromatically to all visible objects and lights" being based on "the most elementary physiological response to luminous flux" (*op. cit.* p. 3).

31. For a fuller discussion of the relation between the "natural" and the "cultural", see Sahlins, *op. cit.*
32. Berlin and Kay, *op. cit.* Chapter 3.
33. Though, see Hage and Hawkes, *op. cit.*, for a modified procedure.
34. See any "upmarket" paint manufacturer's charts and charts presenting shades of eye make-up and nail varnish.
35. "Daytona Yellow" as the colour of a family saloon car.
36. Turner (1967).
37. Though see Sperber (1975).
38. Turner, *op. cit.* Chapter I.
39. Sahlins, *op. cit.* pp. 3 and 12.
40. See Wittgenstein, *op. cit.*
41. Using this word loosely. For a discussion of the term as used in philosophy of science, see works cited by Feyerabend and Kuhn.
42. Or, a "sufficient" number of relevant members, whatever that means.
43. One could regard the "Munsell effect" as a levelling of pertinent cultural differences. Conversely, one could regard it, when the chart is presented in the field, as the introduction of a new, cultural dimension. For an example, see the discussion of the Binumarien category, *akara*, in Hage and Hawkes, *op. cit.*
44. See Merleau-Ponty, *op. cit.* pp. 23–4 and 346–65.
45. See Sperber, *op. cit.*
46. *Ibid.*
47. Turner, *op. cit.* Chapter 3.
48. Compare Sahlins' position.
49. Berlin and Kay, *op. cit.* p. 13.
50. See Wittgenstein, *op. cit.* para. 201–38.
51. Rather than attempting to deny a physicalism, what is urgently called for is a new set of concepts for characterizing the physical basis of our "being-in-the-world". Such a task was initiated by Merleau-Ponty but remains barely recognized.

References

BERLIN, B. and BERLIN, E. A. (1975). Aguarana color categories. *Am. Ethnol.*, **2**, 61–87.
BERLIN, B. and KAY, P. (1969). "Basic Color Terms". University of California Press, Berkeley and Los Angeles.
CASSIRER, E. (1946). "Language and Myth". Dover, New York.
CONKLIN, H. (1973). Review article: color categorisation. *Am. Anthropol.* **75**, 931–942.
FEYERABEND, P. K. (1975). "Against Method". New Left Books, London.
GELLNER, E. (1973). "Cause and Meaning in the Social Sciences". Routledge and Kegan Paul, London.
HAGE, P. and HAWKES, K. (1975). Binumarien categories. *Ethnology*, **14**, 287–300.
HICKERSON, N. (1971). Review of "Basic colour terms: their universality and evolution". *Intern. J. Am. Linguistics*, **37**, 257–270.
JOHNSON, H. (1974). *"Wine"*. Mitchell Beazley, London.

KUHN, T. (1973). "The Structure of Scientific Revolutions". University of Chicago Press, Chicago.
MERLEAU-PONTY, M. (1962). "The Phenomenology of Perception". Routledge and Kegan Paul, London.
SAHLINS, M. (1976). Colors and culture. *Semiotica*, **16**, 1–22.
SPERBER, D. (1975). "Rethinking Symbolism". Cambridge University Press, Cambridge.
TURNER, V. (1967). "The Forest of Symbols". Cornell, Ithaca and London.
WITTGENSTEIN, L. (1968). "Philosophical Investigations". Blackwell, Oxford.

11

Classification, Time and the Organization of Production

David Reason

The world is unique. The simple repetition of the aspects which constantly recur in the same way is more like a vain and compulsory litany than the redeeming word. Classification is a condition for cognition and not cognition itself; cognition in turn dispels classification.

Adorno and Horkheimer: *The Dialectic of Enlightenment*

I

It is curious that the revival of interest in an "anthropology of knowledge" should have adopted as the emblem and device of consciousness the notion of *classification*. There is no doubt that in much of *our* thinking the notion is indispensable, but this gives us no licence to raise it as an epistemological standard. The remarks, observations and arguments of this essay are intended, in part, to persuade the reader that classification is neither necessarily universal nor, where it is a demonstrable form in a given culture, is it necessarily of any great moment for an "anthropology of knowledge". The motto of a fallen crest is, as so often, *caveat preemptor*.

In one sense, the notion of classification (or one very like it) is indispensable: all discourse must at some point indicate and implicate aspects and events of a presumed actual world, and such nods, winks and nudges, by directing our attention to what they are about, effectively discover a classifying of the world. However, this says no more than that sensible discourse proceeds from and in acts of distinction and demarcation: the limiting case is language. This sense of classification I shall refer to as categorization: it may be taken to be of direct concern to the anthropologist only insofar as it provides a means whereby he might be misled into believing a corpus of utterance to either presuppose or promulgate a classification in the stronger sense, where no such belief is, in fact, warranted (Bousfield, this volume, nicely elaborates this point). The stronger sense of classification (I shall reserve my use of the term for this sense) provides the theoretical armature of the anthropology of knowledge: it emphasizes the conceptual orderliness evidenced by and in all cultures, and classifications figure as privileged and sanctioned (and sanctionable) arrangements of the ("social" and "natural") world, as a hypostasized system of categories. Typically, our attention is drawn to a stable structure of rules for discriminating kinds of entities, but the rules are not at all like those of categorization (wherever it makes sense to consider the latter as being, strictly, rule-governed). Categorization solicits recognition of a kind which depends on no particular features of expression for its correct exercise, whereas classification is not only rule-governed (since it indicates a culture property), but these rules must be articulable in principle and constitute criteria of identity. The rules must be articulable (in the culture) for us to be sure that the arrangement under consideration is stable (hence is an example of *a* classification) and to ensure that the rules themselves relate in a way which assures us that we are not dealing with an *ad hoc* arrangement (such as an inventory, whose organizing principle is outside of itself: cp. Anscombe, 1963, pp. 56–62); they must constitute criteria of identity to ensure that the classification transcends particular occasions and is learnable. These rules must address the features of the entities which are candidates for classification: to be more precise, the rule may be in terms of predicates, no reification of features into attributes being strictly required (Quine, 1961, pp. 65–79) (thus there is no *logical* compulsion to consider classification as arising from intercourse with "natural kinds" (cp. Ellen, Bulmer, Hunn, this volume)). It is a consequence of the nature of rules of classification that we can evince a classification from an arbitrary corpus of utterance—but this is a technical facility of a logical stance, and may have no substantive import (cp. Faris, 1968).

As Goodman remarks:

The object does not sit as a docile model with its attributes neatly separated and thrust out for us to admire and portray. It is one of countless objects, and may be grouped with any selection of them; and for every such grouping there is an attribute of the object. To admit all classifications on equal footing amounts to making no classification at all. Classification involves preferment; and application of a label (pictorial, verbal, etc.) as often *effects* as it records a classification. The "natural" kinds are simply those we are in the habit of picking out for and by labelling. Moreover, the object itself is not ready made but results from a way of taking the world.

(Goodman, 1976, pp. 31–2)

It is a further consequence of the commitment to rules of classification that the sense of the terms of the classification is determined largely by specified contrasts, for if this were not the case the domain of application of the classification would be unspecifiable: to be in ignorance of the relevant classification system in a given case is also to admit all classifications on an equal footing. Moreover, we see here an elementary basis for considering classifications as culture items, for it is necessary to assert a high degree of agreement if we are to allow the possibility of communication, and if the principle of classification is to provide a cultural method of conceptual organization by exploitation of its combinatorial properties (see the claims made for the "totemic operator": Lévi-Strauss, 1966).

Now this version of classification presupposes a mode of signification which at least allows of an analytic operation (Ellen, 1977): it must be possible to conceptually *dissect* entities so that either the truth or falsity of particular predicates may be established in their cases. Furthermore, for classification to be a *principal* form of the organization of consciousness, this mode of signification must be the dominant mode in the culture in question. It is the dominant mode in *our* culture, at least according to many theoreticians: it finds its purest expression in the formal languages of post-Fregean logic, and its most fashionable forms derive from the Saussurian conception of language. A crucial and distinctive feature of all its embodiments is the stipulation of the separation of a sign from its sense, a mark from its interpretation, so that sign, mark and sense are conjoined solely in their conventional application. We, apparently, cannot forego an avowedly arbitrary and absurd basis for our elevated discourse: like the chameleon, we live on air.

Different modes of signification provide different means for conceptualizing time and temporality. The "conventional" mode (as it applies to classification) requires that time be treated as an indexable quality like space; there is no substantial difference between them (Quine, 1961, pp. 66–8, for example), which results in the classic problem of system change (and the apparatus of "diachrony" and "synchrony" —which are not *necessarily* or unequivocally temporal concepts! —in an attempt to cope with it non-trivially). The "conventional" mode, with its absent speaker and its analytic predication, produces an *ahistorical* account of its *ahistorical* discourse.

The "conventional" mode may, of course, generate an acceptable metalanguage for dealing with any other discourse: I think this a mistaken view (on the question of the treatment of time within our own culture, for example, compare Quine (1961, pp. 66–8), Merleau-Ponty (1962, pp. 410–33) and Black (1962, 182–93)), but even if it were not it must be borne in mind that the relation between object and metalanguage cannot be one of translation or paraphrase. Thus, while we may be able to formulate an object-discourse with a view to determining its properties *as if* it were grounded in or on classification, this is, as far as it goes, a specious exercise. In order to establish an adequate anthropology of knowledge, it is necessary to know how to determine in any given case whether the nature of the object-discourse is such as to permit the notion of classification as a principal articulation of social consciousness. In this essay, I provide material that suggests that the way in which production is organized is a prime determinant of the dominant mode of signification in a culture, and thus of the possibility of apprehending the world in terms of classification.

The foregoing remarks will already have suggested some of the characteristics of the argument which follows. Since it is essential to proceed in such a way that the universalization of classification is not prejudicially vindicated, I adopt a form of presentation which enhances the possibility of elucidating a determinate difference between modes of signification, one which proceeds from Marxian premises. The discussion derives from an examination of concrete social organization, the peasant family farm. My analysis of this material refers primarily to the classic study by Thomas and Znaniecki (1958) of *The Polish Peasant in Europe and America* (hereafter abbreviated to *TZ*), but the referring is accomplished with the help of commentary and analysis drawn from other authors' studies of other concrete situations with, so far as I can judge from their reports, essentially similar forms of production organization. I have also quoted the words of authors who have so well expressed a point relating to my understanding of the peasant family farm that it would be superfluous and needlessly provocative to have provided my own formulation. Thus, whilst all the comments made may be substantiated with respect to *TZ*, it is an important *practical* part of my argument that the reader should be aware of a community of allusions, and the corresponding suspicion that any sufficiently rich ethnography chosen from within an exceedingly broad range of societies would have grounded identical conclusions.

The presentation of the material on the peasant family farm may seem unnecessarily tedious to those familiar with economic anthropology as a corpus of literature—indeed, the use to which the material is put may remind such readers overwhelmingly of the so-called "formalist–substantivist" debate which until recently formed a theoretical axis of that enterprise. Presentation in such seeming detail is necessary since I wish to substantiate not simply an interpretation, but an argument which requires a possible shifting of emphasis, reconsidering a detail as possessing warrantable significance, and articulating an implicit theoretical structure. In this respect, the choice of *TZ* is not simply dictated by considerations of its compendious information but equally because, dealing as it does with an account of peasant life in Poland *and* with the contribution of this life to the subsequent disorientation and "social pathology" of the Polish immigrants to the United States at the beginning of this century, it throws into sharp relief the essential differences between host and home cultures, between the peasant family farm and capitalism.

II

Consider, then, the way in which members of "peasant family farms" conduct their lives. Such farms are worked by the household, production being oriented primarily to household subsistence rather than commodity exchange. Here, I am concerned with the character and consequences of that subsistence organization.

Two points should be borne in mind throughout this discussion. First, my argument neither makes nor requires any claim which regards the "peasant family farm" as constituting a specific mode of production (cp. Sahlins, 1972, p. 77). Such a claim *may* turn out to be justifiable, or it may not: I do not believe that we have a sufficient understanding of the concept "mode of production" to enable us to decide anything more than that a given society is, or is not, character-ized by a "capitalistic-mode-of-production". It is clear that peasant family farms share the negative characteristic of not being capitalistic, and this is a sufficient common feature for exploring the thesis that such subsistence economies cannot be understood by employing categories specific to capitalism. Secondly, there seems to be a striking degree of similarity in central aspects of "social consciousness" among those societies in which the peasant family farm exists as a productive unit, from twentieth century Colombia to mediaeval Germany. Whilst it is incorrect to argue from a similarity of "phenomenal forms" to an identity of "essence", the extent of the empirical correspondences serves to establish the concrete immediacy of the problem I am about to address, where analysis can but demonstrate the abstract necessity of confronting it.

The peasant family farm is a unit of both production and consump-tion: production is primarily oriented to the subsistence of the produc-tion unit. Wherever such a production unit is either, in large measure, able to satisfy the consumption "needs" of the household, or where it serves as the only means of satisfying them, the organization of produc-tion will be primarily determined by consideration of the use-values of the anticipated product. The peasant family farm seeks to realize use-values, not exchange-values, even when the "peasant economy" exhibits, to a quite considerable degree, forms of institutionalized exchange. Use-values, being qualitatively distinct, are not generally substitutable, and hence are not strictly commensurable; they may be so "on occasion", or in some restricted social domain, but this is insufficient to form the basis of extensive commodity exchange, and thus of general commensurability. The relative specificity of use-values is expressed in the organization of the subsistence economy as the *qualitative* character of the production process.

The economic generalization based upon the principle of quantitative equivalence has not been consistently elaborated, and we therefore find distinctions between phenomena of this class which are economically meaningless but have a real social meaning. The same lack of quantitative generalization leads to another result—a lack of calculation, which has sometimes the appearance of stupidity, but is in fact only an application of the sociological instead of the economic type of reasoning to phenomena which are social in the eyes of the peasant even if they are merely economic when viewed from the standpoint of the [capitalist—DR] business man or the economist.

(*TZ*, 1958, p. 157)

In the nonmonetary [i.e. non-commodity-oriented—DR] farm, the activity of the man that ran it["peasant family farm"—DR] was directed to a whole series of separate consumer demands and in many ways had a *qualitative* hue. It was necessary to obtain for family consumption such and such products, precisely those and no others. The *quantity* could be measured only for each demand separately: "there's enough", or "there's not enough", and is there much "not enough"? . . . Therefore, in the non-monetary farm the question of whether it is more advantageous to sow rye or mow hay, for example, could not arise, since they could not replace each other and thus had no common scale for comparison. The value of the hay obtained was measured in terms of the need for fodder, and the value of the rye in terms of feeding the family. You could even assert that meadows increased in value the poorer they were and the more labour they required to obtain each pud of hay.

> (Chayanov, 1966, p. 124. Ortiz (1971) suggests a
> counter-argument, which unfortunately begs the question)

When he[the farmer] is free to work he will decide on the spot whether to plant more, or weed the existing fields, etc. . . . The amount produced is more critical in subsistence agriculture than the cost of production[*sic*] . . . When a farmer makes his decision as he is planting, the obvious is of a very different nature from that of decisions made in advance, and he focusses on the obvious. It is the size and quality of the stem of manioc which he is planting that will make him decide whether or not it will produce and how many tubers it is likely to bear. He will plant more tubers if the stems he is using are not of good quality, if rains do not hamper his work, if he is not exhausted, and so on. This is what I mean when I say that Indians plant until they *see* they have enough; there is no exact measure of how much is enough.

> (Ortiz, 1967)

It is the *household* as a whole that, to all intents and purposes, participates in production, and both production and the product have an irredeemably social character.

Instead of a division of labour, such as is necessarily created with the exchange of exchange values, there would take place an organisation of labour whose consequence would be the participation of the individual in communal consumption.

> (Marx, 1973, p. 172)

This familial character of the farm should not be interpreted as if the family were an association holding a common property. The members of the family have essentially no economic share in the farm; they share only the social character of members of the group, and from this result[s] their social right to be supported by the group and their social obligation to contribute to the existence of the group. The farm is the material basis of this social relation, the expression of the unity of the group in the economic world.

> (*TZ*, 1958, p. 159)

The social character of the "peasant family farm" is nowhere better expressed than in the absence of the categories of "housework" (e.g. *TZ*, p. 1694) and "surplus product", and in the treatment of loans (financial and material) as subject to moral regulation.[1]

For the peasant family farm, then, the orientation of production to use-values, and the consequent qualitative character of the production process, precludes the possibility of apprehending this economy through the application of categories derived from capitalist forms. So far as subsistence production is concerned, there are no prices, no wages, no capital, no rent, no interest—no profit. Capitalist accounting practices are inapplicable to the peasant family farm, and this is correlative with the claim that the apprehension of the organization of work cannot be in terms of the capitalistic division of labour (Chayanov, 1966; Kula, 1976).

This should not be understood to suggest that the categories which need to be developed in order to comprehend the peasant family farm would *signify like* prices, wages and profit, only differing in their specific denotations, their content. The rub of the problem in studying non-capitalist societies lies in the possibility that the appropriate categories are *essentially* different from those relevant in the capitalist domain: those entities which signify for us signify not at all there. I shall attempt to elucidate this riddle by considering land, labour and time in the peasant family farm.

The land, as the prime instrument of labour, is the material basis of the peasant family farm, and is consequently implicated in the social consciousness of the farmer. First, the land serves both as the immediate site of uncertainty and as the means of its amelioration: generally, for example, the more land there is to be cultivated, the less the cultivator is at the mercy of local conditions (of fertility, drought, disease, etc.), and the more assured the satisfaction of consumption requirements. One widespread expression of this state of affairs is to be found in the tendency for the plots of any one peasant family farm to be appreciably scattered, horizontally (e.g. Russian peasants in the late nineteenth century) and/or vertically (e.g. in so-called "Andean economies").[2] Secondly, land "is evidently the main condition of the social standing of the family" (*TZ*, 1958, p. 162), and would be regarded as a "personal attribute", the capacity to regulate it being both dependent upon, and productive of, the social status of its owner (Gurevich, 1977; Bourdieu, 1963, 1977; *TZ*, 1958, throughout). Finally, the land is the specific and direct object of labour, a situation which is conducive to the formation of a "special relationship" between man and the natural world. This is manifested in the ubiquitous employment of measures "of space by man's body, his movement and his ways of acting on matter", a practice which generates "no absolute and abstract standards of measurement" but a system indexed to each production unit (Gurevich, 1977; see also Thompson, 1967; Bourdieu, 1963, p. 60). In other words, the unit of measurement is generally not an object but an effort, work-time.[3]

Since there can be no relevant concept of socially necessary labour time (for this concept presupposes the category of abstract labour, and hence of the determining influence of exchange in order to realize exchange-value), work-time is founded solely upon concrete labour, and thus is intrinsically variable through its dependence upon the intensity of work, the nature of the task, the qualities of the means of production employed, and so on. More precisely: work-time is not *variable* as a *measure*, since particular concrete labours are incommensurable by virtue of the qualitative differences of works and workers. In this respect, work-time, although employed *as if* a unit of measurement *of* land, is in fact better grasped as an idiom of experience, as indicating a physiognomy of subsistence: certainly, there is little point in the abstract comparison of land sizes (or, for that matter, crop yields) when a question of subsistence consumption presides, when that which needs doing must needs get done.

Conversely, concrete labour in the capitalist economy presupposes a superordinate, abstract and reified temporal framework. Wage–labour is always subject to a time-rate, either explicitly or implicitly, as with piece-rates (Marx, 1976, pp. 683–92): the expansion of capital is plotted with G.M.T. Time, separated from the experience of work and reflexed to situate, measure and mark it, is an essential flux in the dissolution of the qualitative character of working that is the hallmark of abstract labour, the measure of value. Time does, indeed, appear to be money: the history of capitalism can be told in terms of the increasing incorporation of the timing of work operations into the structure of the machinery used in production. The qualitative experience of work may remain, but is of no account to capital and, indeed, tends to become imbued with the temporal framework of capital. The category "work-time", as used here, is inimical to "capital-logic", and is to be found as a central economic category only within the interstices of capitalism; for example, in the domestic economy.[4]

Abstract time (as I shall refer to this superordinate temporal order of capitalism) is often characterized as *linear*, in contrast to the *cyclical* time regularly attributed to the societies anthropologists tend to study.[5] This characterization is misleading, its rhetorical geometry obscuring the problem of how it is possible to live the difference indicated, given that both must employ notions of succession and essential similarity. If I were to epitomize the distinction between capitalist and non-capitalist temporal orders, it would be in terms of how concepts of *again* appear. Under the rule of abstract time, *again* is appreciated as "repetition", the reappearance of an event whose "inner constitution" proclaims its substantive identity; such events indeed mark time. Non-capitalist societies, on the other hand, and specifically the peasant family farm, operate with a conception of "recurrence", in which all events are qualitatively distinct and yet owe their particular identity to their essential affinity to previous events; such events may be understood as standing in relation to history as commentary and exegesis stand in relation to a text.[6] I shall refer to the temporal order distinguished by "recurrence" as *textual time*.

Textual time constitutes, and is constituted in, the narrative account as the prime formula for reflecting (upon) the courses and causes of events, and provides the essential means of explicating the sense of the accomplished facts of life. The world is steeped in immanent utterance, and time "is filled with—indeed, composed of—a rich texture of acts, words and thoughts of personal and social beings" (Pocock, 1971, p. 151): it is as though the manner of the text is that of the authorized biography (cp. Garfinkel, 1967, p. 166; Merleau-Ponty, 1962, p. 410; Bourdieu, 1963, p. 56). The intentionality with which the world is imbued, inscribing immediate significance in everyday occurrences, is ascribed in any particular case and precise sense in virtue of its bearer's place in a socially (and thus naturally) warrantable narrative: intention is revealed in a configurative sense (cp. Anscombe, 1963; Von Wright, 1971), and social agents are condemned to understanding. Now, a notable feature of narrative is that, whenever plausible, acceptable and compelling, indeed, whenever a narrative account is (usually tacitly) treated as coherent, then integrity of the account derives not from the narrative's standing proxy for some explicitly law-referencing explanation scheme, but from its covert dependence upon a practical knowledge of the organization of that social life providing the narrative medium or milieu (Gellner, 1971, p. 16; Gallie, 1964; Sacks, 1974). Narrative accounts cannot compel acceptance through their adherence to canons of logical conduct (and are generally more than sufficient, yet less than necessary, by formal criteria), but by the mutual observances of, and regard for, the customs and procedures of social life: rejection of the good form of the narrative account entails the denial of a sociable commitment, and marks a surrender to estrangement and dis-enchantment—indeed, commitment is usurped by enigmatic calcu-lation. Narrative accounts merge events, sequence, intentions and institutions, and what emerges in textual time is a corpus of collective belief rendered both authoritative and necessary (cp. Bourdieu, 1977, p. 167). (In the circumstances, it proves equally natural to employ an idiom of social arrangements of kinship, production or seasonal variation to indicate and correlate events and occasions: these ways-of-speaking are compatible in principle and, where the temporal order is that of textual time, they are qualitatively equivalent (cp. Evans-Pritchard's 1940 distinction between structural and ecological time).) In consequence, the-way-it-is-now has as a major aspect that of memorandum—of *aide-mémoire* and reminder. There is with textual time—as with all situations demanding the interpretative "reading" of texts—a markedly shallow but palpable temporal reach, as it were, an accented presentness of remembering: it is a quite striking characteris-tic, familiar enough for it to pass unremarked in our own biographies but extraordinarily difficult to evoke when, as with textual time, it pertains to a cultural order (cp. Bourdieu, 1977, p. 166; see also Geertz, 1975). It is as if our sense of the historical past as a Sisyphean recital of numbered years, the massive and unremitting tedium of that number-ing chore echoing in the passage of time, was replaced by that of paraphrasing *Finnegan's Wake*, or of establishing an original reading of Marx's writings: in such cases, time's recoil consists in the weight of allusion, in the volume of interpretation which has to be mastered before one is equal to the task. The sheer bulk of all-that-has-happened is condensed into the belief that there is nothing to be said that has not been said already, and the supreme and impossible novelty is to recre-ate the past without in any sense copying it (as with Pierre Menard's attempt to write *Don Quixote*; see Borges, 1970). With textual time, we deal not with a dimension but with a way of grasping one's living.

Texts are reticent about their origins (it is notorious in most circles that the method of analysis and the method of exposition are perplex-ingly and ironically related), and textual time is similarly modest. Where a question of origins does arise it tends to be only elliptically related to the common social discourse, but there are many devious devices for dealing with—or, more accurately, evading—the question. Conversely, all texts are hostages to the future, and none more so than those texts which are constituted by social life itself. "The anticipation of the peasant . . . consists of reading the signs to which tradition furnishes the key" (Bourdieu, 1963, p. 69), a practice which is possible since development—coming-to-pass—is immanent in the given configuration of the world. To remember is here to lay claim on the future (conceived as the realization of the present) but not to coerce it (Bourdieu, 1963, p. 63; see also Pocock, 1971, pp. 168–9): an eloquent and apposite development of this conception is due to Benjamin:

> The soothsayers who found out from time to time what it had in store certainly did not experience time as either homogeneous or empty. Anyone who keeps this in mind will perhaps get an idea of how past times were experienced in remembrance—namely, in just the same way. We know that the Jews were prohibited from investigating the future. The Torah and the prayers instruct them in remembrance, however. This stripped the future of its magic, to which all those succumb who turn to the soothsayers for enlightenment. This does not imply, however, that for the Jews the future turned into homogeneous, empty time. For every second of time was the strait gate through which the Messiah might enter.
>
> (Benjamin, 1973, p. 226)

In many ways, textual time is the cruellest time, mixing memory and desire.

Textual time refuses the possibility of treating separate occurrences as repetitions of identical events or objects: at the most, occurrences may be citable as instances of a more general category which yet preserves (but cannot articulate) their individuation. (The same thing is never said twice, even, or especially, when "the words remain the same", a circumstance which does not prevent—although it may make contentious—our remarking the recurrence of sentiments: similarly, the Freudian "compulsion to repeat" belies its catch-phrase by providing an example of recurrence, and we celebrate recurring, not repeating, anniversaries.) It is in virtue of the inability of textual time to deal with and yet to respect uniqueness that it must stop short of being able to recount its origins: textual time arises from the ground of production to mystify the producers.

Just as abstract time may be regarded as a necessary concomitant of an economic organization oriented to the realization of exchange-value, so textual time is consequent upon an orientation to use-value. Work-time cannot provide a basis for the organization of work in the "peasant farm economy"—it is, as it were, too self-regarding to serve in the comparison and co-ordination of household activities. Yet *some* form of task allocation is both logically necessary and empirically observed in the peasant family farm for the objective of subsistence to be met at all. The social division of labour, whilst not subject to the temporal order of the technical division of labour manifested under capitalism (Marx, 1976), none the less presupposes negotiative processes, and hence the temporal space in which they can be realized. The character of such a *socialized time* is that it is marked by the presence of an awareness of the social character presupposed by the peasant family farm economy, an awareness which takes the form of solidarity; and, an insistence upon reproduction—of the household (its members and its subsistence product) and of nature (the reproduction of the "material basis" of the household). Socialized time, if it is to provide for the accomplishment of co-ordination, must, if not transcend, then *frame* work-time predicated upon the experience of particular concrete labour. It is within socialized time, pre-eminently, that use-values can be recognized, and in so far as nature both corresponds to and dictates the manner of existence of the household we can identify the basis for the reification of a temporal order founded upon and founding "recurrence"—textual time. (These relationships are schematized in Fig. 1.)

Textual time and abstract time are categories which arise from the organization of production. They do not refer directly to any

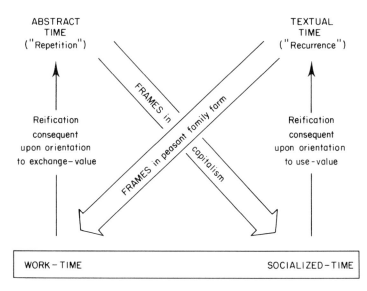

Fig. 1   The production of temporal orders.

phenomenological account of social existence, although they do suggest some of the requirements such accounts must satisfy to be intelligible and of consequence in this, rather than that, form of social organization. Another way of putting it is that temporality must be experienced and expressed in a culturally significant manner, and textual time and abstract time are summary terms for two types of discourse, constituting different subjects, experiences and expressions. But these discourses, these temporal orders, are not wholly autonomous. The dialectic of particular and general, of concrete and abstract may result in work-time and socialized time differing both as concept and as experience under the different dominating temporal orders, but these must be differences of nuance only, for no distinction of "place" within the social organization would be sufficient to dislocate the sense of terms which are conjoined in basic human activity. Pedantically, people do have different "concepts of time",[7] but this does not prevent our communicating since there are common, necessary, real presuppositions of social existence which compel us to reach out for and grasp another's meaning as a reflex of the human condition (cp. Bloch, 1977; Merleau-Ponty, 1962): it would be otherwise if translation and communication were fundamentally a matter of correspondences, of matching, of the comparison of worlds labelled piecemeal (Bousfield, this volume, and the references cited there: cp. Quine, 1964). As it is,

nothing could be more misguided than to conceive of [the peasant's] attitudes to time as radically opposed to that of the occidental. Admitting that industrialised society tends to impose on its members an attitude to rational calculation with regard to the abstract and imagined future, it remains true that most daily actions are undertaken with reference to a concrete future anticipated in preperceptive consciousness like the real horizon of the perceived present

(Bourdieu, 1963, p. 60)

thus providing a point of reciprocal intelligibility.

However, it is a different story when we consider the matter from the other side, and note the influence that different organizations of production and their induced temporal orders exercise on the constitution of immediate social living. Work-time is "essentially different from a measurement of exchange-values (labour or products) by labour time" (Marx, 1973, p. 163), a circumstance which accounts for the absurdity of attempting to use time-spent-working as a proxy for "value" in non-capitalistic economies (see, for example, the discussions of Firth, 1975; Frankenberg, 1967). With the transition to capitalism, abstract time—which is the further aspect of the orientation to exchange and calculative appraisal of capitalist enterprise—appears as the control of social life.

> The concept of time in the modern sense began to develop. Minutes became valuable . . . Too many holidays began to appear as a misfortune . . . A new attitude towards work developed and was so strong that the middle class grew indignant against the economic uproductiveness of the Church. Begging orders were presented as unproductive and hence immoral.
>
> (Fromm, 1960, p. 49)

> Since our Time is reduced to a Standard, and the Bullion of the Day minted out into Hours, the Industrious know how to employ every Piece of Time to a real Advantage in their different Professions: And he that is Prodigal of his Hours is, in fact, a Squanderer of Money.
>
> (Franklin, 1751)

> Those who are employed experience a distinction between their employer's time and their "own" time. And the employer must *use* the time of his labour, and see it is not wasted: not the task but the value of time when reduced to money is dominant. Time is now currency: it is not passed but spent.
>
> (Thompson, 1967, p. 61)

> Remember how gainful the Redeeming of Time is . . . in Merchandize, or any trading; in husbandry or any gaining course, we use to say of a man that hath grown rich by it, that he hath made use of his Time.
>
> (Baxter, 1673)

> The discovery of labour [as distinct from working] presupposes the constitution of the common ground of production, i.e. the disenchantment of a natural world henceforward reduced towards an exclusively economic end, the end which money, henceforward the measure of all things, starkly designates. This means the end of the undifferentiatedness which makes possible the play of collective and individual misrecognition: measured by the yardstick of monetary profit, the most sacred activities find themselves constituted negatively, as *symbolic*, i.e. in a sense the word sometimes receives, as lacking concrete or material effect, in short, *gratuitous*.
>
> (Bourdieu, 1977, pp. 176–7)

Time and money: these are the crucial terms in the capital formulae, and these global abstractions state the terms of the relationship between capital and labour on the shopfloor (Thompson, 1967, pp. 70–86; Hobsbawm, 1964). Aphoristically, it seems that social relationships of production are expressed in the idiom of time in capitalist societies, whilst time is expressed in the idiom of social relationships of production in non-capitalist societies: Evans-Pritchard's (1940) remark that "time-reckoning is a conceptualisation of the social structure" is of general pertinence.

III

The nature of "signification" and "consciousness" in socities in which textual time predominates is central to the argument of this essay. There would seem to be considerable agreement that the central features of the social consciousness in the peasant family farm economy consist in the lack of a profound separation between man and nature, and in the constitution of the cosmos as a "world of deeds" (Gurevich, 1977, p. 10).

The incomplete dissociation of man and nature remains an essential fact of the culture, while the vast majority of the society lived by natural exploitation and while the main source of the satisfaction of their basic needs lay in direct exchange with nature.
(Gurevich, 1977, p. 7)

Far from placing himself face to face with nature as an effective agent, the Kabyle peasant is part of nature, immersed within it . . . The profound feelings of dependence and solidarity towards that nature whose vagaries and rigours he suffers, together with the rhythms and constraints to which he feels the more subject since his techniques are particularly precarious, foster in the Kabyle peasant an attitude of submission and of nonchalant indifference to the passage of time which no one dreams of mastering, using up, or saving . . .
(Bourdieu, 1963, p. 57; cp. TZ, 1958, p. 215)

The "solidarity" of man and nature is expressed in the anthropomorphization of nature, and in the assimilation of man (and the social world) to nature. Nature is "socialized", the natural world is subject to a moral regulation identical to that of the household: there is co-operation between men, animals, plants and the inanimate world, a mutual respect and a common sentience—the cosmos is steeped in intentionality and knowledge.

The bees will never stay with a thief, the stork and the swallow leave a farm where some evil deed has been committed . . . [The earth] consciously rewards the labourer's well-intentioned and sincere work. Every field knows its real owner and refuses to yield to a usurper. The earth is indignant at any crime committed upon its face . . . It sometimes refuses to cover a self-murderer, particularly one who has hanged himself.
(TZ, 1958, pp. 209–210ff.)

This solidarity, whilst pervasive, is not homogenous: a special affinity exists within distinguishable groups (between all plants, or between animals (TZ, 1958, p. 217)) and between particular categories (cuckoos and corn (TZ, 1958, p. 216), cuckoos and wealth (TZ, 1958, p. 218)). Calendrical time itself is drawn into the ambit of sociality ("At least one-third of the days of the year are individually distinguished, and the peasant never uses numbers for these dates, but always individual names" (*TZ*, 1958, p. 207)) and similarly exhibits solidarity relations with man (" . . . each day returns the next year and can then avenge a bad action or reward a good action committed last year" (*TZ*, 1958, p. 211; cp. Bourdieu, 1977)).

Anthropomorphization may also involve encorporation, conceiving nature after the fashion of a "grotesque body" (Bakhtin's apt phrase: quoted in Gurevich, 1977).[8] Whereas the above examples of the socialization of the natural world have tended towards an emphasis upon the *individuating* movement of peasant consciousness, which stresses the qualitative distinction of particular entities (*TZ*, 1958, p. 209), the "grotesque corporeality" of the world manifests the obverse tendency of *universalization*.

> The "grotesque body" appeared as unindividualised, imperfect and always tied to the earth which gave it birth only to swallow it up again. The generic body, always renewed, was cosmic, universal and immortal . . . earthly space itself became carnal because it too was conceptualised in terms of the "'grotesque body".
>
> (Gurevich, 1977, p. 8)

Individuation and universalization are not contrary, but complementary aspects of the peasant consciousness. Indeed, one might say that the peasant consciousness is delineable as precisely that form of consciousness in which they amount to the same thing.

> Mediaeval society did not deprive the individual of his freedom, because the individual did not yet exist; man was still related to the world by primary ties. He did not yet conceive of himself as an individual except through the medium of his social (which then was also his natural) role. He did not conceive of any other persons as "individuals" either.
>
> (Fromm, 1960, p. 35)

> In the Middle Ages both sides of human consciousness—that which was turned within as that which was turned without—lay dreaming or half awake beneath a common veil. The veil was woven of faith, illusion, and childish prepossession, through which the world and history were seen clad in strange hues. Man was conscious of himself only as a member of a race, people, party, family or corporation—only through some general category.
>
> (Burckhardt, 1921)

The trick here is to conceive of this world as composed by *exemplification*—for example, *polysyllabic*—that is, the production of signs which "possess" that to which they refer (Goodman, 1976, pp. 52–7 especially, and see the discussion in Scruton, 1974). (The trickiness of the device derives from the problematic use of "refer" in this connection. Exemplification, like all signifying practices, must be announced in some way before its particular referring can be attended to—one must *do exemplification*—but in a world composed of exemplification, *doing exemplification* is itself an unannouncable exemplification! The resolution of this problem lies in our abandoning the universal application of the fashionable account of signifying which holds that signifiers and signifieds stand in some sort of relation one to the other: after all, my angry gesture does not exemplify anger, it is anger (cp. Merleau-Ponty, 1962, p. 184).) The assimilation of man to nature devolves upon the axis of regeneration and reproduction. "The 'grotesque body' is subject to the metamorphosis of death and birth, old age and rejuvenation" (Gurevich, 1977, p. 8), and, indeed, all aspects of the cosmos conform to the natural imperative of the successions of fecundity and decay. Hence "it [is] not time but eternity and the repetition [recurrence] of natural cycles which [make] up the determining categories of thought" (Gurevich, 1977, p. 11; cp. Gurvitch, 1964, pp. 30, 89–90). It is the permanence of the world which may be reflectively articulated, as in mediaeval philosophy "it was not the part but the whole, not individuality but *universitas* which were ranged in the foreground" (Gurevich, 1977, p. 11). Individuality is inexpressible *(Individuum est ineffabile)* but open to exegesis in relation to the universal, the typical, the general: and this precisely because individualizations—concrete, particular entities—are not given to reflection, but to existence, and their appropriation to thought implicates the world.[9]

The world is organized by a principle of dependence, the cosmic reflection of the personal dependence which characterizes social production (Meillassoux, 1972; cp. Bourdieu, 1977, pp. 163–5 especially, where a *technical* division of labour seems assumed, however), and governed by affinity, resemblance and analogy (cp. Ellen, Morris in this volume). This observation applies to the realm of discourse as to any other: there is no arbitrary relation between the world and the word—"words have a meaning" (Merleau-Ponty, 1962), signifying and the signified are inalienable (and, consequently, *that* formulation points a difference from our conception of these matters, but does not grasp it). There is "unwillingness to change the pronunciation of words or to play with them . . . Nor should words ever be misused, great words applied to petty things, etc." *(TZ,* 1958, p. 211). If the word can be said to "stand for" anything in this context, then they "stand for" gestures, acts, deeds: but, of course, they are these also and above all.

During the high Middle Ages many Germanic peoples followed the custom of *levatio cartae*: before drawing up the deed [of land transfer], the piece of parchment and the

writing implements to be used were placed on the land which was to be the subject of
the transaction.

(Gurevich, 1977, p. 10)

This act of unification of parchment and land rendered the title sealed
on this piece of parchment "unchangeable and potent" (Gurevich,
1977, p. 10). If by "symbol" we understand a signifying which may be
realized in virtue of that which is signifying possessing a *prior*
significance, then the *peasant consciousness is not symbolic* and is not organized by symbolism: rather, we must consider the texture of this consciousness as dependent upon a "process of signification in which the
thing expressed does not exist apart from the expression, and in which
the signs themselves induce their significance externally" (Merleau-
Ponty, 1962, p. 166). (Consider music, or the angry gesture, which
"does not make me think of anger, it is anger itself" (Merleau-Ponty,
1962, p. 184).) Thus, the constitutive feature of this discourse is its
"speech act" (see Searle, 1969; Sacks and Schegloff, 1973) quality, we
are dealing with the word as deed, as *logos*: the "logos of the aesthetic
world" (Merleau-Ponty, 1962, p. 428). What we typically encounter as
early stages in our children's acquisition of language (stages in which
uttering enacts its own significance, in which every "thought" is hear-
able and nothing noticeable is unmotivated) is here characteristic of the
dominant mode of discourse (Piaget, 1969; Vygotsky, 1965; Luria,
1971). Utterance is a *revelation* of meaning, and the typical mode of
intellectual apprehension is by exegesis and "glossing practices",
which are inherently never completely formulated (can never precisely
duplicate or, better, reproduce that which is expressed by the object of
contemplation) in virtue of the inexpressible, unarticulable but (exis-
tentially) incontrovertible individuality of the expressive object itself. A
corollary of this state of affairs is that "oral hygiene", a proper respect
for words, is a potent *but inconspicuous* regulator of social conduct.

IV

The "forthcoming" is the concrete horizon of the present and, in virtue of this, it is
given in the mode of presentation and not that of representation.

(Bourdieu, 1963, p. 62)

The concept of representation is commonly taken to suggest that the
"represented" exists independently of the process of "representation",

and that that process expresses or reflects the "represented" (with more or less verisimilitude, depending upon the particular process employed). In order that we may recognize *this* as a representation, one of two conditions must obtain: either, the represented is recognizable (knowable) independently of the mode of representation and in a way which itself does not rely on representation, or the "represented" itself must determine the process of representation to be of such a nature that the relation of "representation" to "represented" is that of "appearance" to "essence" and there exist means of examining appearances so as to discover their essence (cp. Hirst, 1976). The first condition poses the classical problem of the anthropology of knowledge, as found in the Durkheimian discussion of the social origin of conceptual structures and continued into, notably, those studies in ethnoscience which seek to account for the deviation of folk knowledge from scientific knowledge. The second condition poses the classical problem (or rather, dissolves it!) in the epistemology of the natural sciences: the essence of the real is that it determines its effects in consciousness. Now, whatever else might be the case, it is clear that both conditions invoke an empiricist conception of a subject–object dichotomy, and that this dichotomy, and hence any epistemology derived from it, is unavailable in the social consciousness of the peasant family farm.

If, therefore, we are committed to a theoretical understanding grounded upon empirical enquiry, we need to develop an analysis which proceeds from the given social consciousness and respects the nature of that consciousness. This entails that the folk consciousness is not considered as either "false", "*mis*representative" or "distorted", but as practically adequate and to that extent constituting continually corroborated knowledge; and that "classifications", in particular, are not taken as "representing", in the above sense, anything at all. The analysis required necessarily involves the reconceptualization of the phenomenal (empirically given) world through the analysis of the conditions of existence of that phenomenal world.[10] Such an approach is capable of confronting a discursive practice which presupposes "representation" as a function of the practice itself, and this essay, in part, offers a discussion which seeks to ground the proposition that the separation of modes of production and modes of signification is not given *a priori* and ahistorically. That understanding of signification which regards the sign as the unity of a signifier and its signified standing in arbitrary and conventional relationship mimics in its form the orderly anarchy of capitalist production; indeed, Saussure asserted that in linguistics "as in political economy we are confronted with the notion of *value*: both sciences are concerned with *a system for equating things of different orders*—labour and wages in one and signified and signifier in the other" (Saussure, 1974, p. 79). Capitalism, the social order which accomplishes and is accomplished by the one, is historically specific, and so is a mode of signifying founded upon and founding the binary conception of signifying. The binary conception permits us to identify, but not to disclose, different modes of signifying; from this perspective, different modes of signifying appear as the employment of different relations of signifier and signified (cp. Williams, 1974). Thus Foucault identifies a "trinitarian formula" for Renaissance discourse,

since it requires the formal domain of marks, the content indicated by them, and the similitudes that link the marks to the things designated by them; but since resemblance is the form of the signs as well as their content, the three distinct elements of this articulation are resolved into a single form.

(Foucault, 1970)[11]

We are here entrapped in the dialectic of being and resembling.[12]

The representation of the structure of non-capitalist social consciousness as consisting of classifications organized by resemblance confronts a problem of analogy that derives from a binary conception of the sign. Using this conception if two distinct entities are analogous, then they cannot be wholly analogous or they would become identical: there must always exist "negative analogies" or disanalogies which separate them (Hesse, 1963). But in so far as the classification is stable and/or potent within the consciousness in question, this entails the existence of a means of suppressing recognition of the disanalogies. Conscious control cannot be employed here, since this would press towards an awareness of the essential arbitrariness of the analogy, and the unmasking of the proper forms of social consciousness as structures of power and interest (cp. Morris, this volume; Bloch, 1977). However, the indirect suppression of disanalogy would suggest that the source of the analogy is outside of consciousness itself, and a return to the "representeds" dicatating the terms of their recognition.

But crucially, classifying involves the adjudication of boundaries, and it is the ensemble of boundaries which signifies the structure of the classification and that this is a classification. In other words, in classifications boundaries are not *part of* what is being classified, they occupy a different space to that of the classified: boundaries and classifications are elements in a binary conception of signifying. Strictly, classifications are unthinkable under modes of signifying which do not allow of a binary reduction. The social consciousness of the peasant family farm economy does not exhibit "classifications".

Once we are given a mode of discourse in which classification can be articulated, then we can always adduce a classificatory structure, that is, we can always analyse as though the object-discourse were organized by classification (cp. Faris, 1968; Carnap, 1956). But this possibility is no more evidence for the attribution of classification to the object-discourse than structuralist analyses are confirmation of the relevant immanent operations of the human mind. The inappropriateness of the classification rendition of the object of analysis may be expected, technically, to throw up puzzles and inconsistencies of precisely the kind that led Chomsky to propose transformational-generative grammars as being more adequate than surface-category grammars in grasping the orderliness of language: which is not to suggest that they could be solved by adopting similar procedures (for I do not believe that transformational-generative grammar has met the core problems) although it is interesting to note that Randall (1976) has recently suggested one form that a generative account of classification might take. More indirectly, classification may function as a methodological device, one may set about eliciting "responses" which, in virtue of the method of elicitation, are determinately interpretable as classifying responses (cp. Coxon and Jones, 1979). However, it is unclear in general what to make of the results of this approach (cp. Bousfield, this volume), as with all experimental methods which would claim an ahistorical applicability. Adorno's comments on social surveys are pertinent:

A social science that is atomistic, and which at the same time works upwards from these atoms to general syntheses by means of a classificatory system, holds a Medusa-like mirror to a society similarly atomised and organised according to abstract classificatory categories—in this case [capitalist societies] administrative ones.

But this *adequatio rei atque cogitationis* only attains its full truth-value when it reflects on itself. Its sole right is that of criticism. As soon as one hypostatizes the state of affairs which these research methods both describe and embody, as the rationale inherent in science itself, instead of making it the object of critical reflection, one is contributing willy-nilly to its perpetuation. In so doing, empiricial social research confuses the epiphenomenon—what the world has made of us—with the thing itself. Its procedure contains a presupposition rooted less in the demands of the method than in the state of the society, i.e. historical factors. The thing-like method postulates a reified consciousness in those whom it subjects to its experiments.

(Adorno, 1976, p. 244)

Classification must be considered as an historical, situated discursive practice, which may become reified under specific conditions. "The denomination of objects does not follow upon recognition; it is itself recognition" (Merleau-Ponty, 1962, p. 177), and recognition is a social act which is not necessarily dependent upon classification (cp. Scruton, 1974, p. 11; Sperber, 1975, pp. 115ff.). To engage in the arrangement of classifications is to take up a particular stance towards the world, a stance that is required in capitalist societies, but for which there is no *a priori* necessity in general, nor, specifically, any concrete necessity in the organization of the peasant family farm.

Notes

1. There is no surplus product as such since any increase in product appears as an improvement of the household's *living*. It is interesting to note that "savings" is typically unavailable as a global category: saving is saving for some particular thing, i.e. different savings are individuated and qualitatively distinct (*TZ*, 1958, pp. 169–70; Bourdieu, 1963, pp. 63–5, 67–8). Loans do not attract interest, but the return of a just share of the results of putting the loan to use (*TZ*, 1958, pp. 178–9): this moral regulation extends to "paid" employment (*TZ*, 1958, pp. 170ff.).
2. I am indebted to Frank Furedi and Barbara Bradby for this observation.
3. Work-time is typically instanced by such forms as "morning's-worth", "day's-worth" (cf. the mediaeval *morgen, journal,* and see the references cited by Gurevich (1977)), but where technological alternatives exist these may be employed in specifying a "unit", as in a "yoke's-worth" (Barbara Bradby, personal communication). We owe our term "plough" to the affinity between the tool and work-time (Jesperson, 1972, p. 65).
4. ". . . it is not true that under capitalism all economic decisions are made on the basis of elements, i.e. on the basis of elements measurable and commensurable with other elements which are measurable in money . . . No common denominator supplies a basis for deciding on an objective basis whether to spend the available money on a vacation trip, on a fur for the wife, on stocks, or to keep it in its most liquid form, for example a savings account." (Kula, 1976, p. 171; and see Thompson, 1967, throughout.)
5. There are a host of typologies of time (for example, Gurvitch, 1964; Lévi-Strauss, 1970; Barnes, 1971; Schutz and Luckman, 1974), but it is rarely clear how the typologies are concretely established. See also Martins (1974).
6. We are familiar with this conception through the heretical methodological devices of Freudian psychoanalysis and Marxian–Hegelian dialectics. In both cases, a textual time is restored to the object of analysis, which testifies to its origins and bears witness against the present. (See, in this connection, Ricoeur, 1970.)
7. Certainly, there are no obvious grounds for asserting that a common conception of time arises from the universal physical and physiological vicissitudes of productive activity (cp. Bloch, 1977): while there are important resemblances between the time-consciousness of the broadcast-sower and the assembly-line worker, there are differences dependent upon whose time it is consciousness of!

8. The significative aspects of the body in capitalist society have been examined primarily by psychoanalysts, phenomenologists, development psychologists and a multitude of artists and critics: it is important to note that it is precisely in these areas that the rejection of the "conventional" mode of signification as the principal mode operating for the object-of-enquiry, and the attempt to conceptualize other temporal orders, have both arisen. The conditions for the Body providing a dominant semiotic paradigm are discussed in Ellen (1977); and in Reason (in preparation).

9. Lewis' (1976, pp. 64–5) account of symptom-expression among the Gnau of New Guinea is of great interest in connection with exemplification:

> Illness is displayed rather than described . . . [this] was one factor behind their apparent indifference to recounting symptoms: I could rarely get beyond learning that they were sick and had pain and fever. [They possessed] a vocabulary which was adequate to the precise and detailed description of pain in its varieties, and of functional disturbances, and so on . . . [which] reveals a perceptual awareness of pain, weakness, nausea, and so forth, which is in essentials like our own . . . Illness is recognised by the Gnau patient subjectively. It is communicated to the others in a conventional manner which relies on non-verbal rather than verbal behaviour. [For example, application of dust and grime to the body, listlessness, etc.]

10. It is not the concept of "mode of production" that is central here (cp. Godelier, 1972, 1977), but the logical character of fetishism (see Sayer, 1975).

11. The resolution of the trinitarian formula into a binary form (as a result of which "the profound kinship of language with the world was . . . dissolved" (Foucault, 1970)) was accompanied by the development of the neo-Platonic interest in mathematics (primarily arithmetic) and the development of routine accounting procedures in commerce: mercantile calculation could now fund a morality. A vice was being made of abstraction, commensality became displaced by commensurability.

12. This mode of signification does funny things to how we take jokes, and in a sense creates a construction of the universe as a straight-faced practical joker: see Douglas (1968) for a fruitful and provoking study of joking, which is relevant to and diverges from the argument of this essay.

Acknowledgements

I am indebted to the following for permission to quote from copyright material:

T. W. Adorno: "Soziologie and Empirische Forschung" (translated by G. Bartram) in P. Connerton (ed.): *Critical Sociology*: Heineman Educational Books Ltd., and the Beacon Press.

T. W. Adorno and M. Horkheimer: *Dialectic of the Enlightenment*: Penguin Books Ltd., Herder & Herder, © S. Fischer Verlag GMBH 1969.

W. Benjamin: *Illuminations*, translated by Harry Zohn with an introduction by Hannah Arendt: Cape Ltd., Harcourt Brace Jovanovich Inc., Suhrkamp Verlag K.G.

P. Bourdieu: "The Attitude of the Algerian Peasant Towards Time", in J. Pitt-Rivers (ed.): Mediterranean Countrymen: Mouton & Co. N.V.

P. Bourdieu: *Outline of a Theory of Practice*: Cambridge University Press and Librairie Droz.

J. Burckhardt: *The Civilisation of the Renaissance*: Phaidon Press.

A. V. Chayanov: *The Theory of Peasant Economy*, translated and edited by Daniel Thorner, Basile Kerblay, and R. E. F. Smith (Homewood, Ill. Richard D. Irwin). © 1966 by Richard D. Irwin, Inc.

E. Fromm: *Fear of Freedom*: Routledge and Kegan Paul Ltd., and Holt Rinehart & Winston Inc.

N. Goodman: *Languages of Art*: Hackett Publishing Co. Inc.

A. Gurevitch: "Representations of Property During the High Middle Ages", *Economy and Society*: Routledge and Kegan Paul Ltd.

W. Kula: *An Economic Theory of the Feudal System*: New Left Books.

G. Lewis: "A View of Sickness in New Guinea", in J. Loudon (ed.): *Anthropology and Medicine*: Association of Social Anthropologists.

K. Marx: *Grundrisse*, translated by Martin Nicolaus: Penguin Books Ltd., and Random House Inc.

S. Ortiz: "The Structure of Decision-Making Among Indians of Columbia", in R. Firth (ed.): *Themes in Economic Anthropology*: Tavistock Publications Ltd.

W. I. Thomas and F. Znaniecki: *The Polish Peasant in Europe and America*: Dover Publications Inc.

E. P. Thompson: "Time, Work-discipline and industrial capitalism", *Past and Present*: T. H. Aston.

References

ADORNO, T. W. (1976). Soziologie und empirische Forschung, Trans. *In* "Critical Theory" (Ed. P. Connerton). Penguin, Harmondsworth.

ADORNO, T. W. and HORKHEIMER, M. (1973). "Dialectic of Enlightenment". Allen Lane, London.

ANSCOMBE, G. M. (1963). "Intention" (2nd edition). Blackwell, Oxford.

BARNES, J. A. (1971). Time flies like an arrow. *Man (N.S.)*, **6**, 537–52.

BAXTER, R. (1673). "A Christian Directory" (quoted in Thompson, 1967, p. 87).

BENJAMIN, W. (1973). "Illuminations". Fontana, London.

BLACK, M. (1962). "Models and Metaphors". Cornell University Press, Ithaca, N.Y.

BLOCH, M. (Ed.) (1975). "Marxist Analysis and Social Anthropology". Malaby Press, London.

BLOCH, M. (1977). The past and the present in the present. *Man (N.S.)*, **12**, 278–92.

BORGES, J. G. (1970). Pierre Menard, author of the *Quixote*. *In* "Labyrinths". Penguin, Harmondsworth.

BOURDIEU, P. (1963). The attitude of the Algerian peasant towards time. *In* "Mediterranean Countrymen" (Ed. J. Pitt-Rivers). Mouton, Paris.

BOURDIEU, P. (1977). "Outline of a Theory of Practice". Cambridge University Press, Cambridge.

BURCKHARDT, J. (1921). "The Civilisation of the Renaissance". Allen and Unwin, London.

CARNAP, R. (1956). "Meaning and Necessity". University of Chicago Press, Chicago.

CHAYANOV, A. V. (1966). "The Theory of Peasant Economy" (Translated and Edited by D. Thorner, B. Kerblay and R. E. F. Smith). Richard D. Irwin, Homewood, Illinois.

COXON, A. P. M. and JONES, C. L. (1979). Images and predication: the use of subjective occupational hierarchies. *Quality and Quantity*, **14**,121–40.

DOUGLAS, M. (1968). The social control of cognition: some factors in joke perception. *Man (N.S.)*, **3**, 361–76.

ELLEN, R. F. (1977). Anatomical classification and the semiotics of the body. *In* "The Anthropology of the Body" (Ed. J. Blacking). Academic Press, London and New York.

EVANS-PRITCHARD, E. (1940). "The Nuer". Clarendon Press, Oxford.

FARIS, J. C. (1968). Validation in ethnographical description: the lexicon of "occasions" in Cat Harbour. *Man (N.S.)*, **3**, 112–24.

FIRTH, R. (Ed.) (1967). "Themes in Economic Anthropology". Tavistock Publications, London.

FIRTH, R. (1975). The sceptical anthropologist? Social anthropology and Marxist views on society. *In* "Marxist Analysis in Social Anthropology" (Ed. M. Bloch). Malaby Press, London.

FOUCAULT, M. (1970). "The Order of Things". Tavistock Publications, London.

FRANKENBERG, R. (1967). Economic anthropology: one anthropologist's view. *In* "Themes in Economic Anthropology" (Ed. R. Firth). Tavistock Publications, London.

FRANKLIN, B. (1751). "Poor Richard's Almanac" (quoted in Thompson, 1967, p. 89).

FROMM, E. (1960). "Fear of Freedom". Routledge and Kegan Paul, London.

GALLIE, W. B. (1964). "Philosophy and Historical Understanding". Chatto and Windus, London.

GARFINKEL, H. (1967). Time structures the biography and prospects of a situation (an excerpt from "Studies in Ethnomethodology". Prentice-Hall). *In* M. Douglas (ed.) (1973). "Rules and Meanings" Penguin, Harmondsworth.

GEERTZ, C. (1975). Person, time and conduct in Bali. *In* "The Interpretation of Cultures". Hutchinson, London.

GELLNER, E. (1971). Our current sense of history. *Survey*, **17**, 13–30.

GODELIER, M. (1972). "Rationality and Irrationality in Economics". New Left Books, London.

GODELIER, M. (1977). "Perspectives in Marxist Anthropology". Cambridge University Press, Cambridge.

GOODMAN, N. (1976). "Languages of Art" (2nd edition). Hackett, Indianapolis.

GOODMAN, N. (1976). "Languages of Art" (2nd edition). Hackett Publishing Co. Inc., Indianapolis.

GUREVICH, A. (1977). Representations of property during the high Middle Ages. *Economy and Society*, **6**, 1–30.

GURVITCH, G. (1964). "The Spectrum of Social Time". D. Reidel, Dordrecht, The Netherlands.

HESSE, M. (1963). "Models and Analogies in Science". Sheed and Ward, London.

HIRST, P. Q. (1976). Althusser and the theory of ideology. *Economy and Society*, **5**, 385–412.

HOBSBAWM, E. (1964). "Labouring Men". Weidenfeld and Nicolson, London.

JESPERSEN, O. (1972). "Growth and Structure of the English Language". Blackwell, Oxford.

KULA, W. (1976). "An Economic Theory of the Feudal System". New Left Books, London.

LÉVI-STRAUSS, C. (1966). "The Savage Mind". Weidenfeld and Nicolson, London.

LÉVI-STRAUSS, C. (1970). "The Raw and the Cooked". Harper and Row, London.

LEWIS, G. (1976). A view of sickness in New Guinea. *In* "Social Anthropology and Medicine" (Ed. J. B. Loudon). Academic Press, London and New York.

LURIA, A. (1971). "Speech and the Development of Mental Processes". Penguin, Harmondsworth.

MARTINS, H. (1974). Time and theory in sociology. *In* "Approaches to Sociology" (Ed. J. Rex). Routledge and Kegan Paul, London.

MARX K. (1973). "Grundrisse" (Trans. M. Nicolaus). Penguin, Harmondsworth.

MARX, K. (1976). "Capital", Vol. I (Trans. B. Fowkes). Penguin, Harmondsworth.

MEILLASSOUX, C. (1972). From reproduction to production: a Marxist approach to economic anthropology. *Economy and Society*, **1**, 93–105.

MERLEAU-PONTY, M. (1962). "The Phenomenology of Perception". Routledge and Kegan Paul, London.

ORTIZ, S. (1967). The structure of decision-making among Indians of Columbia. *In* "Themes in Economic Anthropology" (Ed. R. Firth). Tavistock Publications, London.

ORTIZ, S. (1971). Reflections on the concept of "peasant culture" and "peasant cognitive systems". *In* "Peasant Societies" (Ed. T. Shanin). Penguin, Harmondsworth.

PIAGET, J. (with B. Inhelder) (1969). "The Psychology of the Child". Routledge and Kegan Paul, London.

POCOCK, J. G. A. (1971). "Politics, Language and Time". Methuen, London.

QUINE, W. V. (1961). "From a Logical Point of View" (2nd edition). Harper and Row, London.

QUINE, W. V. (1964). "Word and Object". MIT Press, London.

RANDALL, R. (1976). How tall is a taxonomic tree? Some evidence for dwarfism. *American Ethnologist*, **8**, 229–42.

REASON, D. A. (in preparation). "Making sense of the body" (revision of a paper presented at the 1974 Annual Conference of the Association of Social Anthropologists on "The Anthropology of the Body").

RICOEUR, P. (1970). "Freud and Philosophy". Yale University Press, New Haven.

SACKS, H. (1974). On the analysability of stories by children. Reprinted in "Ethnomethodology" (Ed. R. Turner). Penguin, Harmondsworth.

SACKS, H. and SCHEGLOFF, E. (1973). Opening up closings. *Semiotica*, **8**, 289–327.

SAHLINS, M. (1974). "Stone Age Economics". Tavistock Publications, London.

SAUSSURE, F. DE (1974). "Course in General Linguistics" (Introduced by J. Culler). Fontana, London.

SAYER, D. (1975). "Method and dogma in historical materialism". *Sociological Review*, **23**, 779–810.

SCHUTZ, A. and LUCKMAN, T. (1974). "Structures of the Life World". Heinemann, London.

SCRUTON, R. (1974). "Art and Imagination". Methuen, London.

SEARLE, J. (1969). "Speech Acts". Cambridge University Press, Cambridge.

SPERBER, D. (1975). "Rethinking Symbolism". Cambridge University Press, Cambridge.

THOMAS, W. I. and ZNANIECKI, F. (1958). "The Polish Peasant in Europe and America". Dover Publications, New York.

THOMPSON, E. P. (1967). Time, work-discipline and industrial capitalism. *Past and Present*, No. 38, 57–97.

VON WRIGHT, G. (1971). "Explanation and Understanding". Routledge and Kegan Paul, London.

VYGOTSKY, (1965). "Thought and Language". MIT Press, London.

WILLIAMS, K. (1974). Unproblematic archaeology. *Economy and Society*, **3**, 41–68.

Name Index

Subject Index

A

Affinity, logical notion of, 238
Ahistoricism, 136, 224
Alagwa (Tanzania), 48, 55
Alphabetical order, 9, 168, 187
Amboina (and the Amboinese), 146, 149, 157, 161, 164
Analogy, 201, 202, 203, 238, 241
  negative, 241
Anomaly, 4, 7, 9, 13, 14–15, 26, 28, 58, 70–71, 83–84, 103–116, 124, 126
Anthropocentrism, 63, 103
Anthropology, symbolic, 103, 105, 112, 130
  relationship between cognitive and symbolic, 103–104
  theory of, 135
Apache (American southwest), 135
Arabic, 147, 160
Arbitrariness, 7, 8–12, 26, 207
Archaeology, 10
Associationism, 202
Atomism, logical, 198, 242
Australia, 142
  peoples of, 136
Aweikoma (Brazil), 132
Aztec (Mexico), 132

B

Bali (and the Balinese), 157
Banyang (Cameroun), 48
Binary codes (see Dualism)
Binumarien (New Guinea), 219
Biology, 10, 28
  statistical, 3
  theoretical, 5
Body, classificatory, mensural and symbolic use of, 127, 228–229, 244
Botany, modern, 145–146, 149
Britains, ancient, 47

B

Bunaq (Timor)
  history and mythology of, 85–96
  medicinal uses of plants, 92, 94, 95, 96
  plant classification of, 81–101
  prohibitions on use of various plants, 90–93, 94, 95, 96, 97, 98
  ritual of, 87–89, 90, 96, 97, 98
  ritual uses of plants, 98
  war magic, 91, 92, 93–96, 98
Burunge (Tanzania), 35

C

Capitalist mode of production, 225–226, 228, 229, 230, 233, 234, 235, 242, 243
Catalogues, 8
Categories (see also Colour, Ethnobotany, Ethnozoology, Taste, Taxa, Wine)
  boundaries of, 215, 216, 241
  covert, 7, 13, 62, 63, 64, 68, 89, 106
  criteria for distinguishing (see Criteria)
  as fixed points (standards) of reference, 52, 140 (see also Paradigms)
  inclusion of items in by extension, 52, 140 (see also Semantic fields)
  intermediary, 86
  intuition and the assignation of items to, 12
  number of in a domain, 16
  perceptual (see Species, concept of (and natural kinds))
  residual, 111
  ritual, 126
  salient (see Salient (significant) categories)
  simultaneous conditioning of by cognitive processes and the perceived environment, 112
  spatial, 131